Streetwalking the Metropolis

women & masquerade

— women on display / subject of
gaze

↓ more attuned to
modern city life than
men p 26

Streetwalking the Metropolis

Women, the City, and Modernity

Deborah L. Parsons

OXFORD
UNIVERSITY PRESS

*This book has been printed digitally and produced in a standard specification
in order to ensure its continuing availability*

OXFORD
UNIVERSITY PRESS

Great Clarendon Street, Oxford OX2 6DP

Oxford University Press is a department of the University of Oxford.
It furthers the University's objective of excellence in research, scholarship,
and education by publishing worldwide in

Oxford New York

Auckland Bangkok Buenos Aires Cape Town Chennai
Dar es Salaam Delhi Hong Kong Istanbul Karachi Kolkata
Kuala Lumpur Madrid Melbourne Mexico City Mumbai Nairobi
São Paulo Shanghai Taipei Tokyo Toronto

Oxford is a registered trade mark of Oxford University Press
in the UK and in certain other countries

Published in the United States
by Oxford University Press Inc., New York

ISBN 0-19-818683-5

Mine is an urban muse, and bound
By some strange law to paven ground
(Amy Levy)

'My darling, my darling, my darling. Here we have no abiding city'
(Elizabeth Bowen)

Preface

This book owes its inspiration, development, and completion to numerous people. I must begin by thanking above all Laura Marcus for her unfailing intellectual generosity and advice, her incisive critical judgement, and not least her constant encouragement and friendship which remains invaluable to me. At the University of Birmingham, Maria Balshaw, Jan Campbell, Danielle Fuller, and Andrzej Gasiorek have given much-needed friendship and intellectual stimulation and advice, and Tony Davies deserves special thanks for creating a supportive and benevolent research environment as well as for all his words of scholarly wisdom. Chris Willis never fails to inspire with her energy and intellectual vitality. Kaelyn McGregor and Angela Speck know how much I depend upon their ever-open doors and common sense. Thanks also must go to Barrie Bullen, Lionel Kelly, and Anna Robins at the University of Reading for early mentorship, and my parents for their constant support.

Finally, to David Gasca Tucker, I owe a love of cities and a companionship that means more than I can say.

D. P.

Contents

Abbreviations

References to primary works will be noted parenthetically throughout the text under the following abbreviations. All texts refer to the editions cited in the bibliography.

A	Henry James, *The Ambassadors*
AL	Amy Levy, *The Complete Novels and Selected Writings of Amy Levy*
ALMM	Jean Rhys, *After Leaving Mr Mackenzie*
CDN	James Thomson, *The City of Dreadful Night*
DL	Elizabeth Bowen, *The Demon Lover and Other Stories*
FE	Charles Baudelaire, *The Flowers of Evil*
FGC	Doris Lessing, *The Four-Gated City*
GMM	Jean Rhys, *Good Morning, Midnight*
HD	Elizabeth Bowen, *The Heat of the Day*
LB	Jean Rhys, *The Left Bank and Other Stories*
LP	Émile Zola, *The Ladies Paradise*
MD	Virginia Woolf, *Mrs Dalloway*
MHLB	Charles Baudelaire, *My Heart Laid Bare and Other Prose Writings*
Na	André Breton, *Nadja*
Ni	Djuna Barnes, *Nightwood*
ND	Virginia Woolf, *Night and Day*
P	Dorothy Richardson, *Pilgrimage*
PC	Henry James, *The Princess Cassimassima*
PP	Charles Baudelaire, *Parisian Prowler*
PY	Janet Flanner, *Paris Was Yesterday*
Q	Jean Rhys, *Quartet*
RP	Marcel Proust, *Remembrance of Time Past*
SC	Theodore Dresier, *Sister Carrie*
T	H.D. (Hilda Doolittle), *Trilogy*
TN	Elizabeth Bowen, *To the North*
UGB	Anaïs Nin, *Under a Glass Bell*
VD	Jean Rhys, *Voyage in the Dark*
WA	Anaïs Nin, *Winter of Artifice*
WS	Rosamond Lehmann, *The Weather in the Streets*
WW	Rose Macaulay, *The World My Wilderness*
Y	Virginia Woolf, *The Years*
YB	Dorothy Richardson, 'Yeats of Bloomsbury'
YJ	George Gissing, *In the Year of Jubilee*

Introduction: Gendered Cartographies of Viewing

THERE are infinite versions of any one city. The city as a text to be read, the text as a city to be traversed; this formulation has become so common as to be almost a cliché. Not only linguistic terms and figures of speech, but also forms of perception, experience, and communication are predicated on the 'body' and 'soul' of the city. Yet the relationship is not just one of analogy—we are increasingly realizing the significance of the urban map as influential in the very structures of social and mental daily life. A city can be analysed demographically, economically, architecturally, as the result of an urban plan or a history of literary and visual representation. Its landscape can be fixed by the map, the body within it by statistics. Increasingly academic criticism is recognizing that cities have aggregate and multiplicitous identities, made up of their many selves, and geographical, sociological, literary, and art historical analysis are beginning to combine in an interdisciplinary approach to the urban landscape, its influence and human interaction with and within it. The urban landscape needs to be studied as a feature that brings the psychological and the material into collusion, in terms of theories and aesthetics that construct modern subjectivity and modern art from material urban experience. This is to interrelate the observed with the observer, and to assess how the identity of one affects the other.[1]

The urban writer is not only a figure within a city; he/she is also the producer of a city, one that is related to but distinct from the city of asphalt, brick, and stone, one that results from the interconnection of body, mind, and space, one that reveals the interplay of self/city identity. The writer adds other maps to the city atlas; those of social interaction but also of myth, memory, fantasy, and desire. That the city has been habitually conceived as a male space, in which women are either

[1] The paradigmatic discussion of a culture based on vision and observation in 19th-cent. modernity is Jonathan Crary's *Techniques of the Observer: On Vision and Modernity in the Nineteenth Century* (Cambridge, Mass.: MIT Press, 1990), which studies the restructuring of perception as a result of the increasing sophistication of scopic instruments and their pervasive role in all fields of modern life.

repressed or disobedient marginal presences, has resulted in an emphasis in theoretical analysis on gendered maps that reflect such conditions. This study is an attempt to examine women's urban walking and writing from a perspective that looks at the gendered sites/sights of the city, but from a broader context than that of just the politics of power and marginalization that emphasizes the comparative experience of the male and female subject. It walks and reads the literary maps of a range of women writers across customary period and coterie groupings, my route registering their relative and changing relationships with the city. Constraints of space, the boundaries of the book, of course mean that many writers, cities, and trajectories suffer omission. Women's writing within the genres of magazine journalism and urban travel writing demands its own analysis. In this text I deal specifically with London and Paris from 1880 to 1940, roughly the period from the first generation of 'New' women who succeed in gaining access to the spaces of their cities to the second and third generations who faced losing them during the Second World War. The close focus on a number of authors, Amy Levy, Dorothy Richardson, Jean Rhys, Janet Flanner, Djuna Barnes, Anaïs Nin, Rosamond Lehmann, and Elizabeth Bowen, and their differing experiences, perceptions, and literary strategies, is intended to highlight multiple issues with regard to the broad terms of women's social and cultural relationship with the city. As a postscript I turn to Doris Lessing and her protagonist Martha Quest, observing the landscape and possibilities that have been left to a post-war generation.

To consider the ways in which women writers have experienced and/or imagined the connection of their bodies and their pens with the specific urban territories they inhabit or seek, however, we must begin with an examination and reassessment of Walter Benjamin's motif for the writer and writing of urban modernity, the *flâneur*. What is the status of the women who trespass upon his pavement and his page? Can there be a *flâneuse*, and what forms might she take? Answering these questions involves questioning the status and meaning of the *flâneur* as both historical figure and critical metaphor in literary and cultural criticism, in order to reveal the dynamics of its thematic and structural use by a tradition of women's urban writing. How are women writers situated, and how do they situate themselves, in the maps of urban location and literature?

Flâneur/Flâneuse?

Walter Benjamin is the self-acclaimed historiographer of the city of modernity, basing his influential surrealist methodology in a range

flaneur / rag picker

of epistemological and scopic metaphors of which the paradigms are the bourgeois *flâneur* and his vagrant counterpart the rag-picker. Both are historical phenomena of nineteenth-century Paris, yet for Benjamin and the contemporary cultural critics who draw upon him they become retrospective concepts for intellectual debate on the city and modernity. Both are itinerant metaphors that register the city as a text to be inscribed, read, rewritten, and reread. The *flâneur* walks idly through the city, listening to its narrative. The rag-picker too moves across the urban landscape, but as a scavenger, collecting, rereading, and rewriting its history. The two merge in Benjamin's scavenging promenades through nineteenth-century and surrealist Paris. It is with the *flâneur* that Benjamin first attempts the demystification of the city in the arcades project.[2] Yet the *flâneur* as Benjamin first conceives him, the expert observer of the urban scene, translating the chaotic and fragmentary city into an understandable and familiar space, seems to become increasingly detached from his asphalt environment. As Haussmann's imperial capital merges with Benjamin's contemporary city, the bourgeois *flâneur* gives way to the aesthetic rag-picker.[3]

Because the *flâneur* becomes so convoluted in Benjamin's study, and has so many incarnations, this intended agent of demystification has himself become one of the mysteries of the modernist city. Benjamin seems unsure whether to separate or condense the various urban nomads with whose spirit he communes as much as did the poet Charles Baudelaire from whom he inherits them; the dandy, the rag-picker, the prostitute, the beggar. He may attempt to exhaustively catalogue Paris as the 'capital of modernity' but, as Adrian Rifkin warns, 'His arduous process of demystifying Paris has turned into a part of its mystery, and sometimes it looks as if the word Benjamin is just another name for the

---

[2] Benjamin's projected study of Paris in the late 19th cent. was to include sections on, among others, the arcades, spectacle, the prostitute, perspective, panorama, Baudelaire, Proust, and Haussmann. For details of this study I have referred to Susan Buck-Morss, *The Dialectics of Seeing* (Cambridge, Mass.: MIT Press, 1989). Early versions of, and essays related to, the *Passagen-werk* are collected in Walter Benjamin, *Charles Baudelaire: A Lyric Poet in the Era of High Capitalism*, trans. Harry Zohn (London: Verso, 1989).

[3] Benjamin's 'aesthetic' sociology can be regarded as a surrealistic mode of historical materialist discourse. David Frisby, in *Sociological Impressionism: A Reassessment of Georg Simmel's Social Theory* (London: Routledge, 1992), 20, describes Simmel and Benjamin as 'Sociological *flâneurs*', whilst Dana and Michael A. Weinstein continue the methodological metaphor but with a postmodern emphasis in 'Georg Simmel: Sociological *flâneur bricoleur*', in *Postmodern(ized) Simmel* (London: Routledge, 1993), 53–70, p. 56.

anomie of modernity, or for its equivocal pleasures—its fascination if anything intensified through his interventions'.[4]

The *flâneur* is elusive; he literally walks away from Benjamin's definitions into the labyrinth, myth, and fragments of the city. It is this elusivity that provides the theoretical context to this study. The *flâneur* has become an icon of the architextual aesthetics of the modern urban novel. Once an idle observer of the Parisian *demi-monde*, for contemporary theory he is an increasingly expansive figure who represents a variety of 'wanderings', in terms of ambulation, nationality, gender, race, class, and sexuality. The elusivity remains, however. Used to allude to a whole range of urban social identities from shopping-mall consumer to internet surfer, it risks an overload of significance that results in meaninglessness. My concern is to separate out the social and metaphoric descriptions of urban types too often undiscriminated in theoretical discussions of the city. Is the *flâneur* bourgeois or vagrant, authoritative or marginal, within or detached from the city crowd, masculine, feminine, or androgynous? And what does such a redefinition imply for theories of women's place in the urban landscape?

The urban observer, as both a social phenomenon and a metaphor for the modernist artist, has been regarded as an exclusively male figure. The opportunities and activities of *flânerie* were predominantly the privileges of the man of means, and it was hence implicit that the 'artist of modern life' was necessarily the bourgeois male.[5] Raymond Williams, for example, notes that the perspective on the city has always been that of 'a man walking, as if alone, in its streets'.[6] *Flânerie* has thus also become a metaphor for the gendered scopic hierarchy in observations of urban space. Despite defining modernism away from canonical versions towards a recognition of less dominant modes, notably a 'female' modernism, however, feminist literary criticism and cultural sociology has tended to support the masculine definition of the urban observer, employing a conceptual framework that diametrically opposes hegemonic and female modernism. Critics of canonical modernism note that women had a different experience of the modern city to men. Janet Wolff argues for women's lack of freedom to walk and gaze in public spaces, stating, '[t]here is no question of inventing the *flâneuse*:

[4] Adrian Rifkin, *Street Noises: Parisian Pleasure, 1900–40* (Manchester: Manchester UP, 1993), 7.

[5] Charles Baudelaire, '*Le Peintre de la vie moderne*', in *My Heart Laid Bare and Other Prose Writings*, ed. Peter Quennell, trans. Norman Cameron (London: Soho Book Co., 1986).

[6] Raymond Williams, *The Country and the City* (London: Chatto and Windus, 1973), 231.

the essential point is that such a character was rendered impossible by the sexual divisions of the nineteenth century', and Griselda Pollock agrees that 'there is no female equivalent of the quintessential masculine figure, the flâneur: there is not and could not be a female flâneuse'.[7]

That women had restricted access to the public life of the city compared to men is undoubtedly true. It is also true that the self-acclaimed observer of the city has been male. Yet women can be seen to occupy public positions in the city from the mid-nineteenth century that locate them as observers. Rachel Bowlby has analysed women's legitimate presence in the phantasmagoric, consumerist spaces of the modern city, and Judith Walkowitz has described the mobility of women undertaking social and charity work in the slum districts of the East End of London.[8] These positions have remained unrecognized, however, denigrated as immoral, superficial, or vagrant roles in the bourgeois city. Replying to such studies, for example, Wolff argues that, 'to say that women come to have acceptable reasons to be in the street is not to identify them as *flâneuses*', but in so doing limits the *flâneur* to a racial and classed identity as well as a gendered one. Moreover, Wolff ignores the important point that the *flâneur* is not only a historical figure but also a critical metaphor for the characteristic perspective of the modern artist. To infer from the socio-historical position of bourgeois women as confined to private realms that it is therefore a priori impossible to conceive of a female aesthetic perspective in terms of the concept of *flânerie* is false. Wolff and Pollock both overlook the *flâneur*'s inherent contradictions, perhaps as a result of their tendency to blur historical actuality with its use as a cultural, critical phenomenon.

A redefinition of the *flâneur* to acknowledge its related but distinct uses as a conceptual term and as a socio-historical phenomenon, is to clarify a term which is currently at once too vague and too exclusive. Rather than contradicting Wolff and Pollock outright, I question the basis on which they reject the possibility of a *flâneuse*, namely the gender divisions of the nineteenth century and the supposed mirroring of these in the urban environment. My argument that the activity of urban observation is not exclusive to the male will centre around two premisses; first, that the concept of the *flâneur* itself contains gender

*critical of
wolff & pollock*

argument

[7] Janet Wolff, 'The Invisible *Flâneur*: Women and the Literature of Modernity', *Theory, Culture and Society* 2/3 (1985), 37–46, p. 45, and Griselda Pollock, 'Modernity and the Spaces of Femininity', in *Vision and Difference: Femininity, Feminism and the Histories of Art* (London: Routledge, 1988), 50–90, p. 71.

[8] Rachel Bowlby, *Just Looking: Consumer Culture in Dreiser, Gissing and Zola* (New York: Methuen, 1985); Judith Walkowitz, *City of Dreadful Delight: Narratives of Sexual Danger in London* (London: Virago, 1992).

ambiguities that suggest the figure to be a site for the contestation of male authority rather than the epitome of it, and secondly, that a mode of expression can be seen to develop in the late nineteenth and early twentieth centuries that emphasizes observation of the city yet is distinct from the characteristic practice of the authoritative *flâneur*, comparable instead to the marginalized urban familiarity of the rag-picker. Feminist critics need to move away from a focus on the urban observer as leisured *flâneur* to recognize this alternative metaphor for the urban observer, more connected to the twentieth-century city of modernity and to the influence of surrealism, and its possibilities for female urban expression. At the end of her essay Wolff complains of the dominant criticism on modernity and modernism that, '[w]hat is missing in this literature is any account of life outside the public realm, of the experience of "the modern" in its private manifestations, and also of the very different nature of the experience of those women who *did* appear in the public arena: a poem written by "la femme passante" about her encounter with Baudelaire, perhaps.'[9] I shall try to establish that women's fiction does provide such accounts, and that in the modern city of multiplicity, reflection, and indistinction, *la femme passante* is herself a *flâneuse*, just as the 'man of the crowd' is also a *flâneur*.

Of course if this is the case, perhaps the topic of *flâneur/flâneuse* in debate is fallacious—if it is wrong to interpret the *flâneur* as exclusively male, then it is presumably unnecessary to posit the possibility of a female version. However, women's highly self-conscious awareness of themselves as walkers and observers of the modernist city does need to be recognized. A female observer corresponding to the social figure of the *flâneur* can be found in the late nineteenth and early twentieth centuries, when women were achieving greater liberation as walkers and observers in the public spaces of the city. Paralleling this empirical fact, I want to argue for a particular mode of female urban vision. Jonathan Crary states that '[m]odernization effected a deterritorialization and a revaluation of vision'; my argument is that the response to this deterritorialization differed for men and women, resulting in gendered models of modern urban vision.[10] Whereas Benjamin's *flâneur* increasingly becomes a metaphor for observation, retreating from the city streets once the arcades are destroyed to a place of scopic authority yet static detachment, women were entering the city with fresh eyes, observing it from within. It is with this social influx of women as empirical observers into the city street that aesthetic, urban perception as a specifically masculine phenomenon and privilege is challenged.

---

9 Wolff, 'The Invisible *Flâneuse*', 45.   10 Crary, *Techniques of the Observer*, 149.

My aim is therefore to explore the experience of the urban landscape and environment in terms of a fusion of empirical and imaginative perspectives, and to relate this to a gender-related city consciousness. The masculinist ideologies that have dominated the discourses of urban geography and literary modernism are gradually being exposed. But too often the politics of gender difference are concerned with the comparative experience of the male and female subject *in* the city, and overlook their relative formulations *of* the city. Thus Shari Benstock's *Women of the Left Bank* emancipates women writers, artists, and photographers living in Paris in the 1920s and 1930s, but still locates them in terms of the fixed identity of 'expatriate Paris', her book itself acting as a literary Baedeker to the map of the Paris Left Bank.

I have concentrated on those women for whom the city operates as not just as setting or image, but as a constituent of identity, and who translate the experience of urban space into their narrative form. Amy Levy, Dorothy Richardson, Virginia Woolf, Janet Flanner, Jean Rhys, Djuna Barnes, Anaïs Nin, Mina Loy, H.D. (Hilda Doolittle), Rosamond Lehmann, Elizabeth Bowen, and Doris Lessing move the discourse of the *flâneuse* from the Victorian to the modern period, from London to Paris, from the metropolitan aesthetic classes to the cosmopolitan expatriate, and from the wealthy to the vagrant. Yet, whilst writing within and sometimes across different temporal, canonical, racial, national, class, and generic boundaries, each writer is concerned with representing a female city consciousness alternative to that of the male. Gillian Rose has argued that 'Masculinist geographers [and writers] are by and large still demanding an omniscient view, a transparent city, total knowledge. Meanwhile, feminist geographers are understanding the contemporary city not as the increasing fragmentation of a still-coherent whole, but rather in terms of a challenge to that omniscient vision and its exclusions.'[11] Benjamin's geography of the city is indeed marked by an obsessive attempt to know the city in its entirety, a surrealist desire to penetrate the fantasies of its phantasmagoria, and a determined project of reacquisition of its fragments. Although I do not want to argue for a specifically female view of city space, that would at once exclude men and homogenize women's individualities, I agree with Rose's recognition of an understanding of urban space that is not predicated on the model of the omniscient or exclusionary map. I concentrate on a literary geography of the city that, as the range of works considered in this study manifest, is prevalent in the work of women writers and that

[11] Gillian Rose, *Feminism and Geography: The Limits of Geography* (Cambridge: Polity Press, 1993).

involves a concern with the situation of women as modern protagonists in engagement with urban processes and their spatial environment. I suggest through literary analyses that there are certain themes, interests, purposes, and techniques common to women writing about London and Paris in the years 1880–1940, in which social differences yet contribute to a shared position as women entering and seeking legitimate place in the urban and professional landscape of modernity.

Blueprint for the Modernist City

The urban system can be represented through various descriptive metaphors; the semiotics of architecture, maps, demographic patterns, iconic groups. Urban representations assume different viewpoints (more or less authoritative and encompassing) that are part of an implicit discourse of knowledge and power.[12] It has become something of a commonplace that the conditions of the modern city shaped a new observer, whose perspective in turn influenced a new observation of the city itself. Jonathan Crary argues that concurrent with a new urban environment of fragmented and defamiliarized space, 'the discursive identity of the observer as an object of philosophical reflection and empirical study underwent an equally drastic renovation'.[13]

As envisaged by the twentieth-century urban planner, the city falls into two opposing extremes; the modernist, geometrically ordered city of Le Corbusier, and the postmodern, informal and flexible city proposed, for example, by Jane Jacobs.[14] The former is an environment for the rational and purposive figure, the latter for the nomad and lover of the picturesque. The former follows the scopic form of the telescopic panorama, the latter that of the kaleidoscopic myriad. Postmodernism, with its characteristic lauding of that which is disparate as unlimiting, asserts a despotic nature to the ordered city.

[12] Michel Foucault's analysis of the interaction of institutional power and subjectivity in the controlling and regulating (predominantly through overt or implicit observation) of the individual, is one of the paradigmatic philosophies of the social functioning of the visual discussed by Crary, and his analysis of cultural visual power and objectification relates directly to the roles of men and women as observers/participants in the urban field. He conceives of a surveillance state based on the architectural model of Jeremy Bentham's implicitly (yet fallaciously) all-seeing panopticon. See Michel Foucault, *Discipline and Punishment*, trans. Alan Sheridan (London: Allen Lane, 1977).

[13] Crary, *Techniques of the Observer*, 14.

[14] Le Corbusier, *The City of Tomorrow* (1924); trans. Frederick Etchells (Cambridge, Mass.: MIT Press, 1971); Jane Jacobs, *The Death and Life of Great American Cities* (1961; London: Penguin, 1994).

Yet although the city cannot be satisfactorily defined through a total-izing perspective, neither should it become a merely abstract entity within the individual mind of the perceiver. For the fluctuating post-modern city risks becoming a signless place of directionless nomads, as much a mazelike labyrinth of light as its Victorian predecessor was a labyrinth of fog and darkness. In this conception of the city, as Anthony Vidler describes in *The Architectural Uncanny* (1992), we find ourselves lost '[a]midst the ruins of monuments no longer significant because deprived of their systematic status, and often of their corporeality, walking on the dust of inscriptions no longer decipherable because lacking so many words, whether carved in stone or shaped in neon, we cross nothing to go nowhere'.[15] It is this sense of being nowhere that Vidler terms 'posturbanism', an experience of place where 'the margins have entirely invaded the centre and disseminated its focus'. Richard Sennett, in his provocative philosophy of the city in *Flesh and Stone* (1994), regards the city as a positive site for the 'other' and the 'exile', innovatively suggesting that the city should be regarded not as a sanc-tuary but as an open space 'in which people come alive, where they expose, acknowledge and address the discordant parts of themselves and one another'.[16] Michel de Certeau draws attention to the crucial distinc-tion between the urban observer as 'voyeur' and as 'walker'. His con-temporary urban walker constructs the space of the city with his footsteps, which entwine with those of the rest of the urban crowd into a 'poetic geography'.[17] Vidler also focuses on the role of the body within the city, suggesting that the traditional paradigm of the healthy and ordered body as a model for the city is now defunct for postmodern urban experience, but colluding with Sennet in his hope that new urban awareness is more heterogeneous and therefore more socially inclusive. The urban walker is prominent in all three texts, but never as an authoritative and aloof masculine figure. Significantly, the postmodern city is an open and migrational one, available to female as well as male walkers of the city street.

The modernist fascination with the formal structures of urban life, however, can be seen at its two extremes of 'concept' city, the radiant utopia and the degenerate wasteland. Walter Benjamin hinted that he was attempting to combine exactly these Le Corbusian and surrealist

[15] Anthony Vidler, *The Architectural Uncanny: Essays in the Modern Unhomely* (Cam-bridge, Mass.: MIT Press, 1992), 185–6.

[16] Richard Sennet, *Flesh and Stone: The Body and the City in Western Civilization* (London: Faber and Faber, 1994).

[17] See 'Walking in the City', in Michel de Certeau, *The Practice of Everyday Life* (1974; Berkeley: University of California Press, 1984), 91–110, p. 105.

aesthetics in his socio-aesthetics of modernity. Corresponding to these structures are different types of *flâneur*; the authoritative architect with his panoramic blueprint and the marginal rag-picker with his city rubbish. The aim of the former is to ignore, silence, and erase the latter. The tension between valorization of the ordered, planned, and mapped, and the marginal, forgotten, and past, runs throughout the urban representations in this study, women notably taking up the latter perspective in their wanderings in the city streets. The aims of modernism versus postmodernism, and functionalism versus surrealism, form an implicit backdrop to my argument for women's negotiation of the city as a place for them to walk and write. Walking in the city is at once an encounter with modernity and with the past, with the new and unknown but also with haunting ghosts. In the vast notes for his 'arcades' project, the *Passagen-werk*, Benjamin describes surrealism as 'the new art of strolling' and writes that '[t]he street leads the strolling person into a vanished time'.[18] It is an urban aesthetic, that gains its inspiration from the generally overlooked but everyday city landscape of 'roof-tops, lightning conductors, gutters, verandas, weathercocks, stucco work'.[19] The surrealist would seem a natural *flâneur*, wandering a city in which the past uncannily and repeatedly surfaces in the present. In fact Benjamin himself in the twentieth century, in his passionate retrieval and revaluation of the obsolete nineteenth-century arcades, translates into theoretical criticism Louis Aragon's surrealist literary evocation of the arcades in *Le Paysan de Paris* (1926).[20] Perhaps the concept of the *flâneur* as an urban metaphor can be regarded as degenerating with the passage of modernity into that of the rag-picker. As a marginal figure, concerned with the refuse objects of everyday life rather than monumental history, and forming a connective relationship with the city in which the urban landscape is regarded as a palimpsest of layered time, it is the Baudelaire-inspired surrealist rag-picker rather than the autocratic Le Corbusian *flâneur* who would seem to share certain aspects of women's experiences of urban space.

Le Corbusier opens his aesthetic treatise for modern architecture, *The City of Tomorrow* (1924), by correlating city and poetry as man's creative

[18] Walter Benjamin, *Das Passagen-werk*, 2 vols. (Frankfurt: Suhrkamp, 1983), 1000, 524.

[19] Walter Benjamin, 'Surrealism', in *One Way Street and Other Writings*, trans. Edmund Jephcott and Kingsley Shorter (London: Verso, 1992), 225–39, 228.

[20] Although Benjamin does work with similar motifs and themes to the surrealists, I agree with Graeme Gilloch when he argues in *Myth and Metropolis: Walter Benjamin and the City* (Cambridge: Polity Press, 1996), 95, that Benjamin distanced himself from the surrealist belief in dreams and stimulants for sensory exploration. His project is essentially the combination of a surrealist sense of the modern myths contained within the spaces of the city with a more socially concrete, Marxist historical materialism.

acts. For Le Corbusier, the city is a human creation that can be coherently planned and rationally perceived. Man (the modern architect) is at the centre of his creation, dictating its meanings and constructing its 'panorama', as Le Corbusier himself literally did with his panoramic mural 'City of Three Million Inhabitants' for the Salon d'Automne in 1922. As Jacobs asserts, '[l]ike a great visible ego it tells of someone's achievement', one that is notably masculine.[21] For Le Corbusier epitomizes Gillian Rose's 'masculinist geographer', assuming a comprehensive position based on a masculine focus that largely ignores women. His modern city is conventionally surveyable, created for an urban inhabitant conceived along the lines of the authoritative, implicitly male, *flâneur*. In the preface to the first chapter, for example, Le Corbusier asserts, '[m]an walks in a straight line because he has a goal and knows where he is going; he has made up his mind to reach some particular place and he goes straight to it,' and he plans the urban environment accordingly.[22] Le Corbusier's envisioned urbanite is thus not a dallying wanderer absorbed by the impressions of urban experience, he is a rational and purposive man who proceeds directly to a preknown destination.

In *The City of Tomorrow* Le Corbusier compares the paths of the man who walks in a straight line and the 'pack-donkey' who 'meanders along, meditates a little in his scatter-brained and distracted fashion', stating (in a formulation that prefigures contemporary debate between the tenets of the postmodern and the modern) that,

The winding road is the result of happy-go-lucky heedlessness, of looseness, lack of concentration and animality.

The straight road is a reaction, an action, a positive deed, the result of self-mastery. It is sane and noble.[23]

Condemning the former for being the result of ease, an instinctual rather than reasoned and forward-thinking mode of urban passage, he argues that it is all too often on the meandering course that cities are constructed, and that the 'Pack-Donkey's Way is responsible for the plan of every continental city'.[24] Compared to this *ambulatory* metaphor, Jacobs, employing an opposing value system and looking to Europe as a relief from the geometric ordering of centrally planned American cities, defines a related schema of two ways of *observing*; the 'long-view' of

---

[21] Jacobs, *The Death and Life of Great American Cities*, 33.

[22] Le Corbusier, *The City of Tomorrow*, 11.

[23] Ibid. 11, 18.

[24] Interestingly, contrary to Foucauldian theory, this implies that the development of the modern city was very much not based on ideas of authoritative power and reason.

the planner who looks to 'repetition and infinity', abhorring diversity, and the 'foreground-view' of the viewer in the street, 'intimate' rather than 'detached'.[25] Le Corbusier's modernity is based in the enlightenment principles of the past, however, in which the utopian city becomes analogous with the rational mind, and the disordered city with the sickness and degenerative processes of the body. He takes up the conventional bodily system metaphor to assert that a city cannot survive on just capillaries that carry its blood, it also requires arteries and lungs. The modern city 'lives by the straight line', by the functioning of its buildings, pipes, sewers, pavements, highways, and tunnels which allow for the movement of inhabitants, traffic, water, and detritus into and away from it. Lingering, wandering *flânerie* is discouraged as non-utilitarian. The 'healthy' city is built by those who sweep away its undesirable body and replace it with a rational and ordered layout. Le Corbusier's city design thus epitomizes an urban philosophy increasingly concerned with the free (fast)-flow of goods, traffic, and people. Louis XIV is his model planner, but the developments of Nash in London and Haussman in Paris would seem to accord to similar (implicitly classed and gendered) principles. Yet the physicality of the 'donkey's way', compared to the detached rationality of the mind, suggests the place of bodies moving autonomously within cities that is in such need of recognition and has little place in Le Corbusier's utopian city, structured around its perfectly utilitarian transport network.[26]

As a result, the 'city of tomorrow', like most utopias, hardly seems a social environment. It is a city on paper, a literally textual city rather than a space in which landscape and inhabitants interact to form places and significances. People as differentiated, autonomous beings are rarely mentioned; there is only the differentiation of modern, rational man and traditional animality. The cities of the present that Le Corbusier assesses are presented in the form of maps and statistics of population density, traffic movement, and suburb growth. The modern city is repeatedly described as being based on 'man's way', on an exactness of space achieved by an adherence to geometrical law. Where are women in Le Corbusier's urban landscape? Is their 'way' subsumed by, inferior to, or disregarded by that of man? For Le Corbusier's modern city is based in a need to accommodate traffic that must move at high speed to deposit its passengers into the heart of a city in order to begin the work of the day. Yet despite the rise of women in employment, this experience is pre-

[25] Jacobs, *The Death and Life of Great American Cities*, 393.
[26] Richard Sennet argues for the necessity of reassessing the city in terms of our place within them as physical bodies.

dominantly that of the male. Le Corbusier has little interest in the influx of women into the city, their purpose, location, and times of arrival.

Le Corbusier admits that his ideal city, the Paris 'Voisin Plan' of split commercial and residential landscapes, is not a place for the *flâneur* as it discourages leisured or observant walking;

> We should also be right in saying that a straight street is extremely boring to walk through, it never seems to finish; the pedestrian feels he is never advancing. The winding street, on the other hand, is interesting because of the variety of succeeding shapes [...] The straight street is boring to walk in. Admitted. But if it is a street for work, then trams, 'buses and motors can get along it quickly, just because it is straight.[27]

His prime aim is to construct a working and functional city. The curved street for walking in belongs to recreational garden cities. By differentiating the city of the working day from that of repose, Le Corbusier thus entirely reformulates man's relationship to and understanding of urban space. The *urban* walker or *flâneur* belongs on the asphalt and is aesthetically stimulated by the very confusion and clash of the different elements of urban life. Displaced to the park-like garden city, the *flâneur* loses his dynamic relationship with specifically urban streets. In fact the ultimate result of Le Corbusier's city is to prevent human movement over the city map and human contact with the street surface; thus threatening human autonomy. Underground trains carry people into and away from the city, depositing them at its heart, the great station, from which they proceed directly to adjoining skyscrapers that contain their workplaces.[28] Once within the city therefore, the experience is largely one of bird's-eye detachment. Le Corbusier does give way to what he describes as 'human dimensions' to a certain extent, conceiving a lower-level space outside the skyscraper blocks for shops, theatres, and terrace cafés. But these social spaces still seem strangely detached, however, for how are people to reach them across the speeding highways? Le Corbusier's urbanites never actually *walk* through the landscape of the city. They cannot as there are no pathways, only 'vertical concentrations of people, separated by vacuities'.[29]

---

[27] Le Corbusier, *The City of Tomorrow*, 208. The 'Voisin Plan' and panorama was exhibited in the town-planning stand at the *Esprit Nouveau* Pavilion at the Paris International Exhibition of Decorative Art, 1925.

[28] Again Le Corbusier emphasizes the dominant current of 19th-cent. urban growth, in which the railway station and its often prominent clock (indicating the formative role of the railway in ordering and standardizing time) became important orientation points in the city.

[29] Jacobs, *The Death and Life of Great American Cities*, 356.

Mapping a New Subjectivity

Virginia Woolf's statement in *Three Guineas*, that as a woman she has and wants no country, seems to voice a placeless cosmopolitanism for the service of feminism. Indeed cosmopolitanism can be seen as essentially a twentieth-century expansion of the authoritative and panoramic viewpoint of the Benjaminian *flâneur*, the cosmopolitan overseeing no longer just one city but a host of cities, from a placeless and therefore reputedly objective detachment. Moreover, cosmopolitanism implies an era of technical advancement that will permit such international *flânerie*, in terms of the journey by vehicle rather than the journey by foot. But it is important not to overestimate the role of the cosmopolitan or the wanderer as metaphors of emancipation. Jacqueline Rose warns in *States of Fantasy* that the marginal identity can imply 'alternately exclusion from, or belonging to, all possible worlds', and she argues that although Woolf 'offered a vision of feminized migrancy which it is tempting to lift as a solution to the political ills [and personal dilemmas] of the contemporary world', '[y]ou can't, even as a woman, just float off'.[30] There is something detached and overseeing about the cosmopolitan modernist identity that works against social participation and agency.

There is an alternative to this cosmopolitan urbanism, manifest in numerous texts by women writers, in which cities are very much individual entities. The urban landscape of Woolf and Richardson is specifically that of the home environment of London, from which prolonged international shifts rarely occur. Both writers emphasize the tangible and walkable metropolis rather than a conceptual and, by definition, unlocatable cosmopolis, a factor that perhaps offers some explanation for the uneasy position of women writers in canonical accounts of the 'cosmopolitan' nature of modernism. What is important, then, is not to romanticize the position of the wanderer, either as nineteenth-century metropolitan walker or twentieth-century cosmopolitan traveller. For the wanderer never escapes completely from the cultural system of his origins (be it class, gender, or national identity); the expatriate is identified by his different homeland, the Jew is categorized by his racial difference. Perhaps the problem is to do with the dichotomizing of identity as either detached or participant, and as either particular or universal.

The women writers in this study occupy a variety of social, economic, political, and sexual spaces, and their urban narratives are very much

[30] Jacqueline Rose, *States of Fantasy* (Oxford: Clarendon Press, 1996), 129, 13.

rejection of god-eye.

based in these locations, on the pavements of the city rather than floating detachedly above it. They portray a non-fixed, but also located city experience. It is this conception of identity in relation to place that I think is manifest in women writers' use of the urban metaphor. What Caren Kaplan supports when she preaches that 'where [feminists] come to locate ourselves in terms of our specific histories and differences must be a place with room for what can be salvaged from the past and what can be made new', and what Minnie Bruce Pratt expresses in her 'way of looking at the world that is more accurate, complex, multi-layered, multi-dimensioned, more truthful: to see the world of over-lapping circles', is essentially a palimpsestic perception.[31]

Despite differences of psycho-social location, the women in this study do share a concern to validate a place for women in the masculine defined city. Brief analysis of the representation of urban women in the work of George Gissing, Émile Zola, Theodore Dreiser, Henry James, and Marcel Proust, contextualizes the following discussion within the anchor of the male canon and points up the potential con-nections between woman, city, and observation through various aes-thetic perspectives. Focusing on Levy and Richardson, I then consider their self-conscious connection of their place within the late nineteenth- and turn-of-the-century city with their professional identities as specific-ally female writers. In the later part of this analysis, in order to under-stand women's ongoing (non)identity as urban 'strangers' as opposed to the increasingly accepted urban 'cosmopolitan', I attempt to unpack the images of the alien, the stranger, and the cosmopolitan for Rhys and Barnes in the context of the inter-war years. Finally, I analyse how writers such as Nin, Bowen, and Lessing construct heterotopic cities within the pages of their texts, combining the real with the imaginary to create their own psycho-urban space. Across this extended period, and between these different writers, the social and psychic relationship with the city shifts. For all these women the urban map was crucial in opening up the city to exploration, yet within their writing they frequently resist its act of direction, wandering away from planned pathways to back streets, where they find the myths and memories of both the city and themselves. Living in modern cities constructed by and around mascu-line culture, they represented, engaged with, and resisted the narratives for female urban life defined by that culture. In so doing they created an

---

[31] Caren Kaplan, 'Deterritorializations: The Rewriting of Home and Exile in Western Discourse', in *Cultural Critique* 6 (1987), 187–98, p. 195; Minnie Bruce Pratt, 'Identity: Skin Blood Heart', in Elly Bulkin, Minnie Bruce Pratt, and Barbara Smith (eds.), *Yours in Struggle: Three Feminist Perspectives on Anti-Semitism and Racism* (Brooklyn, NY: Long Haul Press, 1984), 17.

urban consciousness modelled on alternative values to those of their male counterparts, and urban narratives that present much more organic cities than the utopian/dystopian representations by hegemonic male modernism; cities that follow natural, temporal, and social rhythms.

1 | Mythologies of Modernity

A NOTABLE feature of the differentiation of male and female modernism is the relative status of the *flâneur*; a conceptual figure related to the
characteristics of the modern artist, his modes of observation, and the
public spaces he portrays. The term *flâneur* was formally recognized at
the beginning of the nineteenth century. Elizabeth Wilson notes a French
pamphlet from 1806, detailing a day in the life of a *flâneur*, M. Bonhomme, in which the concept is already worked out along the themes
that have been accepted as constituting the defining principles of the
figure.[1] The life of M. Bonhomme is characterized by freedom from
financial/familial responsibility, by membership of the aesthetic circles
of café life, by interest in the sartorial codes of society, by a fascination
with womanhood but detachment from sexual relationships, and by a
position of isolated marginality.

In the nineteenth-century *Encyclopaedia Larousse*, the entry '*flâneur/
flâneuse*' describes a figure who loiters in the city, shopping and watching
the crowd. Although predominantly an idler, this *flâneur* can also be an
artist. Significantly, this pre-Benjaminian entry concedes the possibility
of a feminine version and it includes the largely female occupation of
shopping as a characteristic activity, despite then assuming a masculine
gender throughout. In English dictionaries, however, despite Benjamin's
study, the word *flâneur* does not appear until the 1960s. In *Webster's 3rd
New International Dictionary of the English Language* (1961) the term is
anglicized as 'flaneur', 'a) an aimless and usually self-centred and superficial person or b) an intellectual trifler'. The Webster's edition does
attest to a feminine form, the 'flaneuse', 'a woman who is or behaves
like a flaneur', but by the 1990 *Concise OED* the feminine gender has been
dropped and the term reverts to being an appropriated French term,
'*flâneur*', meaning 'A lounger or saunterer. An idle "man about town"'.[2]

---

[1] Elizabeth Wilson, 'The Invisible *Flâneur*', *New Left Review* 191 (1992), 90–110, p. 94.
[2] *Webster's 3rd New International Dictionary of the English Language* (London: G. Bell
and Sons, 1961), 864; *Concise Oxford Dictionary* (Oxford: Clarendon Press, 1990), 445.

17

Neither describes the *flâneur* as a working artist. Between the early usage of the concept *flâneur* in the mid-nineteenth century, and the appropriation of the idea by contemporary feminists, therefore, the term has been masculinized and undergone particular changes in significance. Why should this be and what implications does the ambiguous gendering of *flânerie* pose for defining a *flâneuse*? The two central theoretical questions of my study thus appear. Can the term *flâneur* encompass both male and female observers of the city or is a separate category of *flâneuse* necessary for understanding of a female or feminine (which are different) urban perspective? And, if a separate category is required, how and why is it distinct from that of *flâneur*? Before embarking on a study of the woman as urban observer in modernist literature, it is thus necessary to investigate the reasons for, and implications of, this gendering of the term as specifically masculine.

Ambiguity, Paradox, and Dialectic in the Definition of the *Flâneur*

A concept approaching that of the *flâneur* is in evidence before the nineteenth century, and indeed a detached, urban observer is common in urban art and literature in England with serials such as *Tatler* and *The Spectator*. Richard Steele and Joseph Addison's *The Spectator* depicted a contemporary urban world from a position of self-assumed authority. Frequenting the coffee-houses of London and commenting on London society, the narrator describes himself as a detached observer: '[t]hus I live in the World, rather as a Spectator of Mankind, than as one of the Species; by which means I have made my self a Speculative Statesman, Soldier, Merchant, and Artizan, without ever meddling with any Practical Part in Life [...] I have acted in all parts of my Life as a Looker-on.'[3] He thus explains that his air of omnipotence is justified by his position in life; having lived long and experienced much he is able to reflect on what he observes from an all-seeing, all-knowing perspective. This position also implies certain character traits manifest in later urban spectators; detachment, boredom, world-weariness. Particularly of note is the spectator's depiction of women in the world he observes. Addison states that women have a

Natural Weakness of being taken with Outside and Appearance [...] false Happiness loves to be in a Crowd, and to draw the Eyes of the World upon

---

[3] No. 1, Thursday, 1 Mar. 1711, *The Spectator*, 4 vols. (republished Oxford: Clarendon Press, 1965, ed. Donald F. Bond), i. 4.

her. She does not receive any Satisfaction from the Applauses which she gives herself, but from the Admiration which she raises in others. She flourishes in Courts and Palaces, Theatres and Assemblies, and has no Existence but when she is looked upon.[4]

By the eighteenth century, public/private distinctions were becoming forceful features of cultural ideology. Certainly *The Spectator* did much to promote the idea of woman as belonging to a safe, domestic environment, defining her as weak-willed and open to dangerous temptations in the newly modernizing city of the Enlightenment. The above passage is interesting in that it describes women as being inherently attracted to the newly developing public world of spectacle and yet immediately detaches any value from this attraction. The woman in public is designated as purely a spectacle, who 'grows Contemptible by being Conspicuous'.[5] The commentator of *The Spectator* is supremely assured of his superior position as a bastion of the burgeoning bourgeois order. It is with such a figure of superiority that the nineteenth-century *flâneur* has been equated by Woolf and Pollock.

Addison and Steele's spectator, however, belongs to the ordered, optimistic culture of Enlightenment London, whereas the *flâneur* exists in the chaotic and bewildering environment of the rapidly industrializing and growing cities of the nineteenth century. The *flâneur* is frequently described as a personification of spectatorial authority, yet this interpretation overlooks the tensions and paradoxes inherent within the term, for, as Benjamin notes, the habitat of the *flâneur* was being destroyed just as he was becoming a recognizable social type, making the *flâneur* by definition someone who is out of place. The urban characters evoked in the work of Charles Baudelaire, which, along with Edgar Allan Poe's 'The Man of the Crowd', has become a meta-text for the discussion of '*flânerie*', exhibit this paradox of the scopically authoritative yet wandering and placeless *flâneur*, whose habits result from a mixture of reaction against, dependency on, and anxiety in, bourgeois culture. These complexities are essential to an understanding of the concept of the *flâneur*, and are interlinked with the themes of modernity, spectacle, and gender, implying an instability in his sense of superior, masculine self-identity.

Although the characteristics of the *flâneur* are implied by Baudelaire, the poet never actually defines him as a type, despite categorizing a range of related yet distinct urban spectators; the artist, dandy, collector, 'man of the crowd', prostitute, widow, and rag-picker for example. Male and female, authoritative and marginal, they all have in common a detached

---

[4] No. 15, Saturday, 17 Mar. 1711, *The Spectator* (1965), i. 67–8.   [5] Ibid. 69.

bohemian existence, a lack of place in bourgeois society and an aura of isolation. Part of the difficulty in defining urban spectators in Baudelaire is the result of slippages of meaning in translation. Baudelaire does not use the term *flâneur* but instead that of 'dandy', an English concept taken up and expanded by the French after the loss of favour in London culture of the archetypal dandy Beau Brummell. Yet the English dandy, marked by his attitude of boredom and attention-seeking if unostentatious self-display, is very different from Baudelaire's petty bourgeois. The latter is distinguished by the fact that he works in the city (as artist or writer) and that he is fascinated and exhilarated by the urban experience. To avoid confusion I shall therefore distinguish the two by using the term 'dandy' for the original aristocratic form and *flâneur* for that of Baudelaire. This also seems to be Benjamin's policy, as he relates the concept of the *flâneur* to the art journalists working for the *feuilletons*.

An important difference between the 'dandy' and the *flâneur* is that the latter observes whilst the former displays himself for observation. Ellen Moers's extensive study of dandyism describes the function of the dandy as a reassertion of upper-class superiority in times of challenge to the social order.[6] The concentration on appearance was an attempt to proclaim and justify social position on purely visual grounds. The dandy did not want to merge with the crowd but display his distinction from it. The French dandy or *flâneur* takes on certain characteristics of the dandy (his display of elegance, leisure, and wit) yet combines them with a function. Dana Brand has pointed out that there is no English equivalent to this French 'artist-dandy', Victorianism according little value to the conspicuous display of idle leisure.[7] Rather than elegantly dressed artists populating cafés on grand streets, the London observer tends to be a more shadowy figure haunting the underworld of the working class, a social investigator or rather criminal 'man of the crowd'. It is possibly this distinction that provides another reason for the apparent impossibility of an empirical *flâneuse*. Again the assertion is too broad, as numbers of women did enter such urban spaces as social investigators in the role of health visitors, social theorists, and public officials. However, it must be admitted that Paris offered, if not greater freedom then greater tolerance than London for female *flânerie*, and the female appropriation of the stance of the dandy becomes a feature of modernist works in which women writers assert their position as public artists.

---

[6] Ellen Moers, *The Dandy in Literature: Brummell to Beerbohm* (London: Secker and Warburg, 1960).

[7] Dana Brand, *The Spectator and the City in Nineteenth Century American Literature* (Cambridge: Cambridge, 1991).

Baudelaire's Urban Observers

Baudelaire has been credited with recognizing the aesthetic possibilities of modernity, influencing the Naturalist and Impressionist schools, and with heralding a new sensibility of urban life. In a Western world in which both people and place were classified by a belief in physiognomy, the importance of visual effect resulted in a cultural trope of spectacle/spectatorship. The developing consumer society appealed directly to the visual sense and the 'consumption of the eye' was a crucial element of nineteenth-century commodification. The interest in optics itself became a commodity as entertainment became increasingly aligned with spectacle, resulting in leisure activities such as panoramas and dioramas, 'toys' such as the kaleidoscope and stereoscope, the growth of the tourist industry and the development of large, spectacular department stores. Such features relate to the mass culture of bourgeois society. The city in Baudelaire is marked by three main experiences; ephemerality, transience, and the chance encounter. This latter is highly disconcerting, offering a double of the urban observer that belies his stance of objective detachment, locating him too as merely another face in the crowd. In accordance with his fascination for the spectacle of the modern city, many of the personae in Baudelaire's work are urban observers. Baudelaire's subjects tend to be people alienated from bourgeois society but therefore able to observe it from an external position. Several figures, categorized through their own physiognomy, occur frequently.

Baudelaire's artist is an example of a new urban mentality that coincided with a new physicality of the city, both characterized by fragmentation and ephemerality. In *Les Fleurs du Mal* (1861), the essay on Constantin Guys, 'Le peintre de la vie moderne' (1863), and the prose poems of *Le Spleen de Paris* (1862), Baudelaire depicts the mid-nineteenth-century Paris of spectacle and display and its underside of isolation and dejection, finding material for the modern artist in its inhabitants, structure, and philosophy.[8] The works of Guys depict the social world of modern Paris yet also reflect the modern tempo and structure of everyday life. Rarely accorded much critical attention by contemporary art historians, Guys's drawings are celebrated by Baudelaire for capturing the ephemeral nature of modernity. Many seem little

[8] Quotations throughout the text are taken from Charles Baudelaire, *The Flowers of Evil*, trans. by James McGowan, intro. by Jonathan Culler (Oxford: Oxford, 1993) and *Parisian Prowler*, trans. Edward K. Kaplan (Athens, Ga.: University of Georgia Press, 1989). All quotations from primary works in discussion will be cited parenthetically through the text, with editions referred to noted in the bibliography.

more than sketches, in which figures are outlined against just a hint of setting, their social status or position indicated primarily by the silhouette of their dress and stance. Faces too are not detailed but merely suggested by the outlines of features. This style captures the impressions that strike the mind of modern life, with no time to study carefully the unknown figures that pass by on the street. For it is this position within the crowds on the street that marks Baudelaire's peripatetic 'artist of modern life'. The scenes he portrays reflect the different public areas of Paris experienced during a day's strolling through the city; the fashionable Bois de Boulogne, parks by day, cafés, restaurants, theatres, parks by night, and the world of the *demi-monde*, factories, and brothels. As Griselda Pollock argues, it is in this range of subjects that the artist is definable as male, only the respectable public areas of the gardens in the day, operatic theatre, and bourgeois restaurant being commonly frequented by the female artist.

A specific masculine trait of the artist that Baudelaire emphasizes is his organization of the experiences he receives. Walking through the city and bombarded by the vivid spectacle around him, the artist seems something of a passive figure, his mind a *tabula rasa* open to sensory impressions. Yet Baudelaire constantly notes the critical and selective process of the artist that serves to control and order the mass of impressions and people encountered day to day. The 'automatically amassed sum of physical experiences' is structured by an 'analytical power' (*MHLB* 29). This combination of passive receptiveness and selective re-creation is manifest in Baudelaire's description of Guys as a '*man of the world*' who 'wants to know, understand and appreciate everything that happens on the surface of this globe of ours' (30), and who reproduces the world he perceives in such a way that his experiences are 'classified and rearranged in order, are harmonized and subjected to [...] compulsory formalization' (36). The artist-*flâneur* Baudelaire describes has the same freedoms as Addison and Steele's spectator and also aspires to complacent superiority, his aesthetic style still illustrating a desire for controlling knowledge.

Edgar Allan Poe's story 'The Man of the Crowd' (1840) provided Baudelaire with a paradigm for the experience of the encounter in the city. It anticipates the preoccupations of modernity in its depiction of universal alienation in the city and the isolation of the observing artist. Like Addison and Steele's 'spectator', Poe's narrator begins by justifying his practice of observation and interpretation of the crowd in modern life. Having just recovered from a serious illness, he remains detached from, yet vividly observant of, the events around him, both as a result of his long seclusion from society and of his feverishly heightened senses.

22

Sitting in the window of a café, to relieve the boredom of his enforced leisure he studies the people who pass by, inferring their professions and social status from the outward appearance given by their clothes, stance, and expression. One man, however, confounds the narrator's interpretation, escaping the physiognomist's skill by his anonymity.

Benjamin's writing on Baudelaire and the physiognomies and caricatures that fill the *feuilletons* describes the practice of physiognomy as essentially ideological, categorizing and familiarizing the urban crowd into a coherent, readable, and thus harmless phenomenon. The failure of this practice reveals the opacity of the crowd, making it seem chaotic and fearful, disruptive of the social order. Certainly Poe's narrator is disturbed by this 'faceless' man and follows him, determined to fix his identity. The man leads him on a long journey through the London streets, never stopping in a particular place but moving through a variety of areas. Finally pausing, he looks at the narrator who suffers a moment of disturbing recognition and feels that he is looking at his own reflection. For in this act of mutual observation, the man becomes not just an object for interpretation but a spectator himself, objectifying the narrator. His anonymity also reflects that of the narrator, whose detachment from society (the very thing that caused his sense of superiority and assured his ability to categorize others) has resulted in his own lack of understandable identity, having no professional or familial position. A gap is thus discovered between the social identities attributed to people and their own sense of identity. The physiognomical practice is devalued as an ordering force and the crowd returns to its faceless mass, the masks of identity uncovered. The man the narrator has followed is indeed both the 'man of the crowd' and the 'man in the crowd', and he, the narrator, and the crowd come to form a sort of three-way mirror.

The urban environment of 'The Man of the Crowd' is entirely male populated. Women, however, are central figures in the urban poetry of Baudelaire and often disturbing presences. Considering the relevance of Poe's urban tales to Baudelaire it is surely significant that the chance encounter in Baudelaire's poems is often with a woman rather than man of the crowd. As Baudelaire is acknowledged as a formative influence on both the socio-historic depiction of modernity and the idea of the artist portraying it, it seems crucial for any redefinitions of modernism to recognize the role of female observers in the city in Baudelaire's poems and essays. Benjamin never admits the possibility of a *flâneuse* (and in fact defines it in such a way as to preclude this possibility) but then Baudelaire himself never defines the *flâneur* either. His urban observers display the traits and characteristics of the *flâneur* between them. Benjamin is selective of those he employs. Janet Wolff marks the prominence

encounters with women

of women as subjects for Baudelaire, noting that '[m]odernity breeds, or makes visible, a number of categories of female city-dwellers', notably the prostitute, widow, old woman, and lesbian.[9] Although types, these figures are all marginal in society and observers. Baudelaire treats them ambiguously, sympathetic to the widow and old woman, variously damning and admiring of the prostitute and the lesbian. Particularly disturbing is '*la passante*', the unknown woman who cannot be easily defined and thus controlled. However, despite her perceptive discussion of women in Baudelaire, Wolff accepts the common assertion that his views on women manifest a 'classic misogynist duality'.[10] It is my belief that the complexity of Baudelaire's depiction of women (his contradictory comments on the prostitute and lesbian, the shock experienced during the mutual gaze with the *passante*, the relation of the mannish lesbian to the effeminate dandy) requires further investigation, and that it implies a concern with the place of women in the city and art of modernity that goes beyond personal prejudice. Degraded, marginalized, or alienated as they may be, all the women common to Baudelaire's work are observers, and through them it is possible to question the assumption of the masculinity of public space and to formulate the beginnings of the conceptual idea of a *flâneuse*. Just as Poe blurs the distinctions between observer and object, individual and mass in 'The Man of the Crowd', setting up a dialectical relationship between the two, a similar dialectical relationship marks the encounters of poet and woman in Baudelaire.

Like the narrator of 'The Man of the Crowd', ordering the crowd by categorizing it through physiognomy, Baudelaire sees the artist of modern life as ordering the disruptiveness of the prostitute by observing her and categorizing her into certain spaces and characteristics. Thus he defines the 'young toast of the town', the cynical brothel girls and at the lowest level the women ravaged by illness, age, and alcoholism. Yet there is certainly ambivalence in Baudelaire's attitude to the prostitute and it is useful to distinguish between the prostitute as social figure and the prostitute as concept in this regard. To the prostitute herself, Baudelaire responds with violent loathing, yet, as Benjamin argues, the implications of her theoretical position in relation to modern society fascinate him. In conceptual terms the prostitute exhibits similar characteristics to male urban observers; like the dandy the courtesan displays herself in finery; like the man of the crowd she manifests the 'evil' underside of commercial culture; like the rag-picker the less successful prostitute is destitute, exhausted, and dependent on the scraps left to

---

[9] Wolff, 'The Invisible *Flâneuse*', 41.   [10] Ibid. 43.

her. Most notably the prostitute corresponds to the narrator-poet him-self, a metaphor for the role of the artist as she walks the streets for the material of her profession and offers her constructed body as a com-modity in the same way that Baudelaire regarded the artist as prostitut-ing his work in publication. A dialectical relationship can be seen developing between poet and prostitute, therefore, as certain traits interrelate them.

Despite the conceptual parallels between the prostitute and the *flâ-neur*, however, in his poetry Baudelaire denies her the power of observa-tion, entirely objectifying her. Benjamin notes Baudelaire's equation of the prostitute with the spectacle of consumer society. This is most evident in the poems of *Les Fleurs du Mal* written to Jeanne Duval, in which she is constantly described as an inanimate, purchasable com-modity. Consequently her act of sight is denied. For example, in 'Avec ses vêtements', the poet writes that her 'polished eyes are made of charming stones' that are precious like diamonds, gold, or steel, referring to them as commodities with surfaces that reflect rather than actively see or observe (*FE* 54). A similar image occurs in 'Je te donne ces vers', in which the woman has 'eyes of jet' (80). In Benjaminian terms, a parallel can be drawn between the eyes of the prostitutes in these poems and the windows of the shopping industry. Windows, from which people look out, have traditionally served in literary symbolism as metaphors for eyes and vision. Shop windows, however, are not symbols of active vision. Instead they display and offer themselves to be gazed into, reflecting the desires of those who look into them. In the examples given, the eyes of women resemble the artificially lit windows of the shop, enticing yet unseeing and displaying themselves for consumption.

In 'Le Peintre de la vie moderne' Baudelaire lists the dominant sub-jects of the artist and considers each in turn. Included are sections on 'The Dandy', 'The Woman', and 'Women and Courtesans'. In what is essentially a eulogy on the conception of 'womanhood' he describes the 'woman' as an idealized object, 'a divinity, a star' although, interestingly, this 'ideal' is always clothed, her fashions forming part of delight. This view is not a derogatory one and the female concern with outward display is not a sign of triviality or frippery for Baudelaire. His question, '[w]hat poet would dare [...] to distinguish between the woman and her garb?' (*MHLB* 60), does not, in context, seem ironic. Rather than equating woman with her dress in order to reduce her to the status of fashion, he regards the two as coexistent. The masquerade of dress is thus, for Baudelaire, part of womanhood itself and what increases her fascination. For the woman is consequently a powerful and creative figure and also enigmatic, as elusively transient as her fashions.

[handwritten margin notes: "Women & masquerade"]

[handwritten margin notes: "women more athues? of modern city life [and commodity culture]"]

The positive role of the 'masquerade' as a method for women's public self-presentation has been highlighted by innovatory work by Mary Ann Doane.[11] Through the masquerade women can subvert the superior possession of the male gaze by themselves controlling the image that it objectifies. The male observer is denied possession of the woman because he is only presented with certain façades, fragments of her identity put on display. She too is thus an artist, and through the masquerade of femininity does not so much objectify herself and see herself through the eye of the male, as construct herself and present herself as she wants to be seen. What is also interesting is that this union of inner and outer, of woman and her dress, seems to overcome the distinction between subject and object that leads to Poe and Baudelaire's suspicion of physiognomy. Woman is thus particularly powerful and familiar with the modern city of spectacle, and for Baudelaire, as later for the surrealists, more intrinsically unified than man. It is again suggestive of the actual androgyny of the *flâneur* that this practice of the masquerade and constructing an appearance is a trait of the dandy-artist.

If this self-sufficiency is a reason for Baudelaire's admiration of the woman, it also explains his need to denigrate and condemn her. In the following section of 'Le peintre de la vie moderne', then, 'In Praise of Cosmetics', he trivializes woman's interest in appearance. Assuming an all-knowing authority, he implies that man is always aware of women's 'tricks and artifices' (63) but encourages them for their attractiveness. In 'Women and Courtesans' Baudelaire describes the public women of modernity predominantly available to the male gaze. He notes a moral hierarchy of public spaces and the women who represent them. At the top of the scheme are the upper-class theatres where women are afforded one of their few opportunities to be legitimate observers, but are described as 'as brilliant as portraits, set in their theatre-boxes as if in frames' (65), on display rather than watching the performance. In this respect then the bourgeois woman is equated with women towards the bottom of the scale, courtesans at the music-halls, both displaying themselves for the male gaze. In such places women parade themselves as objects but with the intention of creating a desired effect. Simultaneously, this parading in the interior of the entertainment hall is a displacement of the 'streetwalking' of both the prostitute and the peripatetic observer. For, ironically, Baudelaire describes the courtesan, who makes a commodity of self-display, as actually extremely observant. Of

---

[11] Mary Ann Doane, 'Film and the Masquerade: theorising the female spectator', *Screen* 23/3–4 (1982). Doane's discussion is based on Joan Rivière's essay 'Womanliness as a Masquerade', *International Journal of Psychoanalysis* 10 (1929).

the courtesans of 'Valentino's', 'Casino's', and 'Prado's', he states that, '[t]hey come and go, pass and repass, their eyes wide and astonished like the eyes of animals; they have an air of seeing nothing, but they scrutinize everything' (66). They resemble the scavengers of the urban wasteland (the cat, the pigeon, the rat), with eyes that are quick, observant, and accurate, adapted to the climate of urban life.

It is not only the prostitute who undercuts the stable definition of the male urban observer in Baudelaire's work. In *Le Spleen de Paris*, at the beginning of the prose poem 'Les Foules', for example, he states that the only man who enjoys being within the crowd 'is he whose good fairy endowed him, in his cot, with a bent for disguises and masking, hatred of domestic humdrum, and *wanderlust*' (*PP* 58, 59). A similar desire to escape the confines of the domestic environment, coupled with a wanderlust expressed through forays into the city, or further afield in foreign travel, is a common feature of New Woman fiction and the works of women writers in the early twentieth century. Virginia Woolf's essay 'Street Haunting', for example, epitomizes the perspective of the woman amidst the crowd, empathizing to the point of identification with strangers glimpsed in passing in the city, and becoming 'an enormous eye' that can 'put on briefly for a few minutes the bodies and minds of others'.[12] Woolf's 'enormous eye' seems to follow from Baudelaire's man of the crowd, the 'active and productive poet' who, unlike the 'egoist who is locked inside himself', identifies with the mass, making all its traits his own. He is both the mirror and the soul of the crowd, and 'can enter the personality of anyone else, whenever he likes' (58, 59). One of the most ecstatic identifications the poet performs is 'the saintly prostitution of the soul when it yields itself entire, in all its poetry and all its charity, to the epiphany of the unforeseen, the unknown passer-by'. This passer-by is invoked in the poem 'A une passante' (*FE* 188, 189) as specifically female.

The prose piece 'Les Veuves' (*PP* 60, 61) and the poem of the same year 'Les Petites Vieilles' (*FE* 180, 181) centre on women who have been reduced in old age to the city's waste. Women are objects of fleeting desire as much as other urban commodities, left as rubbish in the gutter when no longer wanted. Part of the detritus of the city, they only retain interest and value for the rag-picker sensibility of a Baudelaire. The poem situates the old women in an explicitly urban setting, as they 'creep' in the 'sinuous coils of the old capitals' and 'trudge' through 'the chaotic city's teeming waste'. These women are themselves part of

---

[12] Virginia Woolf, 'Street Haunting' (1930), repr. in *Collected Essays*, 4 vols., ed. by Leonard Woolf (London: Chatto and Windus, 1967), iv. 71, 81.

this mass of urban excreta, 'dislocated wrecks' and 'hunchbacked freaks'. Seemingly the antipode of the tall, elegant *passante*, they too, however, are briefly passing images and 'part of the swarming tableau of the town'. Empathizing with them as fragile, alienated souls, the poet-narrator follows them, changing from describing them in the third-person narrative to addressing them directly as 'my family! my fellow-minds!'. The material is similar to that of 'Les Veuves', in which the narrator observes lonely widows in the public spaces of the city, two of whom he follows. The first is an old woman who reflects the narrator in that she has a 'masculine character' and 'the habits of an ageing bachelor'. Her solitude has resulted in a certain freedom and she eats in a cheap café, goes to a public reading-room and sits alone in the park. Like the *flâneur* that Benjamin describes, the woman has made of the public world her own personal interior, where she eats, reads, and relaxes. The second woman is younger and elegant, and stands by the rail outside a concert-hall to enjoy the sounds from within, forgoing entry in order to purchase gifts for her son. Both women keep themselves aloof from the crowd, the former sitting carefully away from it and the latter separating herself by ignoring it. They are isolated in their grief, equally alienated whether accompanied or alone. They enjoy a peripatetic existence yet at the price of an outsider status.

Georg Simmel and the Urban Psyche

Baudelaire's urban poetry, commonly employed by critics to assert the maleness of the urban walker/observer/artist, instead introduces paradoxes and tensions that highlight various feminine aspects of *flânerie*, as well as registers a common and constant female presence in the city. This female presence became a subject of increasing interest, and the preponderance of social, cultural, psychological, and medical theories concerned with sexual and gender difference at the turn of the century are evidence for an apparent crisis in gender identity that coincides with the development of an urban modern culture. Andreas Huyssen has interpreted the image of women in the late nineteenth century, and particularly urban women *en masse*, as shaped by male anxiety: '[t]he fear of the masses in this age of declining liberalism is always a fear of woman, a fear of nature out of control, fear of the unconscious, of sexuality, of the loss of identity and stable ego boundaries in the mass.'[13] Popular news and theories tended to equate mass culture with feminization. In particular

---

[13] Andreas Huyssen, *After the Great Divide* (London: Macmillan, 1986), 52.

the crowd in all its strata was depicted as female. *Punch* cartoons of proletarian protests in London in the 1880s and 1890s depicted a raging mob of grotesque women, alluding to stereotypical images of the guillotine mobs of the French Revolution. More frequently the female crowd on the streets were shoppers and prostitutes, indistinguishable both in terms of their adherence to fashion and their uncontrolled desires. Zola's *Au bonheur des dames* (1883) contained evocative scenes of madly desirous shopping mobs, frivolous women who lost their moral sensibilities and were the ruination of their hard-working husbands. Less explicitly, Gustave Le Bon's *Psychologie des foules* (1895) and Freud's *Mass Psychology and Ego Analysis* (1921) continued the identification by describing the mass with highly feminine adjectives. Common to all these studies is the orientation of 'femininity' towards the unconscious, amorality, materiality, and sexuality, and of 'masculinity' towards rationality and consciousness. The opposition of masculinity and femininity was reinforced through this equation of social experiences with biological characteristics. Gender distinctions were thus paralleled with other binary oppositions such as interior/exterior and passive/active.

The theoretical discussions *of* mass culture at the turn-of-the-century are not explicitly gendered, as in fact representations *by* mass culture often are. Georg Simmel, and the 'Frankfurt School' theorists he influenced, presented themselves as advocates of new forms of sociocultural study that were able to observe society and its workings/relations as a structure of discourses. As such they assumed a position outside those discourses (art, politics, psychology), which were informed by, or in reaction to, the ideologies of mass culture. Yet a completely external critical stance, like the *flâneur*'s attempt at an external and objective perspective, is impossible, and such theories of the city and crowd necessarily remain within the parameters of male authoritative thought. Simmel was not insensitive to the position of women in the urban environment. He wrote several articles on the women's movement as a public concern, attracted large numbers of female students to his lectures, and situated himself within 'female' turn-of-the-century culture with his weekly salon engagements. Yet, although cultural criticism identified the materialist spirit of mass culture and the domination of the male, bourgeois controllers of production, in its images and language it accepted the idea of 'feminized' culture *en masse*, and identified with the (intellectual, male) individual standing apart from it.

Baudelaire's urban dwellers have been categorized by Benjamin as the neurasthenic, the big city personality, the consumer, and the rag-picker. These types are also delineated by Simmel in his essay 'The Metropolis and Mental Life' (1905), where he defines certain characteristics as specific to the urban environment and its emphasis on display and ever-changing spectacle. He describes the modern personality as constantly buffeted by the speed and ever-changing variety of the urban experience: 'the psychological foundation of the metropolitan personality type is the *increase in nervous life*, which emerges out of the rapid and unbroken change in external and internal stimuli'.[14] Crucial to Simmel's idea of the neurasthenically inclined city personality is the creative influence of the urban environment, which makes the individual hypersensitive to stimulatory forces. The experience of the Baudelaire protagonist, who perceives the external world through the frame of his own subjectivity, is reasserted in Simmel's statement that 'the essence of modernity as such is psychologism, the experience and interpretation of the world in terms of the reactions of our inner life, and indeed as an inner world, the dissolution of fixed contents in the fluid element of the soul, from which all that is substantive is filtered and whose forms are merely forms of motion'.[15] However, this immediate response frequently is lost in protective reaction on the part of the individual, who distances himself from the attacks of his environment through a psychological detachment or indifference that Simmel cites as the 'blasé' attitude. This distancing seems a biological rather than conscious reaction, however, the result of nerves being dulled from excessive exposure to stimulation. Two states can then develop: normally this is a need for constantly new stimulation for its own sake, that can briefly awaken dulled nerves; pathologically it is the fear of the environment in agoraphobia.

Links with the Baudelairian observer are apparent in Simmel's explanation of the observer's stimulated yet burdened senses, his need for the city experience yet desire to be surrounded by the closeness of the crowd whilst remaining mentally aloof from it. Much of Simmel's theory of the urban personality is concerned with the relation of space and distance (or focus). The urban character retreats to a distanced, private space; psychologically into mental detachment, and, increasingly, literally into the bourgeois interior. The artistic gaze, for Simmel, needs this detachment in order to find formalized beauty in the city, which 'becomes aesthetic only as a result of increasing distance, abstraction and sublimation'.[16] David Frisby, in his fascinating study on Simmel and the relation of protective distance to aestheticist tendencies, suggests that the

---

[14] Georg Simmel, 'The Metropolis and Mental Life' (1905), repr. in Richard Sennett (ed.), *Classic Essays on the Culture of Cities* (Englewood Cliffs, NJ: Prentice Hall, 1969), 47–60.

[15] Georg Simmel, *Philosophische Kultur* (1911), quoted in David Frisby, *Simmel and Since* (London: Routledge, 1992), 66.

[16] Georg Simmel, *The Philosophy of Money*, quoted in Frisby, *Simmel*, 108.

development of the city personality from sensitivity to indifference can be paralleled with the early and later movements of modernity.[17] Whereas the hypersensitive, creative individual in the city street reflects the fascinated, absorbed, wandering '*flâneurs*' of Baudelaire, the self-protective, withdrawn, filtering, and ordering individual is comparable with a more detached and intellectual perspective, that Frisby identifies with Impressionism, as well as Simmel's own theoretical stance, calling him 'a sociological *flâneur*'.[18] This idea of the changing perspective of the modern observer-artist is continued by Benjamin, in his descriptions of the *flâneur* as, first, 'man of the crowd' and, later, 'man at the window'. It is important for the development of the critical metaphor of this urban observer as modern artist that this mental, and metaphorically physical, withdrawal depends on a degree of leisure. As Frisby notes, '[r]eserve and indifference as defence mechanisms in the metropolis are most likely to be used by those social strata, who, from a relatively secure social position, can afford to adopt this response'.[19] Both Simmel and Benjamin, then, can be seen to contribute to the definition of the modern artist as leisured, bourgeois city observer. However, this figural concept, although described in terms of the *flâneur*, is characterized by traits subtly distinct from those of the latter. Detachment, self-assertion and control are now prominent, in comparison to the wandering, subversive ambiguity of the earlier concept of *flâneur*.

Simmel describes a modern psyche that is socially located within the urban environment of the metropolis. It is unsystematic in that it pays little adherence to specific geographic or historical conditions and as such can be applied as a cultural conceptualization of the modern European capital, be it London, Paris, or Berlin. This blurring of boundaries results in a certain continuity of modernity amongst cities and even over time. It is in this same conceptual sense that the *flâneur* can be regarded as unbound by geographical and temporal place. As a social phenomenon, for example, Benjamin can locate him specifically in mid-nineteenth-century Paris, yet as a concept he relates him to the Paris of the Second Empire, Poe's London and Hoffmann's Berlin, as well as making him a metaphor for the modernist artist of the twentieth century. The paradoxes inherent within the *flâneur* correspond to contemporary concerns with the means available to the mind to adapt to the conditions of the modern environment, and the way these were taken up

[17] David Frisby, *Sociological Impressionism: A Reassessment of Georg Simmel's Social Theory* (London: Routledge, 1992).
[18] Ibid., p. ix.
[19] David Frisby, *Fragments of Modernity: Theories of Modernity in the Work of Simmel, Kracauer and Benjamin* (Cambridge: Polity Press, 1985), 83.

into artistic debate over the representation of modernity. It is this debate that has been interpreted as the choice between 'realism' and 'impressionism' or abstract versions of modernism. Urban social theorists such as Simmel and, more recently, Richard Sennett, have diagnosed the experience of modernity and identified an urban consciousness that is highly developed and responds with protective reserve to stimulation. Thus a method of adapting to the urban environment was an intellectualized detachment as opposed to social involvement. This distancing could be manifest in either an analytical or aestheticized response. Examples of the 'artist of modern life' in the late nineteenth century, for example, can be seen in the Naturalist and Impressionist schools, both claiming to depict a 'reality' that differs from conventional realism. Yet this reality is itself still controlled by an omnipotent artist figure. The Naturalist analyses his subject like a physician and details it materially as a long, objectified list. The Impressionist departs from such analysis and constructs reality from his own sensations. The traits of Naturalist and Impressionist emphasis on the perspective of the *flâneur,* for example, are evident in the Impressionist '*flâneur*' figures of James and Proust, the Naturalist observer of Zola, and Benjamin's image of the Naturalist-*flâneur* who 'goes botanizing on the asphalt'.[20]

Richard Shiff's influential study of the ambiguities of Impressionism highlights the fact that although it has been regarded as an art-form that represents nature and modern life through accurate, veridical observation, nineteenth-century critics were also interested in its emphasis on subjectivity.[21] The world of Impressionism is not simply represented, but also objectified according to the subjectivity of the artist. The critic Jules Antoine Castagnary's extensive writing on Impressionism, for example, defined it as an art of sensation but then distinguished between two forms of representing sensation; that resulting from contact with the external world and that which results from extreme subjectivity. The definition of the terms 'subjective' and 'objective' truth in Impressionism is complex, but Castagnary's concern seems to be that Impressionism is 'a mode of expression suitable for some artistic subjects but not for others', and that it is in danger of taking such a detached, subjective position that it breaks with social value and 'becomes incapable of formulating anything other than personal subjective fantasies'.[22]

---

[20] Benjamin, *Charles Baudelaire*, 36.

[21] Richard Shiff, *Cézanne and the End of Impressionism* (Chicago: University of Chicago Press, 1984).

[22] J. A. Castagnary, 'Les Impressionistes', *Le Siècle*, 29 Apr. 1874, quoted in Shiff, *Cézanne*, 4.

It seems plausible to parallel Simmel's social theory with the tendencies of Impressionism, and regard the growing individualism of the artist as stemming from the same cultural climate as the mental isolation of the urban dweller. Certainly this was a connection made by Simmel's contemporaries, David Frisby having unearthed a largely forgotten but insightful text that locates Impressionism in relation to Simmel and the urban context, and associates it with a social detachment that suggests an aestheticized, harmonizing view of life. Frisby quotes Richard Hamann's *Der Impressionismus in Leben und Kunst* (1907) to indicate the hegemonic artistic perspective in European capitals: '[m]odern impressionism in art and life is totally at home in metropolitan centres—Berlin, Vienna, Paris, London.'[23] It seems to me that this is the ultimate end of the *flâneur*; originally both observer and controller of the urban spectacle, as this becomes more and more diversified and fragmentary he withdraws from it, able to assign it coherence only from a panoramic, or detached and totalizing, vantage point and subjectivity. Like the *flâneur*, although rejecting conventional art-forms and conventional society, the avant-garde also depended on it and remained in accordance with its male-individual-public bias.

Walter Benjamin and the Passages of Urban History

A transformation takes place between Baudelaire's representation of city-dwellers and their subsequent theorization by Benjamin. Benjamin approaches a definition of the *flâneur*, equating him predominantly with the Baudelairian artist, yet one that accords as much with his own theories of modernity as with the socio-historical experience of the city. Benjamin's arcade project was an attempt to 'map' the city of modernity, 'a panoramic vision of the city'.[24] Benjamin the surrealist collects together the images of the city that the *flâneur* presents to him, to be left with a vast array of past objects, buildings, and spaces that he then attempts to reassemble into illuminating order. As Susan Buck-Morss illustrates, the arcade work was deeply informed by political interest in contemporary society and should be read as a description of the origins of this society as well as a history of Second Empire Parisian culture. In particular she cites examples of how Benjamin's description of the *flâneur* altered over the thirteen years of his writing on Paris, the version in the late essay on Baudelaire 'Paris of the Second Empire' indicating a stronger Marxist bias than that in early notes for

---

[23] Frisby, *Fragments of Modernity*, 84.   [24] Gilloch, *Myth and Metropolis*, 102.

the *Passagen-Werk*. Benjamin's definitions are not only fragmentary but also essentially incomplete, the *Passagen-Werk* being unfinished at his death. His analysis is a collection of rags and the obsolete, made up of fragments.

Benjamin's study of the *flâneur* begins in the two essays of *Charles Baudelaire: Lyric Poet in the Era of High Capitalism*, 'The Flâneur' and 'On Some Motifs in Baudelaire', the second of which was a revised version of the first in response to criticisms by Adorno. The urban observer of 'The Flâneur' is a 'gentleman of leisure' characterized by a fascination and ability to empathize with the crowd. This definition alters subtly but significantly in the revised version, however, to illustrate the condition of the male urban observer as a middle-class figure of scopic authority who is threatened by the environment of modernity. The first description of the urban observer as 'man of the crowd' is a concept reputedly derived from the urban figures represented in the poetry of Baudelaire, but the later definition transforms Baudelaire's city-dwellers and relates the urban observer not so much to the man *in* the crowd but a man *at* the window. In the later essay the *flâneur* is almost entirely Benjamin's own construction, and is removed from within the city crowd. Having first defined the *flâneur* as a man of the crowd in the manner of Baudelaire or Poe, Benjamin does a U-turn to state: 'Baudelaire saw fit to equate the man of the crowd, whom Poe's narrator follows throughout the length and breadth of nocturnal London, with the *flâneur*. It is hard to accept this view. The man of the crowd is no *flâneur*.'[25]

Whereas in the first essay then, it is the man of the crowd that is most explicitly connected with the *flâneur*, in the second it is the man of leisure, perhaps the result of Benjamin's recognition of a difference between the *flâneur* as a metaphor for the dialectical urban aesthetics (closely related to twentieth-century surrealism) that he was constructing, and as a nineteenth-century urban man of leisure. In the first essay he 'demanded elbow room and was unwilling to forego the life of a gentleman of leisure' (54), yet was also 'someone abandoned in the crowd' which was 'a narcotic that [could] compensate him from many humiliations' (55). In the second essay, however, the 'elbow room' required by the *flâneur* now becomes more extensive and is a more evident detachment and distinction from the crowd rather than empathy with aspects of it. In the revised description, the *flâneur* that Benjamin discusses is more the man of leisure forced out of the arcades, who increasingly retreats away from the crowd of the street, in an

[25] Benjamin, *Charles Baudelaire*, 128.

attempt to retain a certain individual control and self-order over the chaos of the city street.

The perspective of the man of leisure that Benjamin describes resembles the Steele and Addison spectator. His viewpoint on the city is one of comfort from the familiarity of the 'interior'. Benjamin cites Hoffmann's story 'The Cousin's Corner Window' as an example of this perspective, in which the narrator observes crowded streets from the window of an apartment, and is separated from their enticement and threat by his immobility. This detached observer becomes a metaphor for the second version of the urban observer who retreats to the detachment of the interior as a protection against the shocks of the city. The complexity of, and confusion within, Benjamin's idea of the *flâneur* is really made evident through such references and allusions, which compound temporal and spatial distinctions. Hoffman's urban observer belongs to the early nineteenth century, and remains in possession of the scopic authority accorded Addison and Steele's spectator in the ordered, optimistic culture of Enlightenment London.

But the city of modernity that Benjamin chronicles is the chaotic and bewildering environment of the rapid industrial and commercialization. The *flâneur* cannot be a personification of spectatorial authority within this space. Benjamin himself notes that the habitat of the *flâneur* was being destroyed just as he was becoming a recognizable social type, therefore making the *flâneur* by definition someone who is out of place. The fate of the *flâneur* after the loss of his arcade habitat is a desperate attempt to retain an authoritative urban vision, which he attempts through a retreat to the detached and overlooking position above the city streets, implicitly a retreat to the authority of the past, the spectatorship of the eighteenth-century urban dandy. The moving perspective of the walking urban observer, physically within the city street, is exchanged in this act for the panoramic perspective of a static urban observer, who can gain power and authority only in a position of superior detachment. These problematic palimpsestic layerings of scopic positions that Benjamin sometimes conflates and sometimes differentiates in his discussions of the urban observer have been overlooked in the focus on public and private spheres in relation to the city. The passage from involvement in the city streets to detachment from them can be paralleled with aspects of Georg Simmel's explanation of the metropolitan psyche as possessing stimulated yet burdened senses, needing city experience and desiring to be surrounded by the closeness of the crowd whilst yet remaining mentally aloof from it. The hypersensitive, responsive characteristics of the urban figure Simmel defines reflects the fascinated, absorbed, wandering '*flâneur*' of Baudelaire, but the self-protective withdrawn, and filtering characteristics that develop on from this are comparable with a more detached perspective, that comes later. There thus seems to be both a spatial and a *temporal* dimension to Benjamin's study of the urban observer.

In this detached form of observation, the distinctive element of *flânerie—movement—*is lost, and the observer becomes an immobile figure. The act of walking, as a body *within* the city, seems incompatible with the need to be a totalizing, panoramic, and authoritative viewpoint, of being an eye *observing* it. Moreover, the privileged positions of the past cannot be returned to, and mimicry of them only places the urban observer away from the types of scopic authority that relate to the new modern wasteland. Detachment, self-assertion, and bourgeois control are now made prominent, in comparison to the wandering, subversive, and marginal ambiguity of the Baudelairian *flâneur*.

Indeed the mode of urban observation that Benjamin finally emphasizes as expressive of the modern urban consciousness is actually more analogous to this marginal rather than authoritative urban observer. The figure who takes precedence for Benjamin as the dominant walker of the city in the later stages of modernity is the rag-picker or *chiffonier*. For Baudelaire and for Benjamin, the dandy and the rag-picker mark the progressive demise of the bourgeois subject in the city, at once representing and heroically yet vainly resisting the modern.[26] Benjamin's surrealist rag-picker probably resembles Baudelaire's avant-garde *flâneur* more accurately than the authoritative figure he is usually attributed with. Benjamin himself, in his twentieth-century passionate retrieval and revaluation of the obsolete nineteenth-century arcades, acts as a Baudelaire-inspired rag-picker, concerned with the refuse objects of everyday life and forming a connective relationship with the city in which the urban landscape is regarded as a palimpsest of layered time. This form of urban-observer-artist is not a detached voyeur but rather interacts with the city in what is almost a symbiotic relationship, feeding off the city that he creates from its own fragments. Like the modernist artist and the rag-picker, Benjamin makes a collage out of fragments of urban myth. The categorizing and ordering role of the *flâneur* is taken over by the marginal rag-picker, concerned with the old myths of the city rather than its new phantasmagoria.

---

[26] My argument here accords with that of Diane Chisholm in her excellent essay, 'Obscene Modernism: *Eros Noir* and the Profane Illumination of Djuna Barnes', *American Literature* 69/1 (1997), who describes the *détraqué*, or urban vagrant, as the late development of the *flâneur* and 'the last chapter in the history of bohemian conspiracy', arguing that they are to be distinguished by the fact that 'the *flâneur* gets drunk on the commodity, the *détraqué* on refuse', p. 189.

The prostitute and the *passante* are figures in opposition to, rather than reflections of, the *flâneur*, and are objects of his gaze in the city. Benjamin's discussion of these women of the cityscape in 'The *Flâneur*' focuses on their social position and metaphoric role as personifications of the characteristic aspects of modernity, spectacle, and transitoriness. But either way they are regarded as objects of the gaze and their own perspective of looking is not considered. In 'Some Motifs in Baudelaire', which was to replace the earlier essay in the proposed Baudelaire book, the significance of the woman as object is accentuated. She is a figure of erotic fascination for the urban poet, an urban woman who does not parallel him in detached observation but rather is part of the unseeing mass of the crowd. By then relating this interpretation of the *passante* to the character of Albertine in Marcel Proust's *A la recherche du temps perdu* (19), Benjamin serves to extend the role of woman as object of the poetic urban gaze from the mid-nineteenth century to the modernism of the twentieth century. He quotes Marcel's possessive description of (the frequently elusive) Albertine as, 'the type of the fiery and yet pale Parisian woman, the woman who is not used to fresh air and has been affected by living among masses and possibly in an atmosphere of vice, the kind that can be recognized by a certain glance', and denigrates the glance of both the *passante* and Albertine from active observation to merely 'the look [...] of the object of a love' (125). Benjamin's most explicit conflation of woman and commodity is in a fragment from the arcades project, in which, continuing the analogy of *flâneur* and botanist, he states that the arcade presents an 'organic and inorganic world' full of 'the female fauna of the arcades: whores, *grisettes*, old witch-like saleswomen, female second-hand dealers, *gantieres*, *demoiselles*' as well as the inorganic souvenirs in the shops, all of which, it is implied, are equally for consumption.[27]

Despite the prominence of the *flâneur* in Benjamin's discussion, his only contemporary to consider the concept in detail was Siegfried Kracauer, in his parallel yet less theoretically comprehensive study of the Paris of modernity, *Offenbach and the Paris of his Time*.[28] Kracauer describes Paris as a society of spectacle, in which the gaze was a crucial aspect of culture. Kracauer's *flâneur* is less politically significant than Benjamin's, his observation described as less omnipotent and controlling. Rather than categorizing and familiarizing the crowd, this *flâneur* is more leisured, observing the surface pleasures of the city with a mind

[27] Walter Benjamin, *Das Passagen-Werk*, quoted in Frisby, *Fragments of Modernity*, 241.
[28] Siegfried Kracauer, *Jacques Offenbach and the Paris of his Time*, trans. G. David and E. Mosbacher (London: Constable, 1937).

that registers rather than orders. Without the more 'masculine' traits assigned by Benjamin, the *flâneur* as defined by Kracauer is a more open concept, and commodified observation a universal act, although still dictated by leisure. Furthermore, although Kracauer too makes a distinction between the Parisian *flâneur* of the arcades and that of the later Haussmann boulevards, his emphasis remains on the feminine aspects of the concept. He notes that in the apolitical, commercial spectacle of the 1860s boulevards the act of display, enhanced by fashion and cosmetics, led to the mingling of bourgeois city-dwellers and courtesans, often indistinguishable from each other and, inferentially, in conceptual terms all urban observers.

Simmel and Benjamin's writings indicate the difficulties involved in asserting a dichotomy between a feminine mass-culture and masculine high/modernist-culture. The neurasthenic, the city-dweller, and the consumer are all connected with traits described as 'feminine' such as superficiality, hysteria, and covetous desire, yet also connect with the anxiety and thus detachment of the male urban dweller. The problem centres around just what qualifies experiences or phenomena as definable in terms of gender distinctions. The 'spectacle' has been connected with the 'feminine'; presumably due to the idea of women in the nineteenth-century city as displaying themselves as objects of an erotic gaze (as prostitutes, performers, débutantes) and 'for sale'. Yet, in the same period, the crowd that consumes the city spectacle has also been defined as female (the desiring shopper) and enticed to spend. Rather than the female having no place in the city, male writers of the period seemed to emphasize the role of the feminine throughout it. It would almost seem that the intellectual male tried to define himself out of a society that was uncontrollable and thus abhorrent, both the product and the consumer of the commodity world being described as feminine. Nietzsche, for example, compares the urban culture of modernity to the theatrical spectacle, commenting that, 'No one brings along the finest senses of his art to the theatre—solitude is lacking; whatever is perfect suffers no witnesses. In the theatre one becomes people, herd, *female*, pharisee, voting cattle, patron, idiot'[29] (my emphasis). Furthermore, the response of retreat from the spectacle into the subjective self has produced aesthetic techniques that have been interpreted variously as feminine and masculine. The urban figure, who is made a metaphor for the modern artist, is ambiguously gendered as the *flâneur*; masculine as a bourgeois male of privacy and leisure, but feminine as passively

[29] Friedrich Nietzsche, 'Nietzsche contra Wagner', in *The Portable Nietzsche*, ed. Walter Kaufmann (New York: Random House, 1967), 161.

stimulated by the city, dandiacal in dress and on the margins of the public city world.

Feminism and Public/Private Space in the City

The *flâneur* has returned as an object of critical interest only in the late twentieth century, becoming the focus of feminist critiques of hegemonic modernism. Janet Wolff, Griselda Pollock, and Elizabeth Wilson all base their discussion of the *flâneur* within Benjamin's definition, and have been influential in composing the conceptual categories of male modernism and the male artistic 'gaze' that literary and art criticism now employ. Indeed their work has been crucial for encouraging the recognition of the masculine bias of hegemonic modernism, and the subtle techniques and styles women artists used to assert their differing perspectives on the urban experience. For example, Griselda Pollock's study of Impressionist artists and the public spaces of the city argues that women artists such as Berthe Morisot, restricted from involvement in the city, represented their alienation through unconventional angles and perspective that imply enforced detachment (the bars of the balcony for example). However, the straightforward diametrical structure of male/female position she employs means that she overlooks the fact that this use of indirect angles, particularly the high viewpoint, is one characteristic of the Impressionist style and indeed offers a double meaning—it may be a place where the male observer can preserve his visual control and voyeuristic superiority, yet it is also a barrier from involvement with the public spaces observed.

Wolff and Pollock both take up the idea of the *flâneur* as a particularly socio-historical figure, expanding this to cover the characteristics of male modernism. In so doing they conflate the concept of *flâneur* as social figure and *flâneur* as metaphor for the artist. The bourgeois man in the city is described as the 'archetypal occupant and observer of the public sphere',[30] and his characteristic perspective on, and response to, the modern urban world is equated with the artistic style of the male artist. Wolff's seminal essay concentrates on the socio-sexual divisions of the nineteenth century to describe the male domination of the city. Despite noting the social presence of public women in Baudelaire's city—the prostitute and the *passante*—she regards them as diametrically opposed to the position of the *flâneur*, and as commodified objects of his gaze. She does not, for example, reflect that there is a more direct link

---

[30] Wilson, 'The Invisible *Flâneur*', 93.

between the bourgeois woman and the leisure required for *flânerie* than there is for the bourgeois male. The correlation of *flâneur* and artist has resulted in the tendency to overlook the visual perspective of the public woman. For, while adhering to Benjamin's social description of the *flâneur*, Wolff does not follow his subtly distinct use of the concept as a metaphor for a *style* of observation adapted to the modern city. Female artists, as middle-class women, were more restricted in their freedom of the city, and critics have consequently emphasized the representation of the private realm in their work. They concentrate on images of women and domestic spaces in the city (or the lack of them), but do not also examine the connection of women writing and *flânerie* in the urban environment. Wolff states that 'in so far as the experience of "the modern" occurred mainly in the public sphere, it was primarily men's experience', and indeed in so far as the experience of 'the modern' is that delineated by Simmel and followed by Benjamin then her assertion is plausible.[31] Yet Simmel's description of the modern personality is itself an example of the particularly male anxiety over the conditions of public life at the turn of the century. Fragmentary chaos and the bewilderment of the self is indeed the perception of the male observer whose possessive, ordering control of the city is frustrated by the frequent contestation of socio-cultural boundaries. The experience of 'the modern' by women has only been defined in opposition to this gendered version, and hence in acceptance of it. For example, by asserting that female experience concerns the domestic world, critics such as Wolff and Pollock only serve to exclude women from the 'modern' altogether and resituate her in the Victorian home.

Wolff and Pollock's arguments are thus problematic on two counts. Firstly, in terms of the social presence of women in the city, they generally accept the dichotomous public/private structure of gender relations, and this emphasis on the confinement of bourgeois women leads them to disregard evidence of possibilities for female freedom in the city streets as deviant and thus irrelevant (the prostitute) or rare and thus non-representative (cross-dressing artists such as Rosa Bonheur and George Sand). Secondly, as both writers conflate the concept of the *flâneur* with his social manifestation, they fail to distinguish the characteristics of *flânerie* from those of the feminist theory of the controlling male gaze. To accept Benjamin's idea of the *flâneur* as a figure of surveillance is to overlook the fact that Benjamin's text itself is ideological, and based in an attempt to relieve the male anxieties of the turn-of-the-century and modernist period. Wolff and Pollock, therefore, do

---

[31] Wolff, 'The Invisible *Flâneuse*', 37.

not examine fully the concept of the *flâneur* in its transmutations from nineteenth to twentieth centuries. They overlook Benjamin's own admission that the social *flâneur* was a wandering, nostalgic, and dependent figure, both a product and consumer of the society of spectacle. Elizabeth Wilson, in her essay 'The Invisible Flâneur', criticizes Wolff for describing the *flâneur* as a figure of authoritative observation and thus male by definition, as well as for employing the dichotomous concept of separate private/public spheres as evidence for the exclusion of women from the city. Yet all three critics limit their discussion of the *flâneur* by focusing on his identity as a social phenomenon of a brief mid-nineteenth-century period. They disregard the fact that the post-Benjaminian *flâneur* is more influentially a conceptual metaphor for urban observation and walking that extends even to the present day and the *flâneur* of de Certeau's postmodern city. As a metaphor for the experiences and aesthetic styles of an increasingly urban society, characteristics of *flânerie* (adaptability, multiplicity, boundary-crossing, fluidity) place it prominently within a well-established critical debate on masculine/ feminine art-forms.

The motion of *flânerie* reflects the fleeting aspect of the modern, yet this motion is one of walking, of human as opposed to technological movement. In this respect *flânerie* parallels with the idea of the search, and in the abstract wandering in the city this search would seem to be not for place but for self or identity. *Flânerie* can thus be interpreted as an attempt to identify and place the self in the uncertain environment of modernity, what Dorothy Richardson has termed 'pilgrimage', and Virginia Woolf 'street haunting'. Yet a 'pilgrimage' suggests a positive step, the breaking into new territory, whereas 'haunting' is perhaps more forlorn and an attempt to return to something that is lost. To continue this comparison, the 'pilgrimage' is a physical activity that combines walking and hardship over ground and personal fulfilment, the 'haunting' an ethereal one in which the spectre floats above the ground and is detached and immune from the dangers of the cityscape. In these two experiences can be seen the paradoxical aspects of the literary *flâneur*, that so often blurs the walking and stationary urban observer.

The concept of a *flâneuse* that I wish to propound is distinct from the *flâneur* that has been temporally universalized, and has thus become a highly complex concept, as a metaphor for the modern artist. From the examples that I have touched on in this chapter and will discuss in the following chapter, women as observers and artists seem to have increased access to the city as the male artist withdraws from it. The urban landscape of the late nineteenth and early twentieth centuries is even more variable, fleeting, and assaulting than that of the male *flâneur* of nineteenth-century Paris, yet it is a landscape to which women have greater access. The perspective of the *flâneuse* is thus necessarily less leisured, as well as less assured, yet also more consciously adventurous. A reassessment of the figure of the *flâneur* indicates that the concept of the urban spectator is ambiguously gendered. This androgyny undercuts the myth that the trope of the urban artist-observer is necessarily male and that the woman in the city is a labelled object of his gaze, from outside a gendered structure of literature.

2 | The Woman of the Crowd

By the late nineteenth century, women's access to the metropolis was expanding, both in terms of leisure and employment. The New Woman, the working girl, and the female shopper are all types of female presence associated with the city of modernity. They are significant as images of urban women within the city as well as metaphors for female perceptions of the city. Although this new freedom was limited, and subject to the manipulations of employers and the commodity industry, its importance for emancipation should not be overlooked. Women's legitimate participation in city life was an extremely significant divergence from Victorian conventional belief and acquired a great deal of anxious attention from contemporary social commentators, who tended to regard women as becoming overwhelmingly present. Regarded as manifest in huge and growing numbers, the woman in the city was characterized, examined, and theorized into one or more male-authored stereotyped pathological states. I shall argue that the convention of the woman in public as a possessable object continues in these images, which themselves become publicly available tropes for masculine literary and theoretical discourse at the turn of the century. However, I also suggest that the ambiguities of these categories themselves allow for an alternative perception of women's presence in the city, one that suggests the woman as an increasingly autonomous and observing presence.

Pathologizing the Female Crowd

The central position of women in consumer culture, along with an unequally gendered population scale and demands for female emancipation, resulted in widespread concern that expressed itself in the common perception of the female presence in the city as one of a huge, threatening mass. The crowd had been recognized as a potentially threatening political force since the obvious power of the French Revolutions of 1789 and 1848. However, it was not until the 1880s that a discourse of 'crowd psychology' emerged which defined the crowd as a specific phenomenon.[1] Le Bon's *Psychologie des foules*, along with Hippolyte Taine's *Les Origines de la France contemporaine* (1894) and Gabriel Tarde's *On Communication and Social Influence* envisioned the female urban population as a huge, ever-growing mass taking over the streets.[2] Perhaps inevitably, these masses (consumers, workers, spinsters) were then defined in sexualized and pathologized language, dethreatened and made objects for masculine 'scientific' investigation.[3] These 'explanations' of the crowd are not familiarizing, comforting accounts that assure the authority of the onlooker by detailing the outward signs of a type of individual. The crowd is observable but remains frightening, able to subsume the onlooker into its midst.

What is significant about crowd theory is that 'unflattering metaphors were richly sprinkled throughout the writings on crowds' to emphasize the differentiation of the individual from the crowd.[4] These often associated the crowd with the working-class poor, savages, and the insane. Most common, however, were prejudices that were quite explicitly gendered. Women were perceived as increasingly dangerous in the 1890s, evident in large numbers not only in organized groups of the suffrage or strike crowds but also in generalized groups such as shoppers, working girls, and spinsters.[5] Scientific studies of women centred on the

[1] See Susanna Barrows's excellent discussion of social anxiety and the concurrent emergence of sociology, psychiatry, criminal anthropology, and crowd psychology in *belle époque* France in *Distorting Mirrors: Visions of the Crowd in Late Nineteenth-Century France* (New Haven: Yale UP, 1981). She argues that these intellectual discourses arose out of an urgent need for explanation of the perceived conditions of chaos and anomie during the *fin de siècle*. To emphasize the role of crowd psychology as a 'scientific' discipline, theorists employed terminology from other discourses such as medicine and evolutionary science.

[2] Gabriel Tarde, *On Communication and Social Influence*, ed. Terry Clark (Chicago: University of Chicago Press, 1969).

[3] It was Le Bon's study that Freud somewhat idiosyncratically praised as a 'brilliantly executed picture of the group mind' and went on to quote extensively as theoretical basis for his own analysis in *Group Psychology* (1921). *Psychologie des foules* was translated into English as *The Crowd* in 1897, and into thirteen other languages by 1913. It underwent twenty-six reprintings in French by 1920, and sixteen in English by 1926. That it achieved such enormous popularity is an indication of the widespread interest in the crowd throughout European society.

[4] Barrows, *Distorting Mirrors*, 43.

[5] The large number of spinsters in England, largely the result of an unequal male/female birth ratio, were seen as a problematic mass and popularly regarded as the result of the desire of women themselves for emancipation outside marriage. The plight of the numbers of financially unsupported, unmarried women is foregrounded by Gissing in *The Odd Women* (1893). Verbal attacks on spinsters became common after the First World War, when they were described in The *New Statesman*, 24 Sept. 1921, for example, as 'thwarted' and 'superfluous' women. Particularly vitriolic was A. M. Ludovici, in *Woman: A Vindication*

female species as less evolved than the male, and thus less intelligent, less morally reasoning, more emotional, and prone to violence.[6] Tarde and Le Bon, for example, carefully distinguish themselves from the mass by defining their position as that of the detached, rational bourgeois male, and subsequently describing the mass as irrational, excitable, childish, and easily led, all traits they associate with feminine instincts. Le Bon states that 'crowds are everywhere distinguished by feminine character-istics' and Tarde, recalling the sanscullottist crowd of the Revolution, describes the group-mind as at its worst extreme 'when women assemble in the streets [. . .] always appalling in their extraordinary excitability and ferocity'.[7] The *implication* is that women should not be given the oppor-tunity to gather *en masse*. Basically, in the eyes of crowd theorists, women in a group amounted to chaos; if this group was a feminist or political one, then anarchism resulted.

In general, Tarde's theory of crowds can be seen as more discriminat-ing than Le Bon's, as he attempts a distinction between crowds and publics, in which crowds are temporary collectivities of people who have something in common for a transitory period, whereas publics are collectively held sets of beliefs or ideologies. Yet this distinction actually serves to entrench the gendered bias of 'mass', or more appropriately 'mass versus élite' theory. Compared with Le Bon's scaremongering description of the mob crowd, Tarde's definition of a public is tellingly reassuring for a society based on patriarchal norms and values. In intriguing contrast to the raging, changeable female crowd on the streets, Tarde depicts a public as educated, sensible middle-class men in the domestic home: 'they are all sitting in their own homes scattered over a vast territory, reading the same newspaper. What then is the bond between them? This bond lies in their simultaneous conviction or pas-sion and in their awareness of sharing at the same time an idea or a wish with a great deal of other men.'[8] In this image the nineteenth-century male is not part of a primitive mob but neither is he an isolated individual threatened by it. He retains his individuality whilst being supported by the sharing of his beliefs and goals with other, equally educated and knowledgeable men. Tarde does concede the existence of a female public, yet sees it as trivial and less dominant than the male bourgeois public, characterized by the middle-class female consumer

(London: Constable, 1923), who decried them as abnormal and detrimental to the health of society.

[6] Barrows notes that 372 books were written on women in 1890s France alone, half of which were studies of female 'illness', *Distorting Mirrors*, 45–6, 57–9.

[7] Le Bon, *Psychologie des foules*, 44; Tarde, *On Communication and Social Influence*, 287.

[8] Ibid. 278.

absorbed in sentimental novels and fashion magazines.[9] In both cases, therefore, although women's increasing participation in the new semi-public spaces of the late nineteenth-century city is acknowledged, the public woman in a group is also denigrated; on the one hand as part of a mob-like crowd, on the other as an insignificant public manipulated by consumerism.

The tendency to turn the female crowd into a subject for a totalizing, socio-psychological study is one example of the intellectualized detachment diagnosed by Simmel as a means of adapting to the disparate experience of modernity. The social study of the female crowd is the focus of 'Naturalist' novels of the 1880s and 1890s such as Gissing's *The Odd Women* (1893), Zola's *Au Bonheur des Dames* (1883), and Theodore Dreiser's *Sister Carrie* (1900). Yet Gissing, Zola, and Dreiser, in focusing on the significance of the look in the modern city and the influence of gender on perspective, do recognize women's place in the public city. That Naturalism is often dismissed and its interests and techniques regarded as outdated by critics is perhaps the result of its being an aesthetic genre that is dominated by the popular sciences of its time. What is interesting, however, is when art escapes from science and reveals the inadequacies of its theories. I shall argue that Dreiser in particular succeeds to some extent in moving beyond the restrictive conventions of the Naturalist novel form to express the subjectivity of his heroine.

Zola and the Female Consumer

The great nineteenth-century department stores offered an exciting spectacle as palaces of the growing, commercial Western world. However, crowd theorists tend to attempt to disconnect the aesthetic and socio-political possibilities of the department store, rarely reconciling themselves to the new public position of woman unless denigrating them as dupes of commercial industry or hysterical, desirous mobs. The most extended literary survey of the modern social environment of the department store is Zola's *Au Bonheur des Dames*, which compresses the rise of the consumer culture and technologies of the previous

---

[9] Tarde's distinction of 'crowd' and 'public' indicates an alternative conception of society to the simplistic private/public spheres dichotomy. As women entered the streets and public buildings of the city, the private/public ideological model became obsolete. Tarde's distinction reclaims the 'public' as a social and political realm for men by altering its meaning. In doing so, however, it becomes an abstract rather than literal term. The impression left by his distinction is that of women in possession of the streets and men detached in the literally private world of the home.

twenty years into the period 1864–9. Based on the big stores of 'Bon Marché' and 'Louvre' in Paris, and incorporating many of the features of the newly built 'Printemps', the novel depicts the dynamics of a public space permissible, even particularly welcoming, to women. A palace of glass and artificial light, the store is a commercial temple of which woman is both goddess and worshipper. It provides relief from the confinement of the domestic arena and is a place where woman is afforded all the signs of authority. She is served and pandered to, and, as customer, controls the fortunes of consumer society. At the same time Zola implies that this position of authority is merely illusory, and that, rather than controlling the spectacle, the woman is controlled by it, enticed by the careful advertising and arranged displays created by male financiers. Portraying the flood of women entering the city in the legitimate space of the *grand magasin*, Zola also notes the terms on which this new freedom is based; the exploitation of female workers and consumers by a male-dominated commercial world. The spectacle of the department store may provide a feast for the new consuming gaze of the woman, but this gaze is itself controlled and dominated by the masculine institution of the store through its design, layout, and facilities, all structured to entice and guide the female gaze.

Woman's position in the store is thus rendered ambiguously. For the department store owner, Octave Mouret, obsequiousness and subservience to the desires of the female shopper is simply manipulation, for 'if women reigned in [his] shops like a queen, cajoled, flattered, overwhelmed with attentions, she was an amorous one, on whom her subjects traffic, and who pays with a drop of her blood for each fresh caprice' (*LP* 69). Yet the shopper commanded a degree of economic and visual power that should not be seen as negligible. Stores offered a new sensory experience for women, and were liberating for both those working and shopping in them. The balance of positive and negative features of the department store for female emancipation has been the subject of debate of numerous critics, specifically Rachel Bowlby and Anne Friedberg.[10] Bowlby and Friedberg both point to the new access women gained in the city through the department store, the latter even equating the consumer with the *flâneur*: 'the mobilized gaze entered the service of consumption, and space opened for a female *flâneur*—a *flâneuse*— whose gendered gaze became a key element of consumer address.'[11]

[10] See Rachel Bowlby, *Just Looking: Consumer Culture in Dreiser, Gissing and Zola* (New York: Methuen, 1985) and *Shopping With Freud* (London: Routledge, 1993); Anne Friedberg, 'Les *Flâneurs* du Mal(l): Cinema and the Postmodern Condition', *PMLA* 106/3 (1991), 419–31.

[11] Friedberg, 'Les *Flâneurs* du Mal(l)', 420.

The department store represented a spectacle specifically intended for female consumption. Its very existence presumed a female gaze and sensory response, and relied on a female voyeurism and fetishism. In this respect it also allowed for the existence of female desire. Zola's ambivalent representation of the shop crowd shifts awkwardly between support of those who recognize the progress of modernity and can adapt to it, nostalgic sympathy for the values of those who cannot, and voyeuristic delight yet moral outrage at the unleashing of fanatical female desire. The department store becomes a public site for the outlet of previously private desires and the rich fabrics and goods become surrogates for an unattainable desire, Mouret himself. It is perhaps a discomfort with the conception of publicly displayed female desire that resulted in some male writers' apparent need to pathologize the female shopper into a figure with uncontrollable desires, a nymphomaniac of the commodity.

The crowd of female shoppers was popularized by Zola as a mass of 'erotomaniacs', a term coined in the 1880s to define desire for objects of the gaze as a pathological tendency.[12] Zola depicts the customers of 'Au Bonheur des Dames' as overwhelmed by their experience of the goods on display. His evocation of the sensuous female crowd follows the cycle of the sexual act; empty waiting, the ardour of the swelling crowd, the moment of maximum saturation and desire, the discharge of desire in spending, and finally emptiness again. Each morning the sales assistants wait in an almost deserted shop, but by midday the departments begin to fill, increasing to the crush of the afternoon when the women are 'pale with desire' (93) and feverishly pay their 'money from their very flesh' (97). By the dinner hour, the crowd starts to diminish until, at the close of day, as the salesmen count up their earnings, the shop is left in an empty aftermath of 'spent' passion: 'the lace and the underlinen, unfolded, crumpled, thrown about everywhere, made one think of an army of women who had disrobed there in the disorder of some sudden desire' (105). With the store conceived as a place of female desire, its sign flanked by the images of two bare-breasted women, Zola's shoppers are prime examples of female fetishism, rushing to the haberdashery and lingerie departments to remove their gloves and plunge their hands into the luxurious fabrics. Sexual deviance is thus still connected with

---

[12] See Emily Apter, *Feminising the Fetish: Psychoanalysis and Narrative Obsession in Turn-of-the-Century France* (Ithaca, NY: Cornell UP, 1991), 53–5. Apter's fascinating study of the woman shopper as fetishist concentrates on the pathologizing of object fixation once women became voyeurs, displacing their physical desires onto objects of the gaze. Dating the medicalizing of the object-centred gaze as paranoia in the 1880s she notes as a paradigm case Benjamin Ball's 'Erotomania or Erotic Madness', first published as 'De l'éromanie ou folie érotique', in *L'Encéphale* 3 (1883), 129–39.

the 'public woman', extended from the prostitute to the shopper and criminalized for the latter in the psychosomatic disease of kleptomania. Seen as widespread and contagious, arising specifically from the temptations of the consumer spectacle, kleptomania prompted much concern amongst (predominantly male) social commentators. It was a modern, consumer version of the raging desires of the female mob delineated by Le Bon and Tarde.

The presentation of the relation of consumer and commodity in sexual terms is a common one, following from the economic exchange of prostitute and client. One example of this blurring of status is the enigmatic, *passante*-like lady, who sparks the curiosity of the salesmen and who, '[t]all, elegant, dressed with exquisite taste [...] appear[s] to be very rich, and to belong to the best society' (87). The salesmen know nothing about her apart from her appearance, and are unsure whether she is an aristocratic lady or a courtesan. Yet the equation of public woman and prostitute in the world of the department store is a troubled one, and, as Rachel Bowlby suggests, although women in the department store were 'to become in a sense like prostitutes in their active, commodified self-display', they were also 'to take on the one role almost never theirs in actual prostitution: that of consumer'.[13] Mouret himself, for example, is shown as overwhelmed by the sensual crush of the crowd. At one point he leaves his usual position of surveillance at the head of the staircase to plunge into the crowd, where '[h]e lost his breath deliciously, he felt against his limbs a sort of caress from all his customers' (98). He may be the authoritative male figure, yet Zola clearly indicates that the manager is also addicted to, and dependent on, the sensual atmosphere of the store. The metaphor of the prostitute is also extended to cover not only the 'public' woman but also the man who sells to her desiring gaze. In a subtle role reversal, the salesmen take on the traits of the prostitute, vying for customers and trying to attract those most inclined to spend. Moreover, all become 'rag-pickers' in the literal sense, caressing, consuming, or selling the bourgeois 'rags' of rich fabrics.

Zola's meticulous factual research leads to a recognition of the power of the female consumer in the department store, and reveals the tawdry conditions of the existence of the shop-girl, yet it should not be overlooked that he is writing from within the perspective of its own dominant culture. Ultimately his presentation of the female crowd is pathological. Mouret's principle of seduction of his female customers and authority over his female staff is a commercial version of the bourgeois male's belief in his superiority, and it is predominantly

[13] Bowlby, *Just Looking*, 11.

through Mouret's eyes that the crowd is sexualized. By pathologizing the shopper as controlled by the desires instilled in her by the commercial machine, the dominant culture relieves her threat and reasserts its control over the public spaces of the city, and Bowlby perceptively acknowledges that the Naturalist assumption of an objective stance allows writers to 'legitimate their enterprise as properly masculine'.[14] In *Au Bonheur des Dames*, for example, the only woman to escape identification with the desirous prostitute is Denise, a virginal, desexualized working woman who achieves a fairytale marriage with Mouret. The woman in public for Zola, therefore, ultimately remains sexualized or an anathema.

Gissing, Dreiser, and the Shop-Girl

Young, single, and self-supporting, the shop-girl is another subset of the female crowd who represents both a new undefinable class in the city and the commercial culture that has produced her. She is another alienated figure in the city, often an outsider struggling to maintain independence in the submerging crowd, yet also threatening as she cannot be read simply as a manipulated consumer. For although fascinated and attracted by the urban spectacle, the shop-girl is also one of the manipulators. As with the prostitute, she blurs the gendered power structure of the city.

Rachel Bowlby's study of the shop-girl as an alienated worker and part of an undifferentiated urban crowd is important for an awareness of the circumstances of the working girl in the city. However, because of her acceptance of the 'leisured bourgeois' model of the *flâneur*, Bowlby goes on to reject the shop-girl as a viable candidate for a female version of 'just looking'. Yet, as I argued in the previous chapter, the definition of the *flâneur* almost universally employed by feminist critics is problematic, and particularly significant about representations of the shop-girl is that she is often a mobile figure, capably traversing the city. In her excellent defence of the importance of the shop-girl for female emancipation in her article, 'Gissing, the Shopgirl and the New Woman', for example, Sally Ledger calls attention to Monica Madden's frequent and confident travels around London in *The Odd Women*.[15] Whilst working at a drapers in Walworth Road she spends her time off 'in free wandering

---

[14] Bowlby, *Just Looking*, 152.
[15] Sally Ledger, 'Gissing, the Shopgirl and the New Woman', in *Women: A Cultural Review* 6/3 (1995), 263–74.

about London', quickly getting accustomed to the urban spatial environment. Gissing seems to consciously distance himself from the view
that a woman's place is in the home, and portraying it instead through
the conservative Widdowson as the paranoia of the Victorian male.
Widdowson is uncomfortable with Monica's journeys around the city
unless she is under his surveillance, and regarding her desire for unaccompanied travel as socially immoral, he soon suspects her excursions
to have adulterous intent. Gissing implies that his jealousy arises from
Monica's knowledge of the London transport map, and the threat this
freedom poses to his masculinity and authority. Yet Gissing's position is
ambivalent, for although he consciously affirms women's new freedom,
the text tends to continue the connection of the independent and mobile
woman with loose female sexuality. Both the other named shop-girls, for
example, Amy Drake and Miss Eade, make sexually provocative advances in sites of modern transport. Amy Drake seduces Everard Barfoot
in a railway carriage and Miss Eade becomes a prostitute at Victoria
Station.

If Zola's portrayal of women's possibilities in the department store
ends in improbable romance, Gissing in *The Odd Women* offers a more
plausible account of the conditions of the life of the shop-girl whilst still
conforming to Victorian standards with a suitably moral ending of lost
virtue and death. Neither Zola nor Gissing, however, attempt to portray
the subjective response of women to the city they inhabit. Denise Baudu
and Monica Madden are type-cases of the shop-girl who has evolved
with the rise of a consumer environment, and they are regarded as
analysable objects accordingly. They are specimens for examination,
collected by the naturalist writers who, like Benjamin's *flâneur*, go
botanizing on the asphalt of the city streets. Dreiser's *Sister Carrie* can
be distinguished from Zola and Gissing's perception of women by its
attempted engagement with a woman's own angle of vision. Dreiser's
version of Naturalism involves a recognition of the possibilities of
representing modern experience through subjective form as well as
through outward description.

Sister Carrie begins with the familiar scene of a young rural girl
journeying to the metropolis (Chicago in this case) and the authorial
moral warning that accompanies it: 'When a girl leaves home at eigh-
teen, she does one of two things. Either she falls into saving hands and
becomes better, or she rapidly assumes the cosmopolitan standard of
virtue and becomes worse. Of an intermediate balance, under the circumstances, there is no possibility' (*SC* 1). Yet this comment is such a
near-parody that it suggests a satiric tampering with the fallen-girl-in-
city formula of popular nineteenth-century literature. In fact Carrie

Meeber possesses characteristics that indicate a capacity for urban survival: '[a] half-equipped little knight she was, venturing to reconnoitre the mysterious city and dreaming wild dreams of some vague, far-off supremacy' (2). Her immediate search for work in Chicago, and her easy orientation in the city streets despite being a newcomer, displays her tenacity and prompts her open interest in the city spectacle.

In a long day of job-hunting, Carrie conducts a peripatetic observation of the city, which Dreiser articulates through the interactive relationship of the environment she proceeds through and her changing states of mind. Carrie's perception of the crowd is central to her response to the city. At first the sublime vastness of the city streets and imposing buildings overawe her with a feeling of insignificance, and she is intimidated by the seemingly indifferent companies that line the streets, 'gladly [sinking] into the obscuring crowd' (15). Later, following the disappointment of her rejection at the department store, 'The Fair', and weary and forlorn at the futility of her desires, she relinquishes herself to the anonymity in the streets, 'feeling a certain safety and relief in mingling with the crowd' (18). For Carrie in this mood, the crowd is comforting because it seems to engulf and obscure her, relieving her of the responsibility of autonomous action: 'It seemed as if [the city] was all closed to her, that the struggle was too fierce for her to hope to do anything at all. Men and women hurried by in long, shifting lines. She felt the flow of the tide of effort and interest—felt her own helplessness without quite realising the wisp on the tide that she was' (20). Having finally secured a position with a wholesale shoe company, however, Carrie's attitude changes: 'She walked out into the busy street and discovered a new atmosphere. Behold, the throng was moving with a lightsome step. She noticed that men and women were smiling. [. . .] Ah, the long winter in Chicago—the lights, the crowd, the amusement! This was a great, pleasing metropolis after all' (21). The crowd no longer seems engulfing, but instead a mass of positive energy, reflecting the possibilities of the city. Through the mediation of Carrie's changing response to the crowd in this passage, Dreiser attempts to represent the consciousness of his character. This alteration of the physical landscape according to the subjectivity of the female observer will later become prominent in the works of Richardson and Bowen, for example, for whom city and mind are in constant mutual interaction. The intermittent punctuation of descriptions of her position in the city with her appeals for work serves to present her as an active figure negotiating her environment rather than determined by it.

The representation of Carrie's response to the city is complicated by the fact that she is largely inarticulate. Her defining characteristic, however, is her love of stimulation and pleasure, and Dreiser thus registers her excitement at the abundant *visual* spectacle. Carrie avidly observes city life; she gets enjoyment from watching the city streets, for example, when she is forbidden trips to the theatre or tourist attractions by her relatives, the Hansons. Dreiser's ironic portrayal of this family situation points up the unreasonableness of an urban philosophy that is happy for the woman to work to increase the comfort of the home, but is unwilling to allow the enjoyments of urban leisure. Banned from public spaces legitimately available to women, Carrie turns for freedom to watching the street from the doorway. This familiarity is predictably denounced by Hanson, and equated with sexual availability. Strolling briefly from the door, for example, with an 'easy gait and idle manner' (41), Carrie suffers the advances of a man who obviously mistakes her for a prostitute.

That the city is itself a theatre is evident from the show put on by the fashionable bourgeois in the leisure district of Broadway. Like the Bois de Boulogne in Paris, Broadway and Madison Square Gardens of the 1890s was the centre of urban leisure, a 'showy parade' of men and women going 'to see and be seen'. Carrie first experiences the parade by 'fashion's crowd' as she walks with Mrs Vance, yet is painfully aware that she does not participate in this rich show. Dreiser vividly evokes the rich artifice of the scene, and indicates the connection of prostitute, actress, and lady, class differences being transcended in the culture of spectacle. He captures the fascination of the spectacle yet also notes a decadent licentiousness in the display. Both men and women enjoy 'just looking' but their acts of display and voyeurism are only a socially sanctioned version of the disreputable transaction of prostitution. In this environment

glances were not modified by any rules of propriety. To stare seemed the proper and natural thing. Carrie found herself stared at and ogled. Men in flawless top-coats, high hats, and silver-headed walking sticks elbowed near and looked too often into conscious eyes. Ladies rustled by in dresses of stiff cloth, shedding affected smiles and perfume. Carrie noticed among them the sprinkling of goodness and the heavy percentage of vice. (227)

Entry to this society depends on artifice and outward display, and consequently the women create themselves in a particular mould. Bourgeois lady and courtesan mingle in this fashionable place, both free to gaze and observe around them. Yet just as the courtesan is indistinguishable from the lady in her stylish finery, so too is the lady indistinguishable from the courtesan as a figure of vice. All the women are equated as 'affected' and all are consciously out on display. Significantly, however, by portraying this scene through Carrie's excited eyes, Dreiser emphasizes the positive freedom and opportunity of this world as much as a sense of public immorality. It is also important that the fashionable crowd in *Sister Carrie* is not so distinctly female as in *Au Bonheur des Dames*. Both men and women present a public image and the consumption of fashion is not a solely feminine interest.[16] Dreiser does not see society as one of exploitation on gender lines, where women's desires are aroused and controlled by a male production system. He depicts a more complex and dialectical relationship between consumer society and its inhabitants (both male and female) in which commodities and the principle of spectacle become constitutive of identity.

Carrie achieves a position in 'the metropolitan whirl of pleasure' (323) by literally taking up its artifice and forsaking her domestic servitude with Hurstwood for a career on the stage. She conducts a doubled 'masquerade', literally playing a part on stage but also constructing herself into a particular identity off-stage: Caroline Meeber becomes Sister Carrie, Mrs Drouet, Mrs Wheeler, Carrie Madenda. She creates herself in the image of the wealthy women she envies in the street, themselves creating an outward impression through the façades of dress and cosmetics. It seems implausible to suggest that there is something that can be called a more 'real' Carrie beneath these layers of artifice, and it is hard to conceive what such a Carrie could be. She is no longer the country girl who arrived in Chicago, having evolved and changed through her experiences.

Dreiser registers Carrie's consciousness through certain representative images. When living with Drouet, Carrie takes to passing her time in a rocking chair by the window. This position of detached spectatorship is continued throughout the novel, a formal image of Carrie's increasingly introverted identity. For it is through her habit of watching and imitating the attitudes of passers-by in the street that Carrie develops her acting ability. Her growing financial freedom, which allows her to buy clothes and accessories and consequently take on the identity of the city woman, parallels her increasing success on the stage as a professional actress. However, it also coincides with a partial retreat from the vitality experienced in walking the city streets. The first description of Carrie sitting at the window actually prefigures her future, coming just after she has discovered her ability to copy the mannerisms of city women and after she has met Mr Hale, a theatre manager, and his wife: 'It was at that hour between afternoon and night when, for the idle, the wanderer,

---

[16] Chas Drouet, for example, is constantly described as paying great attention to his clothes and the importance of fashion in creating a successful identity. Drouet is an interesting parallel figure to Carrie. Both cheerfully self-interested and increasingly financially successful, they are representative of a modern urban mentality.

things are apt to take on a wistful aspect. The mind wanders forth on far journeys and returns with sheaves of withered and departed joys. Carrie sat at her window looking out' (77). The idle wanderer in a state of melancholy recalls the Baudelaire *flâneur*, living from day to day and searching for something that will be a new stimulation. Carrie has a number of affinities with the *flâneur*. She is an outsider in the city, at first fearful and then thankful of its big crowd, fascinated by the urban spectacle and desirous of its beauty, ending up detached and aloof from emotional commitment as a successful actress who plays many parts. For Carrie is here a wanderer in mind, detached from the external world. At the end of the novel she looks out at the city that is at her feet but does not fulfil her: 'Know, then, that for you is neither surfeit nor content. In your rocking-chair, by your window dreaming, shall you long, alone. In your rocking-chair, by your window, shall you dream such happiness as you may never feel' (369). Carrie's economic position may have changed but the meaning of the rocking still remains. She never really seems to belong to any position, and as she achieves each fresh desire she realizes it to be illusory. Like the *flâneur*-artist, she is constantly in 'pursuit of beauty' (369), and the prospect of her life at the end of the novel is one of alienated walking and searching.

The eloquent description of Carrie as a natural artist betrays a sympathy on Dreiser's part with the mentality of the Baudelairian *flâneur* which does much to explain his perception of the city in contrast to the Zolaesque surveillance mode.[17] It also distinguishes *Sister Carrie* from conventional working-girl novels, and it is one of the strengths of Dreiser's characterization that he does not reduce Carrie to a stereotypical end of fallen woman or satisfied wife and mother. Instead, prefiguring the protagonists of later women writers, Carrie faces the impasse of public success at the expense of emotional fulfilment. Dreiser refuses to detract from his psychological interest in Carrie as a character by confining her within a formulaic, objectifying model of women's experience in the city. Carrie is depicted, through her own response to situations and her contemplative restlessness, as attempting to negotiate her place in the urban world and harmonize herself within her environment. Unlike her husband Hurstwood, who is so used to his authoritative status that he can only sink into inactivity and pessimistic decline

---

[17] Dreiser himself was a peripatetic city-lover, fascinated with the aesthetics of the city expanse. As a reporter for the St Louis *Republic* during the 1890s, he covered the Chicago World Fair of 1893 in a series of six articles (18–23 July, 1893) which express his fascination with the fairytale aspect of the city. This aesthetic trait seems to continue in Dreiser's mediated form of Naturalism. An excellent reassessment of Dreiser's place as a Naturalist writer is Max Westbrook, 'Dreiser's Defense of Carrie Meeber', *MFS* 23 (1977), 381–93.

when it is taken from him, Carrie actively participates in and with the city to create and recreate herself in order to keep up with the transient experiences of urban life.

James and the 'Modern Girl'

Henry James is another important precursor for modernist women writing the city, as he firmly places women as viewers in the urban environment. He registers a new female presence, a modern girl with a modern consciousness, either daughters of the city (Kate Crow, Millicent Henning, Maria Gostrey) or innocents initiated into it (Isabel Archer, Milly Theale). Moreover, this modern female perspective is extended to an aesthetic, evident in the preface to *What Maisie Knew* (1897), James's first novel after a break of six years, and one that heralded the concern with 'point of view' that defines his late style. Speaking of the use of a 'light vessel of consciousness' as the fulcrum of the text, James states that a female consciousness was particularly suitable as 'the sensibility of the female young is indubitably, for early youth, the greater'.[18] James experiments with a consciousness that possesses a receptive perceptual ability yet whose understanding is limited, and that has affinities with the Jamesian and Freudian models of a mind that registers the myriad impressions of experience yet does not operate on a logical, linear level. The perfect subject for James is endowed with a consciousness that is open and receptive and then struggles to relate its immediate subjective response with the accepted conventions of society. In this respect, the young woman fresh to the city is ideal, James's comment on Maisie that '[s]mall children have many more perceptions than they have terms to translate them', being equally applicable to his female characters in the turn-of-the-century city.[19]

The trope of *flânerie* is evident in James's fiction in two ways. First, a huge proportion of his characters are walkers and observers of cities and differences between these observers are suggestive of a distinction between modes of *flânerie*. Judith Feldman has recognized varieties of spectatorship amongst James's characters, suggesting that different observers correspond to different aesthetic standpoints, for example the isolated life of separation, the life of symbiosis and interrelation, and the life of self-involvement.[20] This analogy is astute and suggestive, and can

---

[18] Henry James, Preface to *What Maisie Knew* (1897; Oxford: Oxford UP, 1966), 4.
[19] Ibid. 6.
[20] Judith Feldman, *Gender on the Divide: The Dandy in Modernist Literature* (Ithaca, NY: Cornell UP, 1993).

be extended to correspond to the walking/writing metaphor and the relation of spectatorship to movement. James's own formal style draws on the aleatory perspective (the influence of movement on the spectator) and emphasizes the changing or alternative point of view. This distinction between the fixed and fluid viewpoint also supports a differentiation of positions of spectatorship, in which the aleatory perspective varies from an omniscient, all-encompassing viewpoint. The positions of characters in the city, enclosed in private spaces, wandering public spaces in impressionable reverie, or commanding spaces by imposing the self onto them, become metaphors for aesthetic approaches. Significantly, the fluid, changeable viewpoint is commonly attributed to female or 'feminine' male characters, ideal protagonists because of their 'roving' imagination, expansive consciousness, and capacity for the intuition of nuance. Not only then does James's *œuvre* foreground the visual focus as the basis of knowledge, but he consistently relates a social/ethical/aesthetic vision largely to women. It is feminine characters who invite, see, and try to take advantage of the possibilities of experience.

In *The Princess Cassimassima* (1886) James contributes to the literary image of the newly independent working girl with his depiction of Hyacinth Robinson's childhood friend Millicent Henning. Millicent is sympathetically portrayed as an urban figure. Rather than stereotyped as a neurotic spinster or promiscuous shop-girl, she is remarkably womanly, clear-headed, and confident in her ambition, with a shrewd knowledge of the workings of the city and consequent ability to survive within it. In comparison to the female role-models of her childhood, the Victorian tropes of the working-class woman as spinster, seamstress, and slovenly wife, Millicent raises herself out of her working-class origins, avoiding the choice of female roles open to her, through the new urban space of the department store, 'a more exciting, a more dramatic department of the great drapery interest' than Miss Pynsent's humble room.

On first meeting Millicent, Hyacinth immediately takes her for another type of 'public' woman, making social judgements about her fine clothes and good looks. James thus illustrates the different significance for men and women of the public life of the city; despite the fact that 'he [is] as strikingly as Millicent, in her own degree, a product of the London streets and the London air' (*PC* 71), Hyacinth's assumptions make obvious the discrepancy between male and female conceptions of a woman's place in the public city. James himself, however, is careful not to present a stereotypical model of the female place in the consumer world. Hyacinth and Millicent are both natural observers of the city, Hyacinth taking 'interminable, restless, melancholy, moody, yet all-observant strolls through London' (68), and Millicent possessing an avid 'attachment also to any tolerable pretext for wandering through the streets of London and gazing into shop-windows' (59). A public woman working in the modern department store, Millicent prefigures the modern woman adapted to the consumer city that James was later to develop in Maria Gostrey in *The Ambassadors* (1903). The shop condenses the city into microcosm and provides material for the habit of social observation: 'She had the pretension of knowing who every one was; not individually and by name, but as regards their exact social station, the quarter of London in which they lived and the amount of money they were prepared to spend [...] She had seen the whole town pass through her establishment' (*A* 167).

Millicent is central to the culture of commodity show, yet James indicates that this itself is not a hierarchical relationship. As a 'model', Millicent is the possessed object of the viewer's gaze, and when the reader is shown Millicent at work this is the specifically male gaze of the captain. However, as a 'model of mantles and jackets', it is not her body that Millicent prostitutes to the gaze but the garments she wears, Millicent herself being rather the manipulator of the customer's desire. James therefore highlights the interrelationship of conceptions of prostitution/consumption/female body/value object as they applied to the assessment of women and the consumer culture developing in the 1880s. Millicent's profession as model for a marketable image questions the role of woman as object, implying that the female body is a garment worn and paraded for a purpose. Certainly Millicent achieves independence as a result of a carefully 'sewn' identity, of which her clothes, opinions, and semblance of propriety are part. The irony of her proclaimed belief in the conventions of social manners and morality, yet ignorant enjoyment of the contrary, is indicated by James in several humorous passages, for example when she is perfectly comfortable in the less than salubrious coffee-house to which Hyacinth takes her. Yet James is supremely adept as a male writer of the female mind, and his exposition of Millicent's pretensions is not a dismissal. Rather there is a hint of admiration in his portrayal of her degree of success at life, which can be regarded as paralleling the concurrent rise and success of the department store itself, both the results of a conscious masquerade and paraded spectacle.

Compared to James's mass of 'innocents abroad', Millicent Henning is a rare example of the capable urban woman. He goes on to develop this figure further in the character of Maria Gostrey, the *ficelle* of *The Ambassadors*. James's preliminary outline of *The Ambassadors* describes Maria Gostrey in detail, suggesting that she was originally conceived as a more central focus than she finally became. It is worth quoting at length:

She is inordinately modern, the fruit of actual, intentional conditions of the growing polyglot Babel. She calls herself the universal American agent. She calls herself the general amateur-courier. She comes over with girls. She goes back with girls. She meets girls at Liverpool, at Genoa, at Breman—she has even been known to meet boys. She sees people through. She shops with them in London, where she has a tailor of her 'very own'. She knows all the trains. She meets a want. [21]

Maria Gostrey manifests numerous aspects of the *flâneur*. She is introduced as 'another agent, operative on this expository ground', an active, autonomous figure and a modern woman comfortable and knowledgeable in a female-dominated urban environment. James describes her in the 'Project' as meeting Strether and Waymarsh whilst 'strolling and looking, as they stroll and look: only unaccompanied, detached, with no one to talk of it to'.[22] She is a *ficelle*, a guide or agent, acquainting Strether with the cities and social scene of cosmopolitan Europe as well as the customs of its inhabitants. Ultimately her role is thus as communicator or mediator; she is a human Baedeker helping Strether to find his way round the city and his own response to European society. This capacity for interaction is manifest in her lifestyle and voluntary 'profession', constantly travelling between America and Europe, the old city (Chester) and the quintessential capital of modernity Paris, easily making acquaintances with newcomers and acting as their guide. As an American expatriate in Europe, she stands between two worlds, able to retain a detached perspective on each, and it is this detachment that marks her privileged position and acceptance of multiple viewpoints. She observes on the move, but from a leisured pace that allows for perception rather than a rush that makes everything a blur. As a financially secure spinster, she is independent and has nobody dependent on her. Her detachment seems necessary for James's intention of making her a guiding element, but it also suggests a certain isolation. The American tourists that she takes up are 'customers', in the terms of the new consumer society, rather than friends. The girls to whom she shows London and Paris are not interested in the nuances of her impressions. Maria Gostrey is unique as a strolling, urban woman and therefore she not only has no companions to talk of the city to, but also no satisfactory language for communicating her impressions.

It is useful to compare Maria with Strether's male guide to Paris, Little Bilham, who is a perfect example of the spirit of the traditional male, surveying *flâneur*. Strether first sees Little Bilham watching the street,

---

[21] See Henry James, 'Project of Novel' for *The Ambassadors* in *The Notebooks of Henry James*, ed. F. O. Matthiesen and Kenneth B. Murdock (Oxford: Oxford UP, 1961), 378.
[22] Ibid. 377.

and himself, from Chad's balcony and he envies this all-encompassing perspective. Typical of the Jamesian style, the motif of the balcony reflects Little Bilham's ability to perceive and accept the multiplicity of the social labyrinth of Paris. Yet James finds something unsatisfactory in his detached position, which involves a retreat to the interior tradition-ally associated with female city spaces. Bilham is a constant and intent observer yet also a rather flat figure, whose action is solely the perceptual process. He partners Miss Barrace in a 'power of not being' (124) and lives life indirectly, without involvement. Little Bilham's static detach-ment on the balcony and Maria's busy directions through the streets thus embody different aesthetic perspectives. Both are able to accept the multiplicity of urban Paris and have open viewpoints, but James seems to imply that to live within the world rather than on the margins of it requires choosing something definite from this multiplicity. This de-mands an androgynous conception of *flânerie* in which objectivity and control are merged with subjectivity and flux into positive union. Does Maria Gostrey offer this combination?

As well as epitomizing the traits of the social *flâneur* strolling the commercial city and window shopping, Maria manifests the metapho-rical aspects of *flânerie*. As hostess to the city she too makes the streets her drawing-room, just as her drawing-room becomes a quasi-public space, a museum of curios and collectables, 'an empire of "things"' indicating her role as a modern type, the collector. Such explicit associa-tion belies a gendered definition of the mode as well as the social figuration of *flânerie*. James seems to imply that *flânerie* was never an exclusively masculine point of view and that the growing commercial world was providing the habitat and opportunity for women to join in a particular mode of vision that was already suited to them. James stated that Maria Gostrey is a portrait of 'a highly contemporary and quasi-cosmopolite feminine type'. She is a new figure in the urban environ-ment, representing and epitomizing the new opportunities for women to enter and possess the public life of the city and James emphasizes her role as a guide for the influx of women to the city in his description of her significance. She heralds a female possession of the city, her girls becoming urban voyeurs and consumers as tourists and shoppers. Yet at the same time she continues the image of the natural urbanite, the *flâneur* as someone displaced, as she is rootless and has 'wandered and re-wandered from an early time [...] full of ways and means, full of everything and everywhere'.[23] Any connection with past or background

---

[23] See Henry James, 'Project of Novel' for *The Ambassadors* in *The Notebooks of Henry James*, ed. F. O. Matthieson and Kenneth B. Murdock (Oxford: Oxford UP, 1961), 378.

is suppressed by James in his presentation of Maria, and her life appears to have little sense of structure or progression; it is not a journey with a start and destination but a wander through everywhere that locates her nowhere. It is only with the 'feminine' Strether that she is able to really correspond.

Maria Gostrey's placelessness mirrors that of James himself, and the Paris she exists in is as shifting a place as the narrative form that expresses it. Indeed, Virginia Woolf describes James having 'neither roots nor soil; he was of the tribe of wanderers and aliens; a winged visitant, ceaselessly circling and seeking, unattached, uncommitted, ranging hither and thither at his own free will.'[24] How much of a study of James's own view of himself as artist can be seen in Maria Gostrey? For Woolf makes other parallels of James and the *flâneur* that also relate to the character of Maria. The adjectives James uses to describe Maria's perceptions constantly suggest alertness and interest, and Woolf calls James '[a] spectator, alert, aloof, endlessly interested, endlessly observant'.[25] Other critics have also acknowledged James's affinity with the position of the *flâneur*. Glenway Westcott has compared him to the Baudelairian rag-picker, stating that 'he must have imagined that he could pick up his subjects where he found them, in gutters of this and that metropolis, on refuse heaps of the law, and separate them from their squalid context and deal with them on a higher plane'.[26] The allusion is apt, although perhaps James's fastidious aestheticism is more appropriately described in terms of the antique collector rather than the rag-picker. Maria Gostrey is also a collector; she displaces objects and rearranges them for a new purpose. However, she removes these objects to a private or secluded place. Like the *flâneur*, therefore, she merges both masculine and feminine tendencies, being a moving, mediating figure, but also a possessive, hoarding one. It is this detached possession that prompts Woolf's warning question on James: 'If London [or the modern city in general] is primarily a point of view, if the whole field of human activity is only a prospect and a pageant, then we cannot help asking, as the store of impressions heaps itself up, what is the aim of the spectator, what is the purpose of his hoard?'[27] The hoard of fragments itself, however, not only seems to counter the fluid spirit that collected

[24] Virginia Woolf, 'Henry James' (1919), repr. in Graham Clarke (ed.), *Henry James: Critical Assessments*, vol. i, *Memories, Views and Writers* (Mountfield: Helm Information Ltd., 1991), 356.

[25] Ibid. 356.

[26] Glenway Westcott, 'A Sentimental Contribution', *Hound and Horn* (Apr., May 1934), repr. in Clarke, *Memories*, i. 382.

[27] Ibid. 356.

them, but also is itself denigrated in the novel for its eclecticism, the archetypal ordering 'male' collector having degenerated in the figure of Maria to a frivolous, undiscriminating, and voracious female consumer.

Gostrey's 'little museum of bargains' (145) is fascinating for Strether, but its deficiencies are evident compared to the unity and interrelation of the contents of Mme de Vionnet's spacious house, obtained not through random collection but a tradition of bequeathed accumulation. The gender allusions here are complex and remain unresolved, a sign of James's ambivalence over the status of the 'feminine' in his fiction. Less obviously and thus less ambiguously represented as moving independently in the urban landscape, Marie de Vionnet is also an innately urban figure. Moreover, if Maria Gostrey is the guide then Marie de Vionnet is the architect of the moral and physical maze that Strether stumbles through. Maria Gostrey is a woman of the commercial world but a displaced one, whereas Mme de Vionnet, who suggests the possibility of continuity through the past, becomes the evocative female presence that pervades Strether's response to Paris. It is significant that Maria's awareness and understanding of the streets and social relations of Paris decreases when she loses her superior detachment on falling in love with Strether. For, from being an ordering collector of human types, 'the mistress of a hundred cases or categories, receptacles of the mind, subdivisions for convenience, in which, from a full experience, she pigeon-holed her fellow mortals with a hand as free as that of a compositor scattering type' (21), she is described in James's 'Project' as being, by the end of the novel, only 'poor, convenient, amusing, unforgettable, impossible Gostrey' (403). Indeed it is Strether who then acts as 'expert' guide, 'leading her about Paris' and showing her new sights while she becomes susceptible to 'occasional fatigues and bewilderments' (327).

Proust and the Elusive *Femme*

The female characters in Proust's *A la recherche du temps perdu* (1913–27) are observed through the visually possessive and obsessive consciousness of Marcel. Yet, in relation to Marcel's gaze, women are constantly portrayed as passing, fleeting figures who avoid his possessive look. The women in Proust are examples of the *passante*, the feminine reflection of the *flâneur*-artist. They represent what is fluid and changeable compared to Marcel's attempts to fix and control what he sees. It is significant, therefore, that Odette de Crecy and Albertine, for example, are portrayed as figures of movement. Odette walks daily in the Champs-Élysées and the younger generation of Albertine and her friends are also constantly mobile, although at the faster pace of the bicycle or motor vehicle. This physical mobility is mirrored by a more abstract mobility of identity, both women being adept at taking on a multiplicity of social roles, often simultaneously.

Odette de Crecy is an early object of Marcel's voyeurism, and he waits for her daily walk in the Bois de Boulogne. His obsession is manifest not just in this constant need for observation, however, but also in his attempts to exhaustively describe her. For the reader, Odette in the first volumes of the novel is almost reduced to a fashion template, a mannequin for the display of clothes. As she parades (but also observes) in the fashionable streets of Paris, Marcel details her different costumes. He acts as the 'man of the crowd' evoking Odette's character and indicating her social position by analysis of her outward appearance. In an early description, for example, she is described as a woman of fashion, but the style of fashion itself corresponds to her inner personality. As a young *cocotte*, Odette carefully yet inexpertly pieces herself together to present an image to those who observe her. Her stiff and rigid garments reflect this attempt. Yet what is important about this image is that, although suggestive of Odette's identity, it fails to encompass her. In later volumes Odette is completely transformed, both in clothes and in social identity, as she takes on the roles of transvestite, lover, wife, mother, and mistress. Yet none of these serves to elucidate her completely, and between them she remains elusive. Albertine is another female character who is constantly changeable. Marcel tries in vain to contain her as she first appeared to his imagination. Yet, even more than Odette, she manifests a fluid identity and to Marcel's eyes is so elusive as to seem just a name applied to numerous different girls.

In his sensitive reading of Proust in *Axel's Castle*, Edmund Wilson argues that the central, masculine characters in the novel—Swann, Marcel, and Saint-Loup—all construct women through their perceptions rather than observe them. The visual focus of each is responsive to their imaginations and each thus creates, whilst perceiving, women that accord with their own subjective worlds. By the end of the novel, Marcel comes to realize this collaboration of the imagination and the visual sense, and his practice of 'placing features [. . .] upon the face of a woman seen in the street, when instead of nose, cheeks and chin there ought to be merely an empty space with nothing more upon it than a flickering reflection of our desires' (*RTP 3*, 1103). Women as identities in their own right are absent in the eyes of these figures and exist only as extensions of the male observer's desires. For Marcel, the experience of Paris is constantly equated with a female character as its figurehead; Gilberte, Odette, the Duchesse de Guermantes, Albertine. He attempts to order his impressions amongst the constant transformations around him, and order and control of these women extends to a sense of controlling the modern urban existence. Yet on returning to the Bois he realizes that the fleeting is the main quality of modernity. The static, visual perspective is shown to be unsatisfactory as a way of grasping experience, which includes a temporal as well as a spatial element. Both city and woman are ephemeral, fleeting, and unpossessable.

The female figures in *A la recherche du temps perdu* are thus conceived through the trope of the *passante*; elusive, fleeting figures who effect the observer's imagination. The control of the narrative by Marcel prevents the woman from being anything but an object. She is perceived by the observer as is the *passante*, and is unable to voice her own experience of moving perception as *flâneur*. However, as a moving figure she subverts the traditional conception of the female as possessable object. The *passante* is a fleeting figure observed but with the ability to evade being fixed by the male gaze. In this respect the *passante* becomes a metaphor for the modern, autonomous urban woman.

The woman as *passante* is partly significant for Proust as muse or inspiration for the observing artist. Yet, contradicting Marcel's desire for possession and his belief that by collecting and containing his female muses as aesthetic objects they would 'inspire [him] as a sculptor is inspired when he walks through a gallery of noble antique marbles' (1038), is his realization that their power for inspiration is dependent on their early mysteriousness and lost once they become 'the known, the familiar' (1038). This elusiveness is common to all the women Marcel falls in love with and tends to become a generalized feature of the Proustian love object. The modern generation of Gilberte, Albertine, and her friends are virtually interchangeable presences, their significance being less in their individual characters than in the effect they have on Marcel. Change-able, intangible figures themselves, they yet produce a constant response in Marcel; intrigue, the frustrated desire to possess, a loss of interest at the onset of familiarity, rekindled with the awareness of a new mystery.

Marcel too thus resembles the modern figure of the collector. Obser-ving objects he wants to possess, he attempts to remove them to his own interior environment. The collector impulse involves separating the desired object from its environment and endowing it with a different significance by placing it in a new context. In a similar way, the female figures that Marcel becomes obsessed with do not retain autonomous identities but are collected into a particular meaning structured by his perceiving imagination. Marcel's 'imprisonment' of Albertine is the most explicit example of the collector temperament. He removes her from the modern urban world that defines her and denies her mobility and variability. Both the external world and its representative, Albertine, are elusive and uncontrollable. By removing her to the detached enclosure of the family house, Marcel attempts to reassert the domination of what he can control, his imagination. He creates Albertine in a certain image that accords with his interior haven, and is most happy when she is asleep and not threatening his identity with her own consciousness: 'Her personality was not constantly escaping, as when we talked, by the outlets of her unacknowledged thoughts and of her eyes. [...] In keeping [her body] in front of my eyes, in my hands, I had an impression of possessing her entirely which I never had when she was awake' (64). Yet the irony is that Marcel himself realizes that the achievement of the control he desires does not result in satisfaction.

The essence of fascination for Marcel is that which is unfamiliar, new, or changeable (the 'modern') and these are necessarily fleeting and impossible to retain. This explains his changing attitudes towards Albertine, from desire to boredom and back again as he alternately obsessively desires to possess her and then loses interest until his fascination is aroused by new evidence of her mysteriousness. For example, in *La Prisonnière* (*The Captive*) he admits this interest in the mysterious woman or *passante* and recognizes the impossibility of following her: 'How often, at the moment when the unknown woman who was to haunt my dreams passed beneath the window, sometimes on foot, sometimes at full speed in a motor-car, did I not suffer from the fact that my body could not follow my gaze which kept pace with her.' (20). Proust's distance from Marcel's perspective in this respect can be noted by the statement that immediately follows the above passage: 'Of Albertine, on the other hand, I had nothing more to learn.' There is a certain degree of irony in the comparison with Albertine, as she herself was just such an 'unknown woman' and always mobile or moving at speed. The *passante*, then, is a figure that remains autonomous, indeed is defined by her autonomy. Once she is captured and made familiar she no longer holds the allure of the unknown. Marcel realizes this in an ardent statement to his female muses that, to know them: 'I should have to immobilize you, to cease to live in that perpetual state of expectancy ending always in a different presentment of you, I should have to cease to love you in order to fix your image, cease to be conscious of your interminable and always disconcerting arrival, O girls, O successive rays in the swirling vortex' (58). His predicament is that he wants to hold and define the very element that makes the urban woman elusive and indefinable, a figure of modernity.

The older Marcel realizes that Albertine never actually did lose her autonomy and that his claim to total knowledge of her merely related to the image he created of her. On first meeting Albertine at Balbec, Marcel had remarked on the fluid nature of her eyes. The older, narrator-Marcel, recalling Albertine as the 'captive' in Paris, also describes '[e]yes mendaciously kept always immobile and passive, but none the less dynamic, measurable in the yards or miles to be traversed' (86). These eyes indicate that she is never truly a captive as, '[e]ven when you hold them in your hands, such persons are fugitives [...] we must realize that they are not immobile but in motion, and add to their person a sign corresponding to that which in physics denotes speed' (86–7).

In contrast to Marcel's static, controlling scopophilia, Albertine's eyes suggest a look that wanders and explores possibilities. They are 'kaleidoscopic eyes, far-ranging and melancholy' that 'might enable us perhaps to measure distance, but do not indicate direction' (87). Again they are evasive, suggestive of movement but not of destination. Albertine remains the fugitive *passante* in the city, melancholy yet independent. The *passante*, however, epitomizes the unpossessable figure because to read or interpret her is to destroy what defines her, the fleeting nature of her presence.

The distinction between Marcel's desire to possess the female figures he observes and the ability they have to constantly change and escape possession indicates a difference between the aesthetic of Marcel and that of Proust himself. As obsessive observer, Marcel manifests the perspective of the male, objectifying gaze. This perspective is then undercut by Proust's refusal of the categories and definitions Marcel makes, revealing him to be frequently bad at interpretation. His perception of the two 'ways' as set in opposition metaphorically underlies many other acts of misinterpretation, for example his belief that the Guermantes reject the pro-Dreyfus Swann at their party. These failures of definition result predominantly from the static nature of his perception. As T. F. Petruso perceptively argues, '[i]t is not simply that things are never as they first appear to be to Marcel, but that they are eventually seen as incorporating their opposite'.[28] That static perception is an unsatisfactory position for the artist, in Proust's eyes, is implied by the non-static narrative style. This uses a continuous flow of impressionistic interior monologue to represent the state of the mind as it responds to its environment and influences. Yet because the sensitive mind registers infinitesimal nuances, large sections of representation in language are required to describe one brief moment. Thus, in the stream of consciousness form, Proust, Richardson, Woolf, and Joyce combine stasis and mobility, a captured moment with an awareness of its fleeting

---

[28] T. F. Petruso, *Life Made Real* (Ann Arbor: University of Michigan Press, 1991), 59.

nature, the gaze of the static observer with the ever-moving glance of the *flâneur*.

The novel revolves around the attempt to combine polarities, such as movement and stasis, which at first seem binary opposites but with hindsight are actually interrelated. The basic metaphor for this blurring of opposites is androgyny, which is literally manifested by the sexual relations of various characters and aesthetically in the Proustian style. It is with the elusive, androgynous Albertine rather than the visibly homosexual Charlus that Proust's aesthetic sympathies lie, for example. Frances Pacteau's excellent analysis of the androgyne figure in her essay 'The Impossible Referent' is relevant here, as she contrasts the two artistic tropes of blurred gender, the hermaphrodite and the androgyne, noting that the former, possessing the visible signifiers of biological gender, resembles a man with breasts, whereas the androgyne, as non-sexualized, seems aligned with the female and her association with 'absence', or elusiveness.[29] The trope of the androgyne thus seems to link back to the ideas of movement, elusiveness, and the female; the *passante*. The concept of androgyny, in terms of perceptual mode and aesthetic structure, introduces the experience of the feminine as central to modernity and to art. Far from according with the image of the definitively male peripatetic observer as modern artist, Proust's aesthetic seems to extend that of James and assert the crucial features of the modernist artist to depend on the incorporation of the feminine.

By the conclusion of *A la recherche du temps perdu*, Proust has conducted Marcel on a wandering journey through his memory. This was heralded from the first by a focus on a choice of geographic pathways—the Méséglise way and the Guermantes way in rural Combray—that correspond to Marcel's life acquaintances and influences during his life in Paris. All the characters in the novel belong to one or other 'way', connected to Swann or the Guermantes. Both geographically and socially they are regarded by Marcel as distinct and opposing experiences, one natural and untamed, the other aristocratic and elegant. Marcel, having wandered through these 'ways' in his memory, eventually comes to the position that Proust's own text asserts from the beginning; the falsity of definitive categories of opposition. With the marriage of Saint-Loup and Gilberte, and the birth of their daughter, the two 'ways' are merged. Gilberte reveals to Marcel the original connection of the two pathways: 'Gilberte said to me: "If you like, we might after all go out one

---

[29] Frances Pacteau, 'The Impossible Referent: Representations of the Androgyne', in Victor Burgin, James Donald, and Cora Kaplan (eds.), *Formations of Fantasy* (London: Routledge, 1986), 62–84.

afternoon and then we can go to Guermantes, taking the road by Méséglise, which is the nicest way," a sentence which upset all the ideas of my childhood by informing me that the two "ways" were not as irreconcilable as I had supposed' (711).

However, it is Mlle de Saint-Loup who is particularly significant, as a woman of a new generation standing at the centre of a multiple cross-roads, including the two 'ways', the Champs-Élysées and the front at Balbec: '[n]umerous for [Marcel] were the roads which led to Mlle de Saint-Loup and which radiated around her' (1085). As a representative of a new modern generation, Mlle de Saint-Loup has the possibilities of the *flâneuse* before her and is in possession of numerous trajectories. Significantly, moreover, her position is not only spatial but temporal, as each pathway links with the others as a result of a web of past associations. The roads are metaphors for Marcel's memories, and he perceives that 'between any slightest point of our past and all the others a rich network of memories gives us an almost infinite variety of communicating paths to choose from' (1086). Applying this to the city, it is the involvement of memory that turns the labyrinth of unknown roads into connecting paths. This experience is particular to an androgynous style of *flânerie* and characteristic of the modernist woman writer creating an identity for herself as an urban observer through both temporally and spatially locating herself in relation to the crossroads of the urban environment.

The Wandering Female Point of View

Neither James nor Proust conform to a gendered definition of the urban spectator or *flâneur*, and both tend to collapse gender polarities into a more fluid, interactive aesthetic method. This immediately sets up a distinction between the static, oppositional categories of 'male' and 'female' and the more ambiguous concept of the 'androgyne', which can be extended to an interpretation of the moving observer, the *flâneur*, as an androgynous figure. Among contemporary critics, Lisa Appignanesi claims that James and Proust 'seem to identify *creativity*, some intrinsic aspect of the fiction-making process, and sometimes even their own status as artists, with the feminine' (my emphasis).[30] They thus seem crucial figures in the development of a literary vision that can accommodate the place of women in the urban environment.

---

[30] Lisa Appignanesi, *Femininity and the Creative Imagination: A Study of Henry James, Robert Musil and Marcel Proust* (London: Vision Press, 1973), 2.

What Leon Edel has termed the 'psychological novel' is characterized by an attempt to express rather then describe the activity of the subjective consciousness, achieved through a narrative style that renders thought in terms of movement and flux. Positing Proust, Dorothy Richardson, and James Joyce as its leading proponents, and devoting a chapter to James as a crucial precursor, Edel notes the common trope of the urban walk in their work, stating that their works exhibit 'a curious kinship of search, voyage, pilgrimage' and that 'all were voyages through consciousness'.[31] This would suggest a connection between perceptual consciousness and movement, one that is manifest in *flânerie*. James and Proust were writing within a climate of theoretical discussion on the structure of consciousness that was implicitly linked with an essentially urban modern culture. At the same time, as literary writers, they drew on an artistic heritage of metaphors connecting mind and movement. Both influences were instrumental in the prominence of modes of observation as theme and structure in James and Proust's work, and important for the image of the female observer and the possible concept of a 'feminine' perception that marks their aesthetics.

The urban environment becomes an active presence rather than a situational backdrop in the 'psychological novel'. Exterior and interior life interact as metaphors of the urban scene are used to describe the structure and workings of the consciousness, just as the city is frequently personified and takes on the characteristics of the consciousness. Consciousness and the city are thus mutually interactive and expressive. In James and Proust, for example, the atmosphere of Paris or London is pervasive and informs the mode of vision of the narrative consciousnesses of Strether and Marcel, whilst also being shaped and perceived in terms of their own subjectivity. Interestingly, the point of contact between city and mind for both writers is a female presence. Maria Gostrey guides the understanding of Strether and introduces him to the cities of Europe. She embodies the modern urban consciousness, her influence to be taken over by that of Marie de Vionnet as the embodiment of Parisian culture. In *A la recherche de temps perdu*, Odette de Crecy and the Duchesse de Guermantes embody respectively the cultures of spectacle and society in Paris, to be superseded by Albertine as a figure of the modern, fleeting consciousness. In the later writing of Richardson, Woolf, and Joyce, this interaction of city and subject becomes an almost permanent state of urban experience. What prompts this linking of city and mind, however? Does the concurrence of theories of urban mental life and female psychology, along with experimentation in the form of

---

[31] Leon Edel, *The Psychological Novel, 1900–1950* (New York: J. B. Lippincott, 1955), 16.

the novel, have significance? Each of these have in common the trope of flow, flux, or movement. Can this be connected to the image of the walker as artist, portraying the modern experience of city and self?

Travel and the journey are common literary metaphors for a search for identity or self-discovery, and the 'psychological novel' can be regarded as a reworking of the traditional male *Bildungsroman*. Up to this point, the concept of 'woman' and 'search/voyage/pilgrimage' had been largely incompatible, the *Bildungsroman* being an exclusively male activity. In the modern urban environment, however, the *Bildungsroman* shifted from its traditional form of exotic travel or the Grand Tour to travel within the city itself, the journey becoming orientated inwards as a searching of the consciousness and self. From the complex associations of woman and city (the streetwalker as prostitute/shopper/tourist), a female *Bildungsroman* was able to be conceived; an exploration of the female consciousness based in the urban environment. The Romanticist, male *Bildungsroman* or 'voyage out' is paralleled in the twentieth century with a voyage in, in which the protagonist journeys to or in confined spaces rather than vast, natural landscapes. The city provides a spatial manifestation of this journey, the mind or consciousness a psychological one. Moreover, the city is not only aesthetically but structurally a different environment to the open landscape. Crucially, it is labyrinthine, and, although mappable, is a place of numerous trajectories, along which one can wander. An extension of this city/consciousness metaphor is to imply that the mind is also somewhere one wanders, perhaps that the consciousness shaped by modernity has a particular structure; a relational, socially defined, changing identity rather than a fixed, constant one.

Despite the persistent tendency to interpret the *flâneur* as a metaphor for the male artist, the aleatory perspective often represented by styles of writing termed 'stream of consciousness' is frequently described as a particularly feminine characteristic. Coined by William James as a model of inner mental activity, the term was appropriated for literary criticism by May Sinclair to describe the innovative technique of Dorothy Richardson in *Pilgrimage*. Although Richardson rejected the label, her long psychological narrative does stem from an effort to create a new literary style that will accommodate the experiences of the female consciousness, in contrast to the conventions of technique and subject of the traditional English novel, which she regards as masculine and alienating to female understanding.

The distinction Richardson makes between the traditional realist novel and the new style she attempts to forge is one of masculinity and femininity rather than male writing and female writing. In her retrospective 'Foreword' to the 1938 publication of *Pilgrimage*, she describes both her endeavour, an attempt 'to produce a feminine equivalent of the current masculine realism' (*P* i. 9), and her technique in terms of journeying, specifically walking, evoking a literary 'pathway', a 'lonely track' that becomes 'a populous highway' (10).[32] From the benefit of hindsight she perceives the changing and treading of this path as a collective activity that includes male as well as female writers (Henry James, Marcel Proust, James Joyce, and Virginia Woolf). By attributing to Henry James the role of path-finder, she at once reasserts the idea of the walking artist as male yet also characterizes his perspective as feminine. For Richardson, James and Proust are path-finders of a style that is concerned with, and represents, a mode of consciousness that has been consistently set up as 'feminine' within a dichotomous gender structure.

Fin de siècle cultural thought was marked by a concern with man's consciousness, its interiorization and, consequently, its relation to the phenomenal world. Common to these theories were descriptions of the activity of the mind in terms of movement. William James, in *The Principles of Psychology* (1890), defined the consciousness as something elusive, that is experienced but cannot be examined. For the pragmatist James, identity involves the connection of our experience of the objective world with the subjective associations we apply to it. He thus emphasizes the role of the consciousness as restless, in motion, and non-locatable, as it responds to the stimulation of outer phenomena and inner impulses. He likens thought to a continuous flow of these stimulations that never breaks. The metaphor of movement employed is important, and James considers a number of options (the chain, the train) before settling on 'stream'. Central to his account of consciousness is the notion of differing pace, to suggest periods of rapid glimpses of phenomena interspersed with intermittent captured moments.[33] James's description of the journey by flight can be paralleled, I think, with the journey by foot. It is this idea of moments of focus amidst flux that links with literary experimentation.

[32] *Pilgrimage* was originally published in twelve separate books; *Pointed Roofs* (1915), *Backwater* (1916), *Honeycomb* (1917), *The Tunnel* (1919), *Interim* (1919), *Deadlock* (1921), *Revolving Lights* (1923), *The Trap* (1925), *Oberland* (1927), *Dawn's Left Hand* (1931), *Clear Horizon* (1935), and *Dimple Hill* (1938). A final book, *March Moonlight*, was not published until a collected edition in 1967.

[33] This can be compared to Freud's story in *Beyond the Pleasure Principle* of the nervous system that develops a 'baked crust' that is at once receptive to and protective against stimuli. Although constantly receiving stimuli, the upper layers of the nervous system are desensitized to it, only occasionally letting small amounts penetrate to more sensitive layers of the consciousness that are able to devote full attention to it. A further similarity is with Georg Simmel's blasé urban dweller, occasionally shocked into contemplation.

The walk offers a human version of this 'journey', particularly the urban walk, in which the rapid succession of stimulations is epitomized. This use of movement to define the internal self invokes the role of the walk as a conventional motif for thought in Western philosophy and art. For the Romantics, the healthy constitutional was specifically located in rural surroundings, the release from the stifling bounds of the city paralleling a release of the spirit in a mental search for the self. After the Romantics, the trope of the solitary walker shifts from the rural to the urban environment, to become less a vigorous hike than an incoherent wander. Yet, importantly, the act of walking denies the observer a totalizing, constant perception and a self-absorbed subjectivity. As Jeffrey Robinson states, '[t]he walk is an engaged act of mind', and it forces engagement with a constantly changing environment.[34] It is in this respect that I want to suggest walking as not so much parallel to thinking and writing but rather as extending into thinking and writing in terms of aesthetic engagement with its spatial, situational surroundings. My argument is that this interaction differs from the traditional masculine perspective of detached urban observation.

Dorothy Richardson and the *Passante*

The *passante* is a particularly significant figure because her position in the city streets cannot be denigrated through objectification. She is an enigma, like the man in the crowd, who cannot be placed in the familiarized city of the male *flâneur*. She is also a mirror image of the male observer, however, her height and confidence implying a masculinity that parallels the femininity of the dandy-*flâneur*. The *passante* can perhaps therefore act as a metaphor for the woman as artist-observer of the city.

Baudelaire's 'A une passante' portrays woman as an enigmatic icon of the cityscape. Standing in the street, the narrator is passed by a woman whose grace and figure attract him. Whilst in the process of objectifying her as type (mourner) and erotic object (he notes the line of her leg through the hem of her skirt), she returns his look and he experiences the shock of the mutual encounter. This experience is particular to the modern city—a sudden collision with the unknown, a transient moment of communication and then move away back into anonymity. He is disturbed by the returned glance, which is unusual to the urban condi-

---

[34] Jeffrey C. Robinson, *The Walk: Notes on a Romantic Image* (Norman, Okla.: University of Oklahoma Press, 1989), 42.

tion of isolation and the shock brings him 'suddenly to life again'. Like the artist, the woman walks the night city, yet she cannot be denigrated in sexual or moral terms as her status and actions are ambiguous and defy interpretation. Janet Wolff has suggested that the *passante* is still a prostitute, arguing that a respectable woman of the time would not have met the male gaze. However, Baudelaire rarely misses an opportunity to damn the prostitute or lesbian (even when also admiring them) and the extreme shock the narrator experiences seems at odds with the common sight of the prostitute. Indeed, the woman's dark mourning attire prevents the identification of her as a prostitute in terms of outward appearance and subverts the implications of a woman looking at a man in the night street—two categorizing motifs contradict. Crucial to the idea of the *passante* is precisely the fact that it is impossible to define her as a type and that as a result she is the most perfect reflection of the characteristics of the urban narrator-observer.

It is in the *passante* that it is possible to find one female alternative to the public urban observer of the *flâneur*. It is also with the idea of the *passante* that early twentieth-century women writers pose a challenge to the exclusivity of the male artist-personas in the city of canonical modernism. The concept of the Baudelairian artist-observer, for example, is most directly continued in the urban poems of T. S. Eliot, in which modern women are safely categorized as superficial, neurotic, or of unequal class status. However, the visibility of the woman as object/ invisibility of the woman as subject in Eliot's work is countered by women writers in explicit examples of the middle-class woman's urban experience. In contrast to Eliot's urban women are the examples of observant, peripatetic women in the novels of Dorothy Richardson and Virginia Woolf, both writers manipulating the image of the *passante* to express a female perspective on the city.

Virginia Woolf foregrounds the *passante* in *Mrs Dalloway* (1925), in which a number of female and male characters observe the city from different vantage points, both actual and theoretical. Woolf endows the figure of Peter Walsh, however, with the dominant characteristics of the leisured *flâneur*; an attitude of rebellion yet ultimate conventionality, detachment as a result of his years in India, and a sense of freedom in the streets. In particular, she depicts his attempt to objectify women in the urban environment and uses an encounter with an unknown woman in Trafalgar Square to subvert this superiority. Woolf registers Walsh's visual possession of the woman with an ironic twist, and as he turns the woman into an image that he desires, emphasizes the anonymity and lack of possessable identity of that image. Walsh's perception of the woman is formed by his own subjective desires: 'it was half made up, as he knew very well; invented, this escapade with the girl; made up, as one makes up the better part of life, he thought—making oneself up; making her up' (*MD* 70). A slippage thus occurs between his act of objectification and what is objectified (his own desire rather than the woman). As Bowlby perceptively notes, 'if the *passante* is merely or mostly the man's projection, a creature of the masculine imagination, then the field, or rather the street, might be thought to have been left wide open for women to come along and walk in a way of their own'.[35]

Although unsure of her respectability, Walsh assumes the woman is available, a public woman who would easily accept his proposition of 'refreshment'. Imagining his ownership of her in terms that are highly sexualized, he follows the woman, fetishizing her clothes and accessories in a way that equates her with the articles for sale in shop windows, 'her cloak, her gloves, her shoulders combining with the fringes and the laces and the feather boas in the windows' (69). The woman begins to elude him, however, and he regards himself as a 'buccaneer' in pursuit. Yet Walsh is essentially the passive figure of the pair, following her steps and powerless to prevent her disappearance. For Woolf the woman is triumphant as she takes out the key to her house (indicating her independence and own place in the city) and looks towards him rather than at him, observing him as object. Frustrated in his visual superiority, Walsh's immediate reaction is to revert to the conventional degradation of the public female, associating her building with 'those flat red houses with hanging flowerbaskets of vague impropriety' (70). Woolf, therefore, retains the structure of the 'dominant street story' of the relationship of the male and female in the urban world—the observing male and observed *passante*—yet highlights its limitations by parodying it through Walsh's almost absurd fictions.[36] In *Pilgrimage*, Dorothy Richardson reverses this structure by revealing the urban encounter from the angle of the *passante*. Given a visual perspective, the *passante* becomes a *flâneuse*.

At the beginning of *Revolving Lights*, the seventh book of Richardson's extended novel *Pilgrimage*, the protagonist Miriam Henderson takes a fifty-page walk in the London streets from the City to her room in Bloomsbury. Much of this is taken up with her solitary movement along fairly deserted streets whilst she ponders on the movements of her life itself and the position of independence she has developed. It is a fascinating evocation in writing of a city and psyche explored in walking.

[35] Rachel Bowlby, 'Walking, Women and Writing: Virginia Woolf as *flâneuse*', in Isobel Armstrong (ed.), *New Feminist Discourses* (London: Routledge, 1992), 26–47, p. 32.
[36] Ibid. 34.

It seems to me to directly answer Wolff's call for a description of the experience of the *passante*, and yet also offer a detailed indication of the duality of the *flâneur* and *passante* roles. I shall therefore study it at some length. Twice in her journey home Miriam briefly passes people who prompt shocked recognition; a man standing alone amidst the rush of Piccadilly, and an old woman stooping in the gutter at Cambridge Circus. In Miriam's walk through London, therefore, the reader is offered the experience of the *passante* herself as *flâneuse*.

Miriam's marginality is emphasized as she starts on her walk. Throughout *Pilgrimage* to this point she has struggled to identify herself with a particular place or social group—as a middle-class woman in the city she has had no such place open to her. Richardson vividly evokes Miriam's isolation from the different worlds in her life by emphasizing their separateness and the boundary spaces between them that Miriam is constantly traversing; roads, railtracks, stairs. The walk home occurs in just such a vacuum. On the threshold of 'the busy planning world of socialism', the Lycurgan meeting she has been attending, Miriam observes the vistas of her present life:

[f]ar away in tomorrow, stood the established, unchanging world of Wimpole Street, linked helpfully to the lives of the prosperous classes. Just ahead, at the end of the walk home, the small isolated Tansley Street world, full of secretive people drifting about on the edge of catastrophe [...] In the space between these surrounding worlds was the everlasting solitude. (*P* iii. 233)

The solitude in the streets relieves her from the associations of these classified areas of politics, work, and domesticity. It is almost as if the night streets, even though sites of movement and flux, halt time and hold her suspended, away from the daily pressures of work and the steady progression of days in her meagre room. As with the *flâneur*, who makes a home of the boulevard, for Miriam the street is a natural habitat, soothing and welcoming: 'She went out into its shelter' (235). The androgynous implications of the *passante*, within whom the Baudelaire narrator finds self-recognition, are also present in Miriam, who continually reflects on her sense of masculinity. Here, for example, she sees this masculine quality ('she had a masculine mind') as being responsible for her life's path and her active perception, as well as for her present enjoyment of her walk and visual appreciation of the city:

all the things of the mind that had come her way had come unsought; yet finding her prepared; so that they seemed not only her rightful property, but also in some way, herself. The proof was that they had passed her sisters by, finding no response; but herself they had drawn, often reluctant [...] to a path that it sometimes seemed she must explore to the exclusion of everything else in life, exhaustively, the long way round, the masculine way. (236)

However, Miriam's 'masculinity' is not reaffirming of the inherent maleness of the urban observer, as she often vehemently condemns both the masculine and feminine mind. Rather, her 'masculinity' refers to androgyny, to a maleness that combines with femaleness to cancel the excesses of each.

Finding herself in the West End, Miriam observes the

wide, leisurely shop-fronts displaying in a restrained profusion, comfortably within reach of the experienced eye half turned to glance from a passing vehicle, all the belongings of West End life; on the pavements, the trooping succession of masked life-moulded forms, their unobservant eyes, aware of the resources all about them, at gaze upon their continuous adventure. (240)

This is the city much as Benjamin and other urban theorists describe it, populated by absent-minded spectators, trained to register its myriad sights unthinkingly, and a faceless crowd propelled by purpose. Moreover, like the *flâneur*, Miriam feels an affinity with the crowd and understands the reason for its guarded anonymity: '[t]here was something here that offered her again and again a solution of the problem of social life, a safe-guard of individuality [...] Always to be solid and resistant; unmoved. Having no opinions and only one enthusiasm—to be unmoved' (241). Miriam values the crowd's social method of detachment as a form of self-protection. Yet, at the same time, the crowd implies the disturbing uniformity that results from the widespread adoption of this act and Miriam revolts from it to the more privileged social position of her youth. Earlier I noted that the *flâneur* in Benjamin's revised description increasingly retreated away from the crowd, in an attempt to retain a certain individual control and self-order over the chaos of the city street. The moving perspective of the walking urban observer, physically within the city street, is exchanged in this act for the panoramic perspective of a static urban observer, afraid of and cerebrally aloof from the street's materiality. Miriam may be a supreme example of a female *flâneur* who walks in the streets of her city, but she also shares this tendency to a panoramic position away from the street, in a position of superior detachment. The male *flâneur* gains a position of gendered authority and power from this detachment. In Miriam's case, she is torn between sympathy with the crowd and the constant assertion of independence that is the mark of her feminism. The viewpoint she takes, and the aesthetic perspective that Richardson develops in relation to it, is ultimately impressionistically mobile, shifting, and transgressive, but at the same time remains somewhat isolated. Miriam is always a loner as she wanders the city; like the *flâneur* she refuses to merge with the crowd.

In *Revolving Lights*, Miriam is thus still aware of a certain instability of self. She paradoxically retains an attraction to the stylishness and assurity of the upper classes, whilst feeling associated with the lower classes. Making herself an anonymous figure that belongs to neither category, she takes up a position of detached observation: '[s]he, with no resources at all, had dropped to easy irresponsible labour to avoid being shaped and branded, to keep her untouched strength free for a wider contemplation [...] a *plebeian* dilettantism' (245). This desire for freedom from responsibility in order to enjoy almost Epicurean observation is reminiscent of the *flâneur*. Miriam's struggle to find an identity and define herself objectively is expressed through linguistic shifts in Richardson's text. Miriam's self-reflection moves back and forth between possessives as Richardson changes from third-person to first-person narration and back again. As well as registering Miriam's self quest, however, these shifts also emphasize the doubled role of the *passante*; both object and subject in the city.

Sexualization is an important factor of the Parisian *flâneur*'s relationship to the urban street, as he eroticizes and fetishizes both woman and city. In the tradition of male urban literature in England the explicit equation of London/woman is more rare. However, women writers apply a gender to the city more frequently. There are certainly sexual connotations attached to Miriam's response to the London streets, and, upturning the topological image of city/woman/prostitute, Richardson depicts London as Miriam's 'mighty lover'. Recalling returning to London, Miriam describes the city as welcoming and enclosing her:

No one in the world would oust this mighty lover, always receiving her back without words, engulfing and leaving her untouched, liberated and expanding to the whole range of her being. [...] She would travel further than the longest journey, swifter than the most rapid flight, down and down into an oblivion deeper than sleep [...] tingling to the spread of London all about her, herself one with it, feeling her life flow outwards, north, south, east and west, to all its margins. (272–3)

Richardson thus reverses the tendency to feminize cities and the image of the artist-*flâneur* traversing the city landscape as metaphorical female body. In such analogies the male observer can be regarded as cutting up the body of the city by categorizing it along social distinctions. Miriam's journey decategorizes the city and herself, as she moves and flows through the border areas and streets that are rather the arterial images of the cityscape.

It is immediately after this image of the sexualized city that Miriam reaches the centre of the West End at Piccadilly. The side streets are full of solitary old men 'still circulating, like the well preserved coins of a past reign' (273) (past *flâneurs*?), themselves figures in passing and in the last stages of their transitory existence. The only other women are prostitutes in the shadows, and Miriam herself is approached by a prowling man, evidence that at least at night the woman in public is still deemed an immoral figure. Modernity is heralded by the Circus itself and the noise and hansoms of young people of both sexes. Miriam still belongs nowhere and feels 'the need for thoughtless hurrying across its open spaces', regretting that she has no place, no metaphorical interior or club, 'a neutral territory where she could finish her thought undisturbed' (274).[37] This desire for a version of the private home in the public-private club parallels the *flâneur*'s public-private interior of the arcade. Indeed, the woman developing her independence in the city was negotiating both her own private *and* public space. Yet, actually, at the centre of the Piccadilly island, Miriam feels in a place of 'central freedom' (276) and it is at this point that she sees a man, also 'a watchful habitué' (277), and they come together in a moment of shared recognition, interchanging the roles of observer/observed, *flâneur/passante*.

The moment of recognition is emphasized by being literal as well as psychological; the man is Tommy Babington, an ex-suitor. He preserves aspects of the *flâneur*, dandiacal in his 'dapper' dress and 'pince-nez', and standing in solitude. As Miriam observes him, he is 'expressionless' and anonymous. His face is 'unawakened' and merely the reflection of the people he observes, similar to the way the narrator of the 'Man in the Crowd' realizes he appears to others. The act of passing takes place: 'He had glanced [...] Going on, she must sweep right across his path [...] She rushed on, passing him with a swift salute, saw him raise his hat with mechanical promptitude as she stepped from the kerb and forward, pausing an instant for a passing hansom' (277). Miriam is the active, moving figure, Babington the passive one. Her look is one of challenge, the *passante* defying the male onlooker to objectify her, and celebrating her ability to shock him out of his masculine stability. She rejoices in denying his possession of her; on the streets, of which they are both 'habitués', '[t]hey had met equally at last' (277). Yet, despite achieving her own right to the night streets, Miriam realizes that Babington's reaction will be to reassert his male, bourgeois authority and emphasize her position as an unmarried woman out at night alone: '[a]lready in his

---

[37] In the next volume of *Pilgrimage*, 'The Trap', Miriam joins a female club, 'The Belmont', which provides her with such a place of neutral public territory in the city.

mind was one of those formulas that echoed about in enclosed life. . . . "Oui, ma chère, little Mirry *Henderson*, strolling, at midnight, across Piccadilly Circus"' (278).

However, although Miriam displays many of the characteristics of the *flâneur*, she also criticizes him. She derides Tommy Babington's aura of freedom when he is ultimately conventional and dependent on his home life. In Michael Shatov, the exotic Russian, she criticizes another aspect of the *flâneur*, horrified at his self-assured categorizing of people in terms of physiognomy: '"You don't *see* them; they are not *there* in what you see"' (279). Yet Miriam finds herself adopting a masculine mode of vision, realizing that 'now she herself was interested; had attained unawares a sort of connoisseurship, taking in, at a glance, nationality, type, status, the difference between inclination and misfortune' and questions '[w]as this contamination or illumination?' (279). Having placed herself as subject in the city, she now realizes that she can also act as the *flâneur* and appropriate for herself the 'masculine gaze'. Whether this identification with the male should be the aim of the independent woman, is an essential part of Miriam's 'pilgrimage' of self-discovery.[38] She tends towards a rejection of a male position, however, and certainly Richardson's literary style can be interpreted as a new form of *flânerie*, which she regards as particularly female and in which 'all the practical facts, the tragedies and comedies and events, are but ripples on a stream' (280).

At one point in Miriam's walk, for example, in the commercially developed streets of the West End, the conditions that eradicated the original *flâneur* are brought into focus. Benjamin describes how the building of the grand Haussmann boulevards in Paris, which aided large volumes of traffic moving quickly through the city, ultimately led to an environment unsympathetic to the strolling observer. The 'opening up' of Paris thus reasserted the 'public' space of the city streets that had been metaphorically privatized in the spaces of the arcades and older boulevards. In London, Miriam contrasts late Victorian Oxford Street with Georgian Bond Street in the same way. Oxford Street is unsafe for the walker and constantly bombards the senses in a way that allows no pause for reflection:

[e]ven at night it seemed to echo with the harsh sounds of its obvious conglomerate traffic [. . .] there was nothing to obliterate the permanent sense of two monstrous streams flowing all day, fierce and shattering, east and west.

[38] An example of the familiar liberal/cultural feminist dilemma of whether woman should assert her place within the traditionally male order, denying her femininity, or oppose that order, emphasizing her female difference.

79

Oxford Street, unless she were sailing through it perched in sun-light on the top of an omnibus lumbering steadily towards the graven stone of the City, always wrought destruction. (246)

Faced with a choice between turning into the wide, constantly moving road or the 'sacred pavements [...] the winding lane' (246) of Bond Street, Miriam chooses the latter. It is in the image of the physically as well as mentally detached observer, positioned on the rooftop of a bus, that the decline of the *flâneur* is evident, threatened by the moving flux itself and retreating to a detached, panoramic position.

This ultimate detachment of the masculine *flâneur* is noted by Benjamin in 'On Some Motifs in Baudelaire', when he states that the nineteenth-century *flâneur*, enjoying his superiority and 'unwilling to forego the life of a gentleman of leisure', was 'out of place' in the modernizing city. Benjamin describes a transformation of the *flâneur* into the 'man of the crowd', 'what had to become of the *flâneur* once he was deprived of the milieu to which he belonged'.[39] I would suggest however that, as a conceptual trope, he mutates according to a new conceptual form of spectatorship that is adapted to the city of the turn of the century. As Miriam's allusion to the bus-top observer illustrates, the urban observer as *flâneur* has to make way for the urban observer as high-level spectator. A greater removal from human interaction takes place, as the *flâneur* withdraws mentally and physically (onto the rooftop, bus, or balcony common to the new apartments of Haussmann's Paris) from the tumult of the street. Miriam realizes that the fate of the *flâneur*, protecting himself by choosing 'to live outside the world of happenings, always to forget and escape [...] was certainly wrong' (288). The narrative style that Richardson develops can perhaps be regarded as a negotiation away from this objective detachment. Along with the interior monologue it is a technique taken up by women writers to connect the immediacy of the experience of spectacle with a rendering of the enduring essence of self. Literary techniques that register the personal thoughts and memories of the subconscious, they can be used to combine aestheticizing, Impressionist structures of perception with a concern for human subjectivity.

As she approaches home, Miriam experiences the second 'encounter'. Paralleling her meeting with Babington in Piccadilly Circus, she crosses paths with a grotesque woman in Cambridge Circus, yet the experience is now not so much that of the *passante* as of the 'man in the crowd'. In this passage Richardson evokes a suspended moment in a misty, lamp-lit atmosphere, when an almost mystical encounter of doubles occurs. The poetic rhythm and imagery recalls the intensity of Poe's story and

---

[39] Benjamin, 'On Some Motifs in Baudelaire', in *Charles Baudelaire*, 174.

Baudelaire's prose poems, the imagination taking over from reason in perceiving the relations of self and world. The woman stooping in the gutter, illuminated by the lamp-light is the 'last, hidden truth of London, spoiling the night' (288). Miriam meets her glance and experiences 'naked recognition [...] It was herself, set in her path and waiting through all the years', as if the walk up Shaftesbury Avenue has been an avenue of time between illuminated pools of present and future. In an almost direct female reworking of Poe's tale, the old crone is a stealthy, evil figure (her reddish, nobbled skull is not dissimilar to conventional images of the devil), a lone woman in the city without the fetishizable features of youth or beauty. Yet she is also pathetically forgotten, pushed into a dark passage by the bourgeois world that ignores 'the awful face above the outstretched bare arm'. Miriam is shocked into self-recognition by this confrontation with her 'reflection'. Her youth, job, and room allow her to construct an image of conformity, yet this is really only a pretence, 'a semblance that was nothing but a screen set up, hiding what she was in the depths of her being' (289). Richardson indicates here the precariousness of woman's position in the city and the fear that she will end up as both alienated and alien, a forgotten, unwanted London 'secret'.

In Baudelaire's poem, the *passante* is arguably a metaphor for what can be glimpsed within the urban crowd; the 'feminine' muse embodying what is beautiful, fleeting, and inspiring. Yet she is also a mirror image of the poet-narrator himself, anonymous and with the freedom of the city streets. The *passante* is thus an ambiguous figure in various ways—both observed and observer, part of the crowd and individual in the crowd, a woman yet reflecting a man. This ambiguity suggests androgyny and indeed her outward appearance of austere elegance and grace is similar to that of the androgynous dandy. The *passante* thus seems a female parallel to the *flâneur*. That each possess both 'masculine' and 'feminine' traits suggests an inherent androgyny in the Baudelairian urban spectator that is significant for any discussion of a *flâneuse* and is important in the rejection of the traditional idea of the purely male *flâneur*. Richardson's depiction of Miriam Henderson's walk through the night streets of London offers the perspective of a female urban walker. Miriam's awareness of being viewed as morally questionable, her identification with a male point of view, and assertion of her distinct femaleness, point up issues to be addressed in any discussion of the definition of a female *flâneur* or separate category of *flâneuse*.

3 | The New Woman and the Wandering Jew

THE trope of the male *flâneur* can encompass an urban cultural field, populated with figures that vary from the literary bohemian, the tourist, the exile, and the rag-picker to the institutions of state power. The stretched boundaries of this cultural space are equally permeable to other figures, however. Adrian Rifkin notes of the years after the 1914–18 war that 'a new stratum of single women, who learn their own circuits in the rounds of work and pleasure' enter the city and 'hide, so to speak, in this man-made space, while their pleasures represent a real displacement of its values'.[1] For the city of spectacle and consumption patrolled by the male *flâneur* also provided the necessary conditions for women's greater access to public urban space. I would locate the timing of this phenomenon earlier than Rifkin, however, beginning in the late nineteenth century with the rise of the New Woman.

In social terms, a new female lifestyle became evident in the last decades of the nineteenth century as the marriage age increased and middle-class women began to gain entry into the universities and the workplace, therefore living away from the family home. Moreover, they were increasingly prominent in the city streets as the commercialized metropolis opened up to them as consumers and workers. Although the numbers of such women were relatively low, their position and ambitions were sufficiently unorthodox to provoke widespread debate and criticism. As a result, the New Woman, a social phenomenon and a literary type of the 1880s and 1890s, became a dominant preoccupation for writers of novels, essays, and popular journalism, propounded in her stereotypical form by satirical publications such as *Punch*. As both social figure and literary caricature, she was a specifically urban character, the result of the circumstances and qualities of a growing metropolitan

[1] Adrian Rifkin, *Street Noises: Parisian Pleasure, 1900–40* (Manchester: Manchester UP, 1993), 9.

society. The single woman seeking independence in late nineteenth-century London marks the beginning of a sustained female presence and observance of the urban environment. Furthermore, this 'new woman', 'educated working woman', 'professional woman', or 'odd woman', as she was variously labelled, was to remain a spectral presence for the aesthetic self-consciousness of urban-based writers such as Richardson and Woolf in their writing of the city two decades later.

Although the educated/working woman was high profile in the city of the 1880s, her representation as an urban figure occurred largely in works by men. 'New Woman writers', as Elaine Showalter has termed them, independent women who defined themselves as professional writers and who challenged the conventional subjects and literary forms of the novel tradition, although themselves public urban personalities, rarely concentrated on the city as a subject for their fiction, unless in terms of its interior spaces, notably the enclosure of the Victorian drawing-room.[2] Although women's private journals and letters indicate participation and movement in the city, this is not transferred into their fiction, perhaps suggesting a continued sense of social restraint in urban space. The female characters in the urban-based stories of Showalter's collection, for example, escape the confines of claustrophobic interiors through hashish-induced dreams, or else give up life in the city altogether and leave for foreign exile. Consequently, the city largely remained the domain of the male writer, who observed the New Woman, in the same way as the prostitute, as spectacle and subject for masculinist, naturalistic study. The modern woman, living and working independently in the city, was a new visible presence in its streets. The term 'public woman', therefore, could no longer refer to just the prostitute and was applicable to a new kind of woman who could not be reduced to the category of 'victim' and also seemed alarmingly self-reliant to the bourgeois male. In response, therefore, the meaning of the label 'public woman' was not so much redefined as doubled, and the modern woman was herself classed as deviant.

Moreover, the unmarried, emancipated woman was also judged in sexual terms as threatening to masculinity; either as sexually free and voracious or asexual and androgynous. Meredith, Gissing, Grant Allen, and H. G. Wells all took up the subject of the New Woman and her forays into the public world, yet underlying their interest in and support for her emancipation was a voyeuristic fascination with her sexuality. Marriage remained the ideal occupation for a woman and, if she ultimately

---

[2] Elaine Showalter, *Daughters of Decadence: Woman Writers of the Fin-de-Siècle* (London: Virago, 1993).

rejected this, the novels implied, she was faced with two options of urban life: morally fallen woman or anonymous member of a crowd of 'odd' women. These three choices appear again and again in the male literature of the turn-of the century, and such novels therefore had a rather ambiguous effect on the reputation of the modern woman. They undeniably brought her into focus, portraying her positively in revolt against restrictive social conventions, yet at the same time they ultimately fell back on conventional value judgements in their conclusions.

I have previously argued that Zola, Dreiser, and Gissing portray women working in the world cities of London, Paris, and Chicago with the voyeuristic perspective of the naturalistic *flâneur*. James focuses on the upper-middle-class woman, independent of family or economic ties, who voluntarily enters city life, yet in his novels the relationship of woman and author is not so clearly marked as that of subject and *flâneur*. James's feminine characters are less his 'other' than his mirrored 'double', and it is with their multiple and sensitive experience of the city that he identifies his own. Women now had their own voice in the city. The middle-class working woman could herself be a writer; as novelist, letter or journal writer, essayist or feminist campaigner. As male writers dominated the image of the New Woman in the *fin de siècle*, accounts of women's urban experience from their own perspective have tended to be overlooked. However, they form an important link between the portrayal of women in the nineteenth-century and twentieth-century city.

This ambiguity over the position of the New Woman is succinctly manifest in Gissing's *In The Year of Jubilee* (1894), in which the author alternates the vitality and independence enjoyed by Nancy Lord in the city streets, with vitriolic attacks on her presumption and transgression in entering public urban space. In a novel that ironically depicts the oppressiveness of social conventions at a time of celebration of national progress, Gissing seems at first to commend Nancy's desire to escape from her domestic confines to 'walk about the streets after dark, and see the crowds and the illuminations' (*YJ* 19). The city is a place of opportunity and freedom and 'she resolve[s] to taste independence, to mingle with the limitless crowd as one of its units, borne in whatever direction' (56–7). Yet ultimately Gissing cannot reconcile his rejection of Victorian oppressions with his pessimistic and misogynistic view of the modern city. London is a dangerous place, where the individual is crushed or engulfed, and it is not a place for women, who are regarded as particularly vulnerable to its temptations; 'Nancy forgot her identity, lost sight of herself as an individual. She did not think, and her emotions differed little from those of any shop-girl let loose [. . .] Could she have seen her face, its look of vulgar abandonment would have horrified her' (62).

The middle-class woman walking in the city is a problematic figure for the threatened male, however, as she is not a sexually available object and her economic security protects her from punishment as a fallen woman. Despite Gissing's wishful identification of Nancy with the loose shop-girl, then, in social terms they are very different. The threat of sexual fall as a result of her 'streetwalking' is more in the mind of traditional cultural opinion than a likely actuality. Thus Gissing alters his definition of the public woman; the middle-class woman cannot satisfactorily be identified with the available prostitute, so she becomes instead the self-interested, unavailable barren woman. Nancy's enjoyment and exhilara-tion in the city streets, and her ability to place and guide herself within them, do not accord with Gissing's male, *fin de siècle* aesthetic pess-imism. Into this vision, which views the city as an engulfing, confusing labyrinth in which men become anonymous cogs in a world machine, strides the modern woman, asserting her place, identity, and independ-ence. Gissing's response is ascerbic:

In her conceit of self-importance, she stood there, above the battling millions of men, proof against mystery and dread, untouched by the voices of the past, and in the present seeing only common things, though from an odd point of view. Here her senses seemed to make literal the assumption by which her mind had always been directed; that she—Nancy Lord—was the mid point of the universe. (95)

Gissing's description of Nancy on the Monument exemplifies the male image of the New Woman.

The New Woman was contemporaneous in the late nineteenth-century city with an influx of immigrant Jews from Eastern Europe. As anomalous newcomers to the city in the 1880s, and as they began to adapt and find a professional space for themselves in the first decades of the twentieth century, both were the subject of apprehension, satire, and marginaliza-tion. The Jew is a figure who frequently preoccupies the writer of the urban scene, integral to portrayals of London from Dickens to the Modernists for several reasons; the visibility of Jews in the late nine-teenth-century city, the mythic legend of the 'Wandering Jew' as a symbol of spiritual quest, and the consequent perception of the Jew as both actual and metaphorical embodiment of cosmopolitanism. The 'wandering' identity of the Jew, and the notions of cosmopolitanism, placelessness, and the alien, were influential for the experience of the metropolis.

The 'metropolitan' is a term that surfaces constantly in discussion of the *flâneur*, who makes his home in the 'metropolis', walking and obser-ving a particular urban environment with a particular quality of experi-ence. Nineteenth-century literature is full of metropolitan observers;

Dickens, Booth, Mayhew, and Gissing, for example. The metropolis is a place, the concentration of political and financial power, of both exploited poverty and ostentatious wealth and leisure. It is the capital city, the imperial city—it is named. The figure of the cosmopolitan, the outsider, the foreigner, the tourist, is the dominant observer within this city, exemplified by both the Jamesian protagonist and the novelist himself. The metropolitan is placed as a figure and a quality of a particular city, whereas the cosmopolitan wanders as a figure and quality that extends to many cities or metropolises. There would seem to be no 'cosmopolis', only a series of metropolises. The cosmopolitan is an urban character with no fixed place or identity; on the margins of all cities he yet belongs to none. Cosmopolitanism is thus a decentralized, placeless state and 'stands for a relatively autonomous *discursive* community with its own distinctive values and traditions' (my emphasis).[3]

The position of the Jew in Western culture is problematic, not least due to the frequent confusion of his historical and representative identity. Theorized, like the *flâneur*, into a critical metaphor, he becomes a figure outside history, whose conceptual boundaries can be stretched to encompass various types of exilic discourse. The *flâneur* is something like the Jew as a marginalized, wandering outsider in the city. Unlike the *flâneur*, however, the paradox of the chameleon qualities of the Jew is that ultimately he is also an icon of what is unchanging and immutable, his features making him instantly recognizable, unable to escape into the anonymity of the crowd. The two figures are therefore contemporary but distinct urban types, existing together in literary representations of the city but embodying different attitudes, perspectives, and anxieties. However, the figure of the cosmopolitan Jew in London is a recurring motif at the turn of the century for women urban artists such as Amy Levy and Dorothy Richardson, who frequently write about their experience of walking and traversing the city through a process of identification and self-definition with the Jewish immigrant. The two writers share three common tropes; the spaces of the private room and the city street, and the use of the Jewish identity for paving the way from the former to the latter.

Amy Levy and Paven Ground

The two dominating features common to self-conscious, female representations of the urban landscape are the city street and the private

---

[3] Elizabeth L. Eisenstein, *Grub Street Abroad: Aspects of the French Cosmopolitan Population, from the Age of Louis XIV to the French Revolution* (Oxford: Clarendon Press, 1992), 3–4.

room. The stereotype of the male urban poet was either that of the Romantic in his panoramic garret room or the Victorian walking the streets of a foggy labyrinth. Women employed these tropes in asserting their own position as urban writers, using and portraying the street as place of inspiration and creative thinking, and the room, with its obligatory writing bureau, as place of repose and artistic production.

Amy Levy, both woman in and writer of the 1880s city, is one of the first women writers to consistently adopt the perspective of a female writer-observer or *flâneur*.[4] Levy is a good example of the modern woman of the affluent middle class living in the city. The first Jewish woman to be educated at Newnham, she was friends with Olive Schreiner, Eleanor Marx, and Vernon Lee. Interested in the new experimentation taking place in the arts and social politics of the 1880s, she wrote widely on feminism and politics as well as her own fiction and poetry. Yet despite the high esteem with which she was regarded by contemporary critics, including Oscar Wilde, who published her in *Woman's World*, and Richard Garnett, who wrote her entry for the *Dictionary of National Biography*, Levy has been almost forgotten until recently. Attention has previously focused on her Judaism and representations of Anglo-Jewish society in her controversial novel *Reuben Sachs*, and it is only now that interest in Levy as a writer of the city is growing. The two intersect, however, as her writings self-consciously debate the freedoms and limitations identifiable with her position as a female and/or Jewish urban observer. It is necessary to read Levy's depiction of Jewishness against the context of her position as a Cambridge educated professional writer, interested in the developing social/scientific discourses and staunchly defendant of the needs and abilities of the New Woman. She is caught between her own Anglo-Jewishness and her belief in woman's suffrage, between her restricted social position as a woman and her need for personal and racial identity, between the urban character of the stereotypical Jew and the domestic role of the Victorian woman.[5]

---

[4] Levy has been shamefully neglected as a feminist writer, even by Elaine Showalter in her re-establishment of previously forgotten women writers in *A Literature of Their Own: Women Writers from Charlotte Brontë to Doris Lessing* (London: Virago, 1978). Although supported by Oscar Wilde, who published her work regularly in his *Woman's World*, she fell into relative obscurity after her death (suicide, by gas inhalation) in 1889. Contemporary interest in her writing is now growing, as a result of the republication of her work in *The Complete Novels and Selected Writings of Amy Levy 1861–1889*, ed. and intro. by Melvyn New (Gainesville, Fla.: Florida UP, 1993), and Deborah Nord's assessment of her writing in *Walking the Victorian Streets: Women, Representation, and the City* (Ithaca, NY: Cornell UP, 1995). Parenthetical references refer to New's edition.

[5] Perhaps one strategy for reconciling Jewishness and feminism was to adopt and manipulate the Decadent discourse that identified the modern New Woman with the

Levy's parents were wealthy middle-class Anglo-Jews with traditional values. Although Levy's father was reputedly proud of his daughter's writing, her mother was less enthusiastic. Isobel Levin Levy agreed with society that the primary aim of young women was to achieve a good marriage and she objected to her daughter's independence, preventing her from undertaking work as a private tutor for example, because of the impropriety of teaching men. In her London home Levy was expected to conduct herself as a respectable Victorian lady, and her friend Clementina Black recalled that she rarely left the house, and only then if she was visiting friends or going on holiday. Black's statement would seem slightly exaggerated, as Levy obviously had some freedom as a member of both the British Library Reading Room and the University Women's Club. Nevertheless, the scenes that frequently occur in her urban poems and novels—walking in the streets, the bus ride, listening to the street-hawker—would have been rare events for Levy herself and perhaps unsurprisingly prompt moments of concentrated imagination.[6]

London pervades Levy's writings, as a source of inspiration and subject, but also as a place of support and nurture that she is at home within. These are the characteristics that surface in her celebrations of the city. At the same time, however, Levy was greatly influenced by the work of James Thomson (B.V.) whose major work *The City of Dreadful Night* (1874) exemplified the hegemonic *fin de siècle* pessimism of the male urban mind. The struggle to overcome the difficulties faced by the individual women in the late nineteenth-century city in order to enjoy the concurrent opportunities (largely seen as a positive *Bildungsroman*, a journey towards independent identity, by women writers) was thus combined in Levy's viewpoint with the intermittent surfacing of deep pessimism. On the more positive side, however, Thomson's impressionistic writing, his overt presence in his poem as observer of a simultaneously beloved and hated city, and his merging of external scenes and objects with the emotions of the mind, informed her own aesthetic perspective. Thomson is something of a Baudelairian poet of the city,

destructive Jewess or Salome-figure. The actresses Rachel Félix and Sarah Bernhardt, for example, emphasized both their emancipation and their dark Jewishness. Sander L. Gilman's 'Salome, Syphilis, Sarah Berhardt and the Modern Jewess', in Nochlin and Garb (eds.), *The Jew in the Text: Modernity and the Construction of Identity* (London: Thames and Hudson, 1995), 97–120, is a useful starting point for this idea.

[6] The likelihood that she would have some first-hand knowledge of working-class areas is due to her father's position as chairman of the Beaumont Trust, which was established to build a People's Palace in the East End. Although Levy acted as honorary secretary, however, the majority of her duties were presumably conducted at home. 'Notice for Beaumont Trust', *Jewish Chronicle*, 28 May 1886, p. 4, and 4 June 1886, p. 3.

an agonized, spleen-ridden *flâneur*. Can we describe Levy as its first *flâneuse*?

Crucial to an understanding of the place of London in Levy's writing is her self-acclaimed identity as an urban writer. She consciously places herself within the traditional iconography of the male urban poet; in her identification with Thomson, and also the posthumous collection *A London Plane-Tree and Other Poems* (1890), the illustrations to which also exploit urban stereotypes. The *London Plane-Tree* volume is prefaced by a couplet from Austin Dobson's poem, 'On London Stones': 'Mine is an urban Muse, and bound | By some strange law to paven ground.' In Dobson's poem, these words are spoken by the poet-persona who wishes for country air to purify and inspire his imagination but, once there, finds that his muse can only survive in the city. It continues, 'Abroad she pouts;—she is not shy | On London stones!' By appropriating Dobson's lines, Levy immediately upturns the gender associations of the city as a literary subject. The urban muse was consistently the female figure of the prostitute/*passante* for the male poet of the nineteenth century. Levy positions herself as a poet with the city as her muse, avoiding in her choice of preface the lines that gender this muse as female. The muse is now invoked by a woman writer, who describes herself as bound to the city streets, its 'paven ground' rather than its domestic interiors. Levy's own poems reiterate Dobson's discovery that, despite the peace of the countryside, it is the city that provides her poetic muse.

Following Urban Footsteps

Levy was already identifying herself as an urban writer in her essay on James Thomson (B.V.) in 1883. She defines Thomson as a specifically peripatetic artist, whose perspective on London results from his constant walking in its streets. What Thomson does with the city subject is idiosyncratic, creating a city that is both symbol and product of a state of mind. Rather like Baudelaire's Paris, his 'London' is a phantasmal city of ruin that encompasses the urban landscapes of infinite spaces and times. As Isobel Armstrong describes, 'Thomson's endless city holds within itself the landscapes of all and any latitudes, the monumental buildings of all and any cultures'.[7] *The City of Dreadful Night* is a city of limbo and darkness, in which the inhabitants wander ceaselessly.

---

[7] Isobel Armstrong, *Victorian Poetry: Poetry, Poetics and Politics* (London: Routledge, 1993), 466.

Armstrong argues that these wanderers are always male, and that '[w]omen are not visible in the city because they are so entirely subordinated'.[8] Yet Levy identifies herself firmly with the Thomson wanderer. Asserting that the full meaning of his words is lost on those who have not 'trod its streets', she aligns herself with and addresses herself to the urban walker when she states that '[m]ost of us at some time or other of our lives have wandered the City of Dreadful Night; the shadowy forms, the dim streets, the monotonous tones are familiar to us' (*AL* 502). It is this peripatetic as opposed to panoramic viewpoint that Levy particularly commends; '[n]o prophet, standing above and outside things, to whom all sides of a truth (more or less foreshortened, certainly) are visible; but a passionately subjective being, with intense eyes fixed on one side of the polygon of truth, and realising that one side with a fervour and intensity to which the philosopher with his birdseye view rarely attains' (501). The side of truth that Thomson presents is the role of the subjective consciousness in the observation of realities. For Thomson's city of dreadful night is at once real and symbolic, London and a dream city. In Levy's description, the city and the mind are linked by the narrator's act of walking, which is a consistent metaphor for writers experimenting with techniques of expressing consciousness:

The walker goes down in to the city; all is dim and shadowy; the dismal inhabitants [...] are few and far between, holding little intercourse with one another, communing each man with himself [...] The wanderer follows in the footsteps of one sad being who appears to be walking with some intent, and presently stands successively before the spots where Faith and Hope and Love have died. (503)

Levy's preoccupation with the struggle of the independent woman faced with solitude in the city is evident in her concentration on the female personifications in Thomson's poem. Faith, Hope, and Love, traditionally feminine muses, have died on the route of the narrator's walk. In Thomson's bleak vision of London, urban life involves the death of these 'beautiful' and 'inspiring' principles. Their death has added symbolism for Levy as a woman. Walking in the city, which symbolizes the passage of public urban life, incurs on the way the death of those aspects of life deemed irreconcilable with urban existence. Indeed Levy steps outside the subject of the poem to identify it with the world around her; 'The City of Dreadful Night is always standing; ceaselessly one or other human soul visits and revisits the graves of Faith and Hope and Love' (503).

---

[8] Armstrong, *Victorian Poetry*, 467.

The dominant female figure in Thomson's text however, is a huge statue erected to the north of the city. This statue replicates Dürer's figure of *Melancholia* (1514)—he describes her as leaning her cheek on her hand, and holding a pair of compasses and an open book in her lap—but he also identifies her as both a wanderer and as a personification of the city itself. She is a wanderer in spirit, like the urban walker whose outward journey parallels a wandering through his own consciousness, and Thomson describes her as 'wandering in thick mazes of sombre thought' where she 'beholds no outward sight' (*CDN* 69). Despite her compasses, therefore, this woman cannot seem to place herself or to identify her direction. In fact her wandering must be only in spirit because she cannot move and therefore cannot have any direction—made of heavy stone and with her wings folded, she is incapable of movement. In this respect she resembles Benjamin's 'angel of history', developed from the image of Paul Klee's drawing *Angeles Novelus*, into an icon of helplessness in the face of history in his 'Theses on Philosophy of History' (1940). Like *Melancholia*, Benjamin's angel is a despairing and impotent figure. Facing an ever-increasing pile of debris that is the catastrophe of the past, and desiring 'to stay, awaken the dead, and make whole what has been smashed', he is yet propelled unseeingly into the future by a 'storm' that is 'progress'. Benjamin's angel is a highly personal image and, in his ability to perceive the débâcle beneath the illusions of history and his desire to reawaken the past through the restoration of the broken, is characterized by the writer's own historical materialist and surrealist impulses.[9] But in this personal understanding of the angel icon, Benjamin embraces a Judaic tradition in which angels represent the human inner self, a point pertinent to Levy's reading of the angel image in Thomson's text. Indeed, describing the 'angel of history', that quite overtly reflects his public, theoretical aims, Benjamin yet notes that it also 'resembles all from which I have had to part: persons and above all things', the subjective or inner self that is hidden from the public eye.[10]

It might be stretching the metaphor to its extreme, but I think it is possible to connect the image of *Melancholia* in *The City of Dreadful*

[9] The image of angels in the material rather than the spiritual world, observing the broken landscape of urban modernity, is also the central feature of Wim Wenders's film *Wings of Desire* (1987), in which the camera performs a floating *flânerie* over a 1920s-style Berlin. See Robert Phillip Kolker and Peter Beicken, *The Films of Wim Wenders: Cinemas as Vision and Desire* (Cambridge: Cambridge UP, 1993).

[10] Walter Benjamin, notebook entry entitled 'Agesilaus Santander', 13 August 1933, reprinted in Gershom Scholem, 'Walter Benjamin and His Angel', in Gary Smith (ed.), *On Walter Benjamin: Critical Essays and Recollections* (Cambridge, Mass.: MIT Press, 1988), 51–89.

Night to Levy's perception of the position of the woman in the actual London of the later nineteenth century. She has the means to enter the city environment but is weighted down and unable to use them. She can only gaze unspeakingly over a tortured cityscape, impotent to change its continuing process of historical destruction. Given Levy's strong identification with Thomson, and her likely knowledge of the Jewish angel-inner self-identification, along with her consistent interest in feminist issues, the image of the female statue must surely have interested her. Yet the only reference to it in her essay is a non-committal, two-line paragraph: 'I will not attempt to follow further the course of the poem. The passage which closes it on Durer's 'Melancholia' is worthy of its text; I can say no more' (*AL* 505). There is almost a hint of concealment in this conscious absence of discussion. Thomson's later lines on the statue read:

> Baffled and beaten back she works on still,
> Weary and sick of soul she works the more,
> Sustained by her indomitable will:
> The hands shall fasten and the brain shall pore,
> And all her sorrow shall be turned to labour.   (*CDN* 70)

This description of the mythic city and statue could be transcribed to a description of London and the woman writer, with Levy herself as the struggling and ultimately defeated urban woman, wandering the city in her imagination, from her house just before the Euston Road, on the threshold of the north.

The urban woman writer first appears as subject of Levy's work in the novel *The Romance of a Shop* (1888), which follows the basic plot plan of male stories of the modern woman, who, faced with supporting herself, enters the public world of the city, yet approaches it with a different value system. The four Lorimer sisters are left with little financial income after the death of their father, yet reject the conventional options of marriage or teaching posts expected of them, instead planning optimistically to set themselves up in business as photographers. The sisters at first seem to represent different versions of Victorian womanhood; the Victorian angel-of-the-hearth, the New Woman, the aesthetic muse. Yet they cannot actually be read as such simplistic types. Frances is a caricature of Victorian femininity whose passivity and excessive sensibility make her totally dependent on others. Yet Levy also shows her to be a figure who is out of place and time; as an older half-sister of the others, she is differentiated from their modern ambitions yet, still unmarried at 30, she does not really satisfy Victorian domestic values either. She is thus rendered almost useless, a 'superannuated baby' who does not fit into either the occupational or domestic roles and spaces of the Lorimers' Baker Street tenancy. Gertrude and Lucy are the two most unconventional sisters, and although New and Nord regard Gertrude as the classic New Woman and fictional version of Levy herself, I would argue that the sisters between them exhibit different aspects of the modern woman and the role of the female urban spectator and artist. For whereas Gertrude is passionately eloquent in her belief in female independence, and also an aspiring but struggling writer, Lucy is quieter and more systematic in her approach to work, visiting Mr Russell to actually learn the art of photography and eventually taking over the business. Levy seems to identify with features of both sisters, as well as their more affluent friend Conny, herself a 'shrewd, far seeing daughter of the city'. The youngest sister, Phyllis, beautiful, tall and willowy, and consumptive embodies the ideal model of the male artist (as indeed she becomes for Darrell). She shares a desire for independence with her sisters, yet without their determination and will to struggle, exhibiting her modernity instead in flightiness, restlessness, and a constant desire for stimulation and excitement.

Although Levy backs down from the implied female radicalism by concluding the girls' stories with the conventional endings of marriage or fall and death, the novel does offer a female perspective on the city and is an example of Levy's ideal of the female urban artist invoking the city as muse. Both Gertrude and Lucy mirror Levy herself in being female artists in an urban environment, and their work is bound up with the conditions and experiences of modern urban life. Levy herself was interested in the modern art-form of the photographic medium and it is significant, I think, that the Lorimers pursue a career as photographers, appropriating in a modern and commercial form the capturing look of the male artist. Levy's interest in differences in perspective is manifest in the different art-forms practised in the novel. Sidney Darrell, successful and arrogant Royal Academician, paints in the Victorian aesthetic style; Lucy, down to earth and realistic, excels at the photography business; Gertrude, whose perceptions are more impressionistic, turns to writing. Moreover, Darrell and Gertrude are contrasted as artists and are mutually antagonistic. Although little information is given about the style or subject of Gertrude's writing, it is implied that it is inspired, her lack of success in print resulting from the prejudices of publishers and the Victorian reading public. Darrell, on the other hand, is successful and sought after, yet his traditional works lack the spark of inspiration that he recognizes she possesses. Gertrude's aesthetic muse, Levy implies, is the city itself and the sights and sounds of its streets, which she frequently traverses by bus, revelling in the view from its open top:

Indeed, for Gertrude, the humours of the town has always possessed a curious fascination. She contemplated the familiar London pageant with an interest that had something of passion in it; and, for her part, was never inclined to quarrel with the fate which had transported her from the comparative tameness of Campden Hill to regions where the pulses of the great city could be felt distinctly as they beat and throbbed. (87)

The vitality of the city is reflected in Gertrude's pulsating response and the similar emotion that spurs her writing. Continuing this connection, however, Gertrude's writing is implied as a similar infringement of male ground as is her presence in and observance of the public city. Observed by her aunt, who is horrified at Gertrude's exposure on the omnibus, she suddenly sees herself through the disapproving eyes of society with 'a humiliating consciousness of the disadvantages of her own position' (105), literally that of the woman in the public spaces of the city.

Levy's own passion for the pulsing rhythm of city life is evident in the novel, for example through her registering of the changing atmosphere of London according to the interaction of the meteorological and social seasons, and her accurate descriptive details. However, her self-definition as a specifically female writer of London is most fully developed in the poems of *A London Plane-Tree and Other Verse*.[11] That this is the work of a woman writer of the urban scene is meant to be overt, I think, and this is emphasized by the illustrations by J. Bernard Partridge that accompanied the posthumously published collection in 1890.[12] The extent of connection between Levy and Partridge is unknown but I think that it is plausible that he was aware enough of her feminist interests to provide illustrations that emphasize the image of the female urban writer. Wilde had been publishing Levy's work regularly from the start of his editorship of *Woman's World* in 1888. This magazine, produced by Cassell and Co., was originally titled *The Lady's World: A Magazine of Fashion and Society*. When Wilde was invited to take over as editor, he altered the name and subject to appeal to a more independent, educated, and urban female readership. Levy was thus publishing in a journal dedicated to progressive views on women and that included articles on the suffrage, feminism, and the cultural life of the city, mainly by female contributors. As Partridge was a friend of Wilde, illustrating some of his stories as well as for his other journal, the *Lady's Pictorial*, it

[11] In this respect I disagree with Deborah Nord's evaluation of the poems. Although Nord also notes the importance of the female writer, the 'Aurora Leigh' figure, she regards Levy's feminist stance to be subordinated, with the poet expressing her experience of the city through masculine personas.

[12] Amy Levy, *A London Plane-Tree and Other Verse*, illustrations by J. Bernard Partridge (New York: Frederick A. Stokes, 1890).

seems likely that he may have become connected with Levy through *Woman's World*, certainly at least that he would be acquainted with Levy's status as a professional writer concerned with the position of women in the modern city.

'Odds and Ends' portrays a solitary young woman in modern dress writing at a desk in a room overlooking the rooftops and spires of a large city. Behind her, a fully open window allows the air and sounds of the city to flow into the room. The sketch is informed by the iconographic image of the solitary, struggling male urban artist living in a garret room overlooking the city. The image of the paned window open onto the rooftops, and the light of the city spilling into the bare room, can be compared to Henry Wallis's popular painting *The Death of Chatterton* (1856). Chatterton faked his works as those of a fifteenth-century poet, and moving to London in 1770, he committed suicide four months later at the age of 17, in his attic room in Brooke Street, which is just off Gray's Inn Road. Iconized by the Romantics—Wordsworth described him as 'the marvellous boy' and Keats dedicated *Endymion* to him— Wallis's painting turned him into a popular symbol of the Romantic urban artist. I think that the fact that George Meredith posed as the model for Chatterton, and that Wallis sought out the actual Brooke Street room in order to create the setting, also serves to reinforce and continue this image into the Victorian era, constructing the urban artist as a destitute male figure, both inspired and defeated by the London in which he lives.

Given her interest in James Thomson, Chatterton is another male poet whose history may have appealed to Levy's imagination. In fact, the title poem of *A Minor Poet and Other Poems*, which New suggests is about Thomson, actually accords better with the legend of Chatterton. It is split into two parts, the first narrated by the poet as he prepares to commit suicide. Like Chatterton, this poet kills himself with a phial of poison, in a room bare except for a few books. He describes lying beneath the window, with the sunlight falling '[a]cross that endless sea of London roofs' (370) and through the window onto him, as it does in Wallis's picture. The second part is spoken by the friends who break in and describe the scene: the poet lying with his arms outstretched, half-written poems and scattered scraps of letters on the floor, again features of Wallis's painting. Again then, Levy uses the iconography of the male urban poet to express her own voice.

Partridge's drawing is not a romanticized portrayal of a male writer defeated by the ambivalence of the city, however. It depicts a rather androgynous female writer inspired by her urban surroundings. She writes intently and profusely, with paper and books overflowing onto the floor. The other illustration is a plane-tree, a natural urban feature that seems to represent Levy's argument about the status of the female urban writer herself. For in the title poem, the poetic persona identifies herself with the plane-tree, which is gendered as feminine, an object of nature that is yet indigenous to the atmosphere of the town rather than the country. Levy expresses herself as an urban woman with an urban muse through the personification of the tree. The identification, however, is also a wishful one, the poet envying the tree's place in the open spaces of the city. Trapped behind her 'garret-pane', she compares herself to the tree outside, open to the sun, breeze, fog, and smoke of urban life.

The other poems in the collection also express Levy's awareness of her problematic identity as a female urban writer. The poetic voice of the poems tends to be genderless and the theme constantly the gender politics of observing the city. Also, although Levy uses conventional figures of urban iconography (the student-artist in his garret room and the wandering Baudelarian *flâneur*), she is not merely mimicking the male writer, instead challenging gender bias by questioning the implications of these images in female terms. 'The Piano-Organ', for example, continues the image of the attic room, the poet leaving his/her work to open the window to the sounds of street-music outside. Again the solitary artist is a conventional urban image, yet it has a particular emphasis when we consider that the writer of the poem is female. The dominant mood is one of loneliness and loss, and the poet wants the organ-grinder to exchange the cheerful waltz he plays for a dirge or requiem. The implication of the poem is that the life of independent study or art is achieved only at the expense of personal relationships. Similarly, a later work, the short story 'Wise In Her Generation', registers a growing disillusionment with the sacrifices and demands made of the urban woman. A young, educated woman is disappointed in love by an ambitious barrister (the common literary type for the educated, single male in the turn-of-the-century city) and, giving up on any possibility of reconciling romance and city life, shuts off her heart and sympathy in order to survive in the middle-class urban world. The city in this story is no longer an inspirational muse but a power system, and although the woman is quite able to exist in it, this capacity is achieved at the expense of her femininity. The girl is an urbanite, who listens to 'the distant murmur of the Great City' (497) and understands and can replicate its operations, yet she bitterly recognizes what it takes from her; 'Black, black in its heart is the City; the blackness of man's heart is revealed in its huge, hideous struggle for existence' (497). Levy's depiction of the city here is similar to the sombre pessimism of Thomson but poignantly imbued with a sense that the depression she feels results at least in part from the restrictions of a male dominated society. Indeed, much of the ambivalence that female writers manifest in their sometimes contradictory stance on women's emancipation is a result of the struggle to reconcile independent occupation in the city and romantic relations, the two being seen as incompatible for a woman. It is a common concern of women writers of the city and is taken up in the 1880s as well as by Richardson and Woolf in the early twentieth century.[13]

Levy's most positive expressions of her urban identity occur when she describes the atmosphere and influences of actually being out in London's streets. Here it is with the urban artist as *flâneur* that she identifies. In 'Ballad of an Omnibus', in an image reminiscent of Gertrude's experience in *The Romance of a Shop* the speaker rejoices in 'The city pageant, early and late' that, from the top of the bus 'unfolds itself, rolls by, to be I A pleasure deep and delicate' (386). The omnibus, supreme symbol of commercial London, is frequently employed by women writers as an expression of their entry into once restricted public spaces. The bus offers 'the freedom of London' as contemporary slogans advertise, as well as a panoramic yet moving view from its top deck, a means of traversing the city that passes through different social and class-defined spaces, independence amidst a crowd, and shelter from both the elements and the appropriating gaze of others. For Levy's poetic persona, a bus ride is appropriate for all seasons, purposes and all moods, as she registers by the repeated refrain 'An omnibus suffices me'. The bus provides a contemporary development from the moving perspective of the walking *flâneur*, and allowed the woman of the 1880s and 1890s to move in and observe the city without threat on the street.

In another poem, 'London in July', Levy directly confronts the figure of the male *flâneur* in the persona of a man wandering in the city in the hope of seeing a woman he loves, although the idea that for the male observer every woman in the city street is a desirable or sexual object is implied by the fact that every woman he passes seems to possess the face of his beloved. All women in the city thus become condensed into the one that he desires to possess. What I think is important, however, is that unlike the male persona of Baudelaire's '*La Passante*', the man in 'London in July' does not see his beloved and therefore cannot capture her in his gaze. Rather than being at home in the city, an omniscient male observer who can map his landscape, the man wanders lost in its streets, disorientated and unable to understand the labyrinth. The gendered

---

[13] See e.g. Olive Schreiner's short story, 'The Buddhist Priest's Wife', in Showalter, *Daughters of Decadence*, 84–97, p. 88.

power relationship of observing male, observed female in the city is thus complicated in the poem, with the woman that he seeks seemingly the figure of urban knowledge and identity. She 'dwells in London town' and would seem to have a better knowledge of its labyrinthine streets. The fact that she stays in London in July, when the city empties of the upper class and tourists, also suggests that she is a working woman and in tune with the city itself rather than the social season. This sense of an 'organic' city is common to women's perceptions of the city, Richardson, Woolf, Lehmann, and Bowen also expressing the cyclical nature of its atmosphere over the passing year; the bustling summer Season, high summer period of desertion, and relaxed Autumn Season. All are also particularly appreciative of the late summer months of August and September, during which the London beneath the social veneer of the Season surfaces. Writing in 1903, for example, Ada Leverson notes that '[t]here is a sort of Freemasonry about Londoners who meet in London in September—old friendships are renewed, slight acquaintances become almost intimate, affectations are forgotten, and ceremony put aside. It is a cosy season.'[14]

Perhaps the most self-conscious poem of the volume is 'London Poets (In Memoriam)', in which an again genderless poetic persona walks the city thinking of its representation by past writers. Levy takes on the role of the *flâneur* to observe not a female object but a heritage of writers walking the city: 'They trod the streets and squares where I now tread' (389). She is a female writer positioning herself as following both the literary and geographic footsteps of male writers of the urban scene. The evocation of these literary ghosts, each with their own vision of the city, results in a recognition of their different perspectives and the different images of the city that result. Not only, then, is there no one authoritative, male perception of the city but also each vision is as appropriate as any other, and therefore that of the speaker (implicitly Levy herself) is equally legitimate. The famous reputations of the past are ghosts that haunt the female writer but she also sees herself as according with them in the melancholy and weariness of their souls. This simultaneous experience of difference from and yet identification with the walking male writer becomes the central feature of the self-reflexive modernism of Dorothy Richardson, who can be interpreted as progressing from merely borrowing or identifying with the masculinized tropes of attic room and street, to constructing them as the spaces of the woman in the city, the *flâneuse*.

---

[14] Quoted in Julie Speedie, *Wonderful Sphinx: The Biography of Ada Leverson* (London: Virago, 1993), 129.

Dorothy Richardson's Urban Pilgrimage

Dorothy Richardson's work is a constant wandering of memory, at once autobiographical and fictional, as the author attempts to establish her identity both in the past and the present. Living and walking in London at the turn of the century, the young Richardson sought a coherent self-identity; retracing her past and her steps in the persona of Miriam Henderson in *Pilgrimage* she sought to express and thus define and confirm this identity; remembering both the 1890s and her fictional reworking of that period, her writing in the late 1930s is a conscious and self-reflexive analysis that establishes the identity of the past from the authority of the present, whilst simultaneously using that identity as the basis of the self-knowledge of the present itself. Richardson's *œuvre* is thus palimpsestic. The time periods of the 1890s, 1910s–1920s, and late 1930s are layered, connected by the thread of imaginative and physical wanderings through the same mental and urban space. In the 'Preface' to *Pilgrimage* written in 1938, and the article of the following year 'Yeats of Bloomsbury', Richardson both describes and displays her identity as an urban and specifically female writer through the metaphor of walking and its cultural associations with the alien outsider and the transgressive female.[15]

Bloomsbury, an 'oasis to the north of the British Museum' (YB, 60), was a perfect site for the modern woman defining her independent identity and the female writer defining her creativity, as it provided both street and room in a central urban area that was yet conducively peaceful. Edwardian Bloomsbury, as Richardson describes it, was 'comfortably modest', its eighteenth-century buildings having been turned into apartments and boarding-houses offering 'a noble heritage for those of the inhabitants who in square, or in street linking square with square, for a modest outlay could enjoy their exceptional surroundings' (61). For Richardson, Bloomsbury was a place of stability amidst the tumult of the capital, one that reconciled 'London's exhausted prisoners' to its daily grind by its cool stillness at night. When Miriam Henderson, and also Woolf's Mary Datchet, Katharine Hilberry, and Eleanor Pargiter, walk in London at night they observe an impressionistic landscape of moon and lamp-lit streets where they can walk in quietly serene squares or along a silently flowing river. In a section deleted from *The Years* (1937), for example, Woolf describes that Eleanor 'liked walking in London, at night especially, when the outlines of buildings showed; the detail that

[15] Dorothy Richardson, 'Yeats of Bloomsbury', *Life and Letters Today* (Apr. 1939), 60–6.

distracted one by day was lost; and it became larger and more digni-fied.'[16] The formative function of walking for the urban writer is also registered by Eleanor as she walks through the 'relief' of a foreign quarter of eighteenth-century houses (presumably Bloomsbury). Replicating the constructive effect of Bloomsbury walks on Richardson and Woolf themselves, Eleanor's thoughts—'[h]er mind was full; her being brimmed populous with sights, with sounds, with half realized ideas [. . .]. She had been bringing things together; building up new combina-tions as she walked; adding fresh to old ones'—suggest the creative influence of streetwalking that they experienced.[17]

The city does not seem external and indifferent in Richardson's essay, even when she is inside, as '[s]oon after sunset a message would reach even the most stifling attic, brought by the evening air stealing in at its open window' (61). Her room above the city is open to the air and noise of the streets, unlike a detached ivory tower. The female writer does not mourn for a rural simplicity but, like Levy's plane-tree, thrives on 'the familiar, inorganic air of London' (62). Indeed, Richardson implies, the occasional fresh breath of trees is to be appreciated more in the middle of London's humidity, and, reversing Simmel's concept of the blasé me-tropolitan, she argues that it is instead the rural dweller who has only 'a habitual or a deliberate receptivity' to his surroundings, accepting trees just as a matter of course.

'Yeats of Bloomsbury', as the title suggests, situates the poet firmly within an urban milieu that Richardson also sees as her own home territory and she devotes as much space to her perceptions of the area as she does to Yeats. Retracing the steps of a night walk in which a passing stranger (the iconographic 'urban encounter') turns out to be Yeats himself, she thus also creates a symbolic metaphor for the relation-ship of male and female writer with the city and each other. Returning home after an evening of discussion with friends (possibly Elsie Schleussner and her flatmate, the originals of Jan and Mag in *Pilgrimage*) Richardson goes out of her way to extend her walk and aesthetic enjoy-ment of Bloomsbury—'[t]he surrounding buildings became mere re-flectors of moonlight, infinitely far away. The giant trees mingled their breath with mine, their being with my own'—an urban artist, wandering and perceiving the night city. In a pool of light, that urban phenomenon that is so frequent in Richardson and Woolf's writing, she comes face to face with an urban *doppelganger*, 'a fellow-lover of nocturnal solitude',

---

[16] Appendix to Virginia Woolf, *The Years* (1937; Oxford: Oxford UP, World's Classics, 1992), 423.

[17] Ibid., 454.

distinguished from him by gender and his status as a famous poet compared to hers as a developing writer of the 'feminine consciousness'. Yet both are city-dwellers, and walkers who perceive 'Bloomsbury's deepest enchantment'. How are they to relate in the city? The immediate reaction is one of confrontation; '[i]t was *my* chosen path. It was *his*' (63). Richardson as walker holds her ground, refusing 'skipping into the gutter to make way for men' (the gutter of course being the place of the traditional female 'streetwalker'), but is unable to move anyway, recognizing the famous presence and wanting to 'acknowledge [her] debt' to this fellow worshipper of the city. Richardson as woman writer is in a similar position of confrontation with a masculine literary tradition, refusing to deny her own literary ability yet remaining in respectful awe of the male urban writers before her.

Although Richardson and Yeats as walkers presumably passed somehow in the street, the female writer remained struggling with the obstruction in her path and Richardson notes that '[f]or memory, we stand permanently confronted on either side of that lake of moonlight' (64). Yet ultimately it is not a position of subservience or confrontation that Richardson takes in relation to Yeats but one of identification. For in this essay, which in its subject, setting, and even its language (the first paragraphs replicating passages from 'The Tunnel') exemplifies the continuity Richardson emphasizes between the stages of her urban and literary life, she notes that, later in life, Yeats repudiated the results of this period of *his* creativity, in direct contrast to her own practice. But she hopes that, 'despite his protests' against the 'Bloomsbury solitary' of the past, he secretly regarded him as 'not a regrettable wanderer in a self-made darkness, but the hesitant younger brother of the author of *Michael Robartes*' (66), just as the Richardson portrayed in the character of Miriam Henderson was a younger sister of the author of *Pilgrimage*.

Cosmopolitan Wanderings

Levy and Richardson's attempts to resolve or at least find a plausible alternative to the impasse of their position as female urban walker-writers are inflected by the social and political context of the period, as well as the characteristics of the Jewish acculturated and immigrant populations. Levy is a Jew who is feminist, Richardson a feminist who considered becoming Jewish—both find in the Jew a spiritual identity and a restriction on the free expression of that identity.

The East European Jew was a particularly visible feature of late nineteenth-century London, alien in looks, cultural practices, and nationality. The Jewish immigrant thus embodied racial 'otherness', just as the New Woman was the embodiment of gendered 'otherness'. Their significance within the city should be seen within the socio-political context of an overabundant labour supply, as many of the immigrants were also skilled artisans who were yet cheap to employ. These qualities, attractive to employers, were defined as innate characteristics rather than socially caused. Charles Booth described the Jew as 'more fit, pliant, adaptable, adroit' to working in the city, and David Feldman stresses that in the social and literary writing of the time '[t]he Jewish immigrant was represented as the mirror image of the sturdy countryman; a figure who had adapted so well to the demands of urban life that he was inevitably the victor when competing with the London-born'.[18] The idea of the Jew's innate urban identity was thus reinforced and became a worrying threat to British custom, religion, and livelihood in a period of anxiety over degeneration. As Linda Nochlin describes, the 'modern construction of the Jew'—the Jew as the modern cosmopolitan—'and the establishing of a coherent Jewish identity may be said to have begun with the construction of modernity itself, in the nineteenth century'.[19]

In response to this new Jewish stereotype, the post-emancipationist Anglo-Jew emphasized his Victorian middle-class liberalism, his acculturation to the West, and the middle-class orthodoxy of his merchant and financial status, in contrast to the foreign Jew so menacing to national purity.[20] Up until the 1870s the Jewish community in London was largely upper-middle-class, composed of Jews anglicized by assimilation or marriage. This community became the subject of a trend of liberalist apologetic fiction, in which the Jew was depicted in terms of his similarity rather than his difference from Englishness. Underlying this 'semitic discourse' is an aim to redeem both Jewish and English society to a moral and ordered promised land.[21] Yet the late nineteenth-century

[18] David Feldman and Gareth Stedman Jones (eds.), *Metropolis. London: Histories and Representations Since 1800* (London: Routledge, 1989), 59. Feldman discusses the *fin de siècle* response to the 120,000 Jews who came to Britain between 1880 and 1914, over half of whom settled in London.

[19] Linda Nochlin, 'Starting with the Self: Jewish Identity and its Representation', in Linda Nochlin and Tamar Garb (eds.), *The Jew in the Text: Modernity and the Construction of Identity* (London: Thames and Hudson, 1995), 7–19, p. 10.

[20] The anti-alien sentiment of the time cannot be simplistically equated with anti-Semitism as the Anglo-Jewish community itself operated an effective scheme of immigrant management and repatriation through the Jewish Board of Guardians, one of the communal institutions overseen by the leading mercantile Anglo-Jewish class.

[21] The term 'semitic discourse' is coined by Bryan Cheyette in *Constructions of 'the Jew' in English Literature and Society: Radical Representations, 1875–1945* (Cambridge UP, 1993), 8, to refer to racial representations that are detached from the post-holocaust, moral connotations of anti-Semitism.

Jewish question was marked by uncertainty and tension over stereotypes of the Jew, as the value of these characteristics could be upturned. The Jewish novel of revolt took a different slant on the Jewish issue and presented Anglo-Jewry as materialistic, hypocritical, and concerned primarily with social success rather than racial purity. On this view it is the immigrant who accords with the icon of the spiritual pilgrim, upholding a pure Zionism and searching for a moral homeland amidst the disordered city. This was the position taken by novelists who promoted the spiritual and national purity of the Russian student and artisan in contrast to the hypocrisy and mercantile greed of the financiers. For Levy and Richardson, writing and working in London during the mass immigration before the Aliens Act of 1905, the Jew was therefore a prominent and topical feature of modern urban life.

Israel Zangwill's *Children of the Ghetto* (1892) begins with the rejection by Anglo-Jews of a revolt novel written, although they do not know it, by one of their own party. This passage is an allusion to Amy Levy, who was regarded by the Anglo-Jewish establishment as exhibiting racial self-hatred in her novel *Reuben Sachs* (1886), which focuses on the beliefs and hypocrisies of an extended family in the Anglo-Jewish community of Kensington and Bayswater. Zangwill recognized Levy's importance for the modernization of the Anglo-Jewish novel, acknowledging that his own study of the tensions within stereotypes of the Jew were 'pioneered' by her 'genius', but for decades Levy had few other defenders.[22] Even recently, Linda Zatlin, although suggesting that Levy distinguishes Judaism as a religion and Jewishness as a social trait in order to attack the latter, accused Levy's Jewish generalizations as evidence of 'bigotry'.[23] Yet Levy's position is less clear than this, and made complex by her feminism, which rejects both religious and social aspects of Anglo-Jewish tradition.[24] *Reuben Sachs* is part of a whole body of work in which Levy explores her racial and cultural origins, and it needs to be read

[22] Israel Zangwill, 'A Ghetto Night at the Naccabæans', *Jewish Chronicle*, 25 Jan. 1901, p. 19. Although applauded in the national press and by the Jewish community in the USA, *Reuben Sachs* was steadfastly ignored by reviewers in Jewish periodicals and journals. (Rachel) Beth Zion (Cohen) Lask (Abrahams) speculates in 'Amy Levy', *Transactions of the Jewish Historical Society of England* 11 (1926), 168–89, that it is largely this strategy of neglect that resulted in Levy's fall into obscurity after her death.

[23] Linda Zatlin, *The Nineteenth-Century Anglo-Jewish Novel* (Boston: Twayne, 1981), 97.

[24] Nadia Valman, 'Women and Jews in an Age of Emancipation (1845–1900)', MA diss., (University of Leeds, October 1991), interprets Levy as writing from a radical feminist perspective and gives an excellent account of the similarity in the status of women and Jews in the late 19th cent. Bryan Cheyette, *Constructions of 'the Jew'*, makes a similar association between Levy's dissatisfaction with the demands of Jewish custom and her support of women's suffrage.

alongside both her essays on middle-class Jewish society and the poems that refer to the Jew in his relation to the city. Across these works Levy makes a distinction between her own Anglo-Jewish community, which if anything accentuates the patriarchal confines of Victorian society, and the immigrant population, loyal to its spiritual roots and thus closer to the iconic figure of the 'Wandering Jew'.

If Levy identified herself as an essentially urban writer, she also regarded the Jewish as an intrinsically urban race. The 1880s witnessed the development of the social sciences, as evidenced by Le Bon and Tarde's crowd theories and Simmel's definitions of the urban psyche for example, in which interest in mental processes combined with social prejudices under scientific terminology and medical discourse. Levy was well read in these new sciences and in 'Jewish Humour' defines the modern Jew as 'a very delicate and elaborate organism' (*AL* 530), 'descendant of many city-bred ancestors' and the result of 'centuries of city life' (531), with a high rate of mental and nervous disease, accords with Simmel's description of the characteristics of the urban dweller. This assertion is repeated in *Reuben Sachs*, when a doctor describes Reuben's nervous illness as a common affliction among Jews. Yet, although she accepts the psychological effects of urban living, Levy's discussion does not continue the negative connotations and dooming prophesies applied by male theorists. The hypersensitivity of the modern Jewish child may predispose him to 'self-consciousness, arrogance and other worse vices' (531), but the development of such are only allowed by indulgent parents. The highly developed nervous system of the city-dweller brings with it a certain toughness and vitality. What is required is that these urban qualities are trained and directed into profitable channels.

The essay 'Middle-Class Jewish Women of To-Day', published in the *Jewish Chronicle* anonymously under the pseudonym 'A Jewess', suggests that for women at least this certainly was not the case. It clearly indicates the tension she felt between her Jewish identity and her feminist beliefs, and condemns the practice of Jewish parents in encouraging their daughters to regard marriage as their sole objective in life.[25] The consequent plight of those Gissingesque 'odd women' who do not achieve this aim is that they have developed no skills or knowledge for 'making [their] way about the world' (525). This is all the more distressing when one considers the waste of potential in these women, who Levy considers are naturally inclined to be 'more readily adaptable, more eager to absorb the atmosphere around them', and more cultured than their financially absorbed male counterparts, and suffer all the more because

[25] This essay is attributed to Levy in New's collection.

'with greater social capabilities they have far less social opportunity' (526). For she notes that the improving status and opportunities of the single woman, as described in 'Women and Club-Life' for example, does not extend into the Anglo-Jewish community, in which '[t]he assertion even of comparative freedom on the part of a Jewess often means the severance of the closest ties, both of family and of race; its renunciation, a life-long personal bitterness' (527). Given Levy's own status as a university-educated, single, Jewish woman, it would seem plausible that her depressive tendencies can therefore be linked to her political and social awareness as well as to her innate temperament.

For Levy (as Richardson and Woolf would also depict) the independent woman, and the Jewess in particular, achieves public freedom only at the expense of personal relationships. She describes such eager women as 'beating themselves in vain against the solid masonry of our ancient fortifications, long grown obsolete and of no use save as obstructions; sometimes succeeding in scaling the wall and departing never to return, to the world beyond' (527). Breaking out into the public world of the city, they are also breaking away from their Jewish heritage, the racial identity that has collaborated in their suppression. The emancipated Jewish woman is doubly alienated, even more the homeless wanderer as the spiritual stereotype becomes also an actuality. Perhaps, however, the perceived freedoms of the gentile woman were only relative. Virginia Woolf uses a similarly architectural image in her memories of her life at Hyde Park Gate and its fictional treatment in *Night and Day* (both, like *Reuben Sachs*, Kensington based), the Victorian home, with its drawing-room, thick plush curtains, and relics of the past standing in turn for a tradition that the young Woolf must break out from if she is to develop her own independence. As with Levy's Jewishness though, Woolf's Victorian background provided her with origins and an identity that she never totally repudiated.

In *Pilgrimage*, Miriam Henderson comes into contact with Jewish immigrants during her residence in Tansley Street, where Mr Mendizabel and later Michael Shatov are fellow boarders. These two friendships characterize two levels of interest and response to Jewish identity in its various forms. Through Mr Mendizabel, Miriam is introduced to the café world of the cosmopolitan, to placelessness as bohemia, to the modern, degenerate Jew. With Michael Shatov, who identifies with a spiritual community based in the past, she learns about Jewish doctrine and begins to develop her own views on women's emancipation during their discussions of his socialist Zionism. Both are *flâneurs* who enjoy walking in the city and extend Miriam's freedom. Yet with both she undergoes two stages of relationship, at first identifying with their outsider status and thus their wanders in the city streets, but later recognizing that she is still ultimately 'other' to them. As Carol Watts has argued, Miriam's exploration of new or previously restricted spaces in the city involve 'a metamorphosis that is either an index of her alienation, or a means by which she is freed to make the space her own'.[26] Miriam's pilgrimage is a constant process of identifying with groups that promise to expand her autonomous ego, and then of distinguishing herself from them once their demands conflict with and threaten this independence. The two Russian Jews are crucial to Miriam's self-development in that they are influential in her practice of extensive wandering walks, but their friendship is dropped or reduced when they reassert their male authority over her—Mendizabel by treating her as a female spectacle in a bohemian café, Shatov by attempting to make her his wife.

It is through walking with Mr Mendizabel that Miriam gains a new and unconstrained masculinized perspective on the city. In Mendizabel, Richardson draws upon the stereotypical iconography of the Jew, equating him with the rat and the dark underworld, to emphasize his familiarity with the multidimensional city. A foreigner and outsider, like Miriam herself, he acts as her guide and educates her in understanding the connections of the streets as 'they [thread] their way together, meeting and separating and rejoining, unanimous and apart'. His gaiety and ease, along with a swinging cane and hat, suggest the characteristics of a latter-day *flâneur*, with which Miriam feels at one: '[w]e are both *batteurs de pave*, she thought. Both people who must be free to be nothing' (*P ii.* 391–2). It is Mendizabel who takes Miriam to the bohemian café Ruscino's, a forbidden place, 'a spectacle she could not witness without contamination'. A fictional Café Royal, it is a place where the cosmopolitan, rootless, and degenerate congregate. She responds to this café life, which satisfies her desire for communities of strangers who are both 'separate and free, united in freedom'. Yet she also recognizes that it is a 'man's heaven', the space of the leisured male *flâneur* in which the women present are not themselves and only approximate freedom by identifying with men. By taking on Mendizabel's mode of perception, Miriam realizes that she too dissembles: '[s]he was there as a man, a free man of the world, a continental, a cosmopolitan, a connoisseur of women' (394). The combination of sharp, bright lights, under which one feels scrutinized, and clouds of smoke, that mystify, results in an uneasy experience of watching and being watched, of revealing and concealing, of identifying and dissembling. A similar feeling will be experienced by

---

[26] Carol Watts, *Dorothy Richardson* (Plymouth: Northcote House, 1995), 48.

Stella Rodney in the cheap Piccadilly café that she is taken to by the espionage agent Harrison in Elizabeth Bowen's *The Heat of the Day*. In both, the categories of alien, cosmopolitan, and observer are unstable. They are places of spectacle, where people conduct masquerades of identity.

In this respect Ruscino's differs from Miriam's other eating haunts; the A B C cafés that are full of workers snatching sustenance during a break in the purpose of the day, and Donizetti's, the little restaurant of strangers, also an assembly of the marginal and the rootless, who yet crave obscurity rather than ostentation. Both seem male territory when she first encounters them, but both are ultimately found to be welcoming, identifying her less as a 'woman' than as a 'Londoner' and thus one of themselves. Ruscino's is sensuously and exotically attractive but not that 'bit of her own London home' (360) that encourages familiarity. Nationality is an important influence on Miriam's urban experience, because her relationship is very much with the particular city of London, the metropolis rather than the 'cosmopolis' of different cities.[27] Miriam's ultimate response to Ruscino's, therefore, involves a rejection of the cosmopolitan Jewish identity that corresponds to popular class and national prejudice. Her upper-middle-class Victorian upbringing (although it progressively surfaces less frequently and dogmatically) remains a framework for her thought throughout *Pilgrimage*, and provides a context against which her feminist rejection of Judaism must be read. Writing in a letter in December 1935, for example, Richardson explained that 'M. [Miriam] was pitched headlong without training or suitable preparation' into the 'bourgeois working-class', where she is a 'sympathetic onlooker' but 'fails to recognise herself as "a worker" always, though quite unconsciously, assuming that life should be leisure and should be lived in perfect surroundings'.[28] Although attracted by Mendizabel's easy companionship and the type of freedom he offers, she is distanced from him by the class prejudices of herself and others.

---

[27] A persistent feature of the writing assessed in this study is women's connection with particular cities (London or Paris), rather than with general or cosmopolitan urban qualities, which are more often the concern of male writers. It is interesting to compare Richardson's representation of London as metropolis, for example, with T. S. Eliot's modern cosmopolis in *The Wasteland*, an 'unreal city' assembled from a series of ruins 'London, Athens, Jerusalem'. Or Jean Rhys's distinctions between the atmosphere of London and that of Paris compared to Ford Madox Ford's description of her urban sketches in terms of the 'Left Banks of the world'. The national identity of the particular city becomes extremely forceful, of course, in the depictions of the wartime city by Bowen.

[28] Gloria Glikin Fromm (ed.) *Windows on Modernism: Selected Letters of Dorothy Richardson*, (Athens, Ga., and London: University of Georgia Press, 1995), 304.

Mendizabel is alien in nationality, his habits seem degenerate, his place of leisure breathes corruption, all of which are coloured by his racial difference. Being seen in his company also endangers Miriam's reputation and discourages the advances of the Canadian doctor. His cosmopolitan Jewish identity she therefore rejects, turning instead to the spiritual wandering Jew, Shatov. Miriam may identify her position as a woman with the wandering of boundaries that the cosmopolitan immigrant Jew epitomizes, but only to certain limits.

Ironically, the aim of the sincere Jew is to lose his cosmopolitanism and discover his own homeland. Michael Shatov follows his own pilgrimage 'from the cosmopolitan, "denationalised" Leubronn [...] to the final vision of a future "national" Jewish Palestine'.[29] This parallels, whilst inverts, Miriam's journey from her roots in the family home to an independent, roaming existence in the city. The two 'pilgrimages' manifest the paradox of the rootless, however, and the paradox that haunts the identification of the woman with the Jew or the cosmopolitan. For Miriam's experience undercuts the binarism of place/nonplace, identity/rootlessness. It is her own family home that is stifling of individuality and progressively unstable, and she leaves it to discover an identity and selfhood through wandering (through the city, and the different political views and religious/social groups she finds there).

Even Michael Shatov's racial identity is sometimes disconcerting for Miriam and, although she commends his 'clear, swiftly manoeuvring encyclopaedic Jewish mind' (*P iii.* 294), she is relieved that his intellectual appearance means that the 'mysterious fact of Jewishness could remain in the background' (193). For, contrary to Mendizabel, who emphasized his cosmopolitanism over his Jewishness, Shatov identifies himself primarily as a Jew. She sees him as a wandering Jew, doomed to continual searching;

Frenchman, Russian, philosophical German-brained, he sat there white-faced, an old old Jew, immeasurably old, cut off, alone with his conviction, facing the blank spaces of the future. Why could he not be content to be a European? [...] In his deeply saturated intelligence there was still a balance on the side from which he had declared to his father, that he was first a man; then a Jew. (168)

Partly xenophobia, Miriam's attitude is also the result of her awareness that the wandering, cosmopolitan Jew that could help express her continuing pilgrimage is an identity that is unavailable to her as a woman. The cosmopolitan is a male prerogative, a 'connoisseur of women' she states. Judaism is a religion that prioritizes the male and,

---

[29] Cheyette, *Constructions of 'the Jew'*, 45.

hence, Miriam rejects it, unable 'to breathe always the atmosphere of the Jewish religious and social oblivion of women' (224).

The simultaneous tension yet connection between the experiences of the woman and the Jew has been revived in contemporary critical discussions.[30] Miriam's sentiments are reflected in feminist terms for example by Adrienne Rich's reminiscence 'Split at the Root', in which she describes Judaism as 'yet another strand of patriarchy', and states that 'if asked to choose I might have said [...]: I am a woman, not a Jew'.[31] Women have been metaphorically equated with Jews as the victims of dictatorial authority. Carolyn Heilbrun has described the continuing paradox of the Jewish feminist, stating that 'having been a Jew had made me an outsider. It had permitted me to be a feminist' yet also that 'if Jews were outsiders, women were outsiders among Jews'.[32] What can be seen in Levy and Richardson's representation of their position is an awareness of this paradox and an exploration of the Jewish identity as a symbol of a marginal urban experience. Thus Levy writes frequently about the characteristics of Anglo-Jewish life, deploring its tendency to disregard its spiritual heritage and assimilate to the conventions of Victorianism, at the same time lauding the potential of the Jewess who has managed to escape from the stifling limitations of the Anglo-Jewish family home. The two come together in her late poetry, pervaded by the experience of the city. Levy, the Jewess who has achieved professional distinction, explores her racial and spiritual roots not only in relation to the plane-tree but also to the East European immigrant population in the ghettos of Whitechapel and the Mile End Road. It is again this literally 'wandering' Jewish immigrant that Richardson and her fictional ego Miriam experience as a symbol and guide to urban freedom. Yet Miriam rejects the option of marrying into the Jewish community. The enthusiastic *flânerie* that she enjoys with her male Jewish friends is open to her as an outsider yet inappropriate for the Jewish wife, who she perceives would be restricted by both the culture and its religion.

---

[30] Interest in the implications of Judaism for women is largely restricted to specific feminist discussions, for example Jacqueline Rose's essay 'Dorothy Richardson and the Jews' in *States of Fantasy* (Oxford: Clarendon Press, 1996). Although a comprehensive and perceptive study of the significance of the Jew for the literature of modernity, Bryan Cheyette's *Constructions of 'the Jew'*, does not consider the role of gender. He consciously omits Joseph Conrad, D. H. Lawrence, Dorothy Richardson, and Virginia Woolf from his discussion, seemingly unaware that in so doing he avoids the gendered racial issue.
[31] Adrienne Rich, 'Split at the Root', in Evelyn Torton Beck (ed.), *Nice Jewish Girls: A Lesbian Anthology* (Boston: Beacon Press, 1989), 89.
[32] Carolyn Heilbrun, *Reinventing Womanhood* (New York: Norton, 1979), 20–1.

At Home in the City

Given the significance of the streets and rooms of London as formative factors for her writing, it is unsurprising that the meaning of different spaces for woman in the city is a common feature of Richardson's novel, and workplace, social space, private room, and the city streets between them are all vividly evoked. Accommodation, area, and relationship to them, differ for women according to class and financial position. Miriam Henderson lives as a lodger in what later is converted into a boarding-house, moves into a shared tenancy, and then later returns to Mrs Bailey's, still on a lodging agreement. Of her female friends, Jan and Mag live together in a college-style atmosphere of easy lounging and evening discussion in rooms in an unrespectable building, and she meets Eleanor Dear whilst both are staying at a 'Decayed Gentlewoman's Hostel', and Amabel at the 'Belmont' where she is a resident member. Mary Datchet, in Woolf's *Night and Day* (1919), rents a fully self-contained flat in the professional area of the Strand, and the Pargiters in *The Years* occupy various types of urban accommodation; Delia lodges in a St Pancras slum, Maggie and Sara rent rooms in the shabby area south of the river, and Eleanor finally moves into a residence block of flats. These different spaces carefully portray the living conditions of women in London at the turn of the century.

The wanderings of these characters, physically between the different social areas of the city, imaginatively between different subjectivities, and personally between different conceptions of self are framed and located within a map of the city and memories of the past. The essential dilemma of Levy's female writer of the 1880s and 1890s remains that of Richardson and Woolf; the attempt to resolve the public/private dichotomy of street/house, independence/company, in a connective relationship of the three realms of street, private room, and workplace.

Women in *fin de siècle* London, theoretically legitimized presences on the city street as workers and/or consumers, were yet still faced with practical restrictions, resulting from a lack of urban facilities catering for women. For, as Martha Vicinus notes of the New Woman, '[h]er greater freedom also brought greater isolation', as she found the spaces of the city open to her to be selective, limited, and fragmented from one another.[33] The educated working woman living in the city, and not financially supported by her family, had to subsist on the meagre levels

---

[33] Martha Vicinus, *Independent Women: Work and Community for Single Women 1850–1920* (London: Virago, 1985), 297.

of female earnings, and at first the living accommodation affordable on such an income was a barely respectable lodging-house. The problem of the lack of informal social spaces affected middle- and upper-class women alike. During lunch hours, tea-time, and the early evening between the end of work or shop hours and the start of evening entertainment such as the theatre, there were few places for women to comfortably pass the time, and it was still not respectable for women to eat alone in restaurants or wander the streets. Leonora Davidoff has noted that 'cafés, the growth of tea-rooms, the use of buses, even the provision of public lavatories for women were as important in freeing middle-class women from strict social ritual as the slow erosion of chaperonage', and indeed it is largely due to the increased provision of such non-familial, semi-public spaces within the city that women were able to develop a legitimate position in the urban environment and to enjoy greater freedom in its streets.[34]

The paucity of acceptable accommodation affordable for the single, working woman, and of respectable public and social amenities, was a constant concern of urban social reformists in the 1880s and 1890s, and journals of the time frequently included articles that called for residential and recreational spaces to cater for the needs of the single woman in the city. The idea of a female community residence was discussed in an article in the *Englishwoman's Review* in 1889, for example. 'Sloane Garden's House', to be built by the Ladies Development Co., was to provide 'suitable house accommodation at reasonable rents to ladies of small incomes, where, while retaining their entire independence, they may live with greater comfort and economy than in lodging houses of the ordinary type'.[35] 'Sloane Gardens House' was one of a number of community residences that offered bed-sits with shared kitchen and washing facilities, along with a number of self-contained flats (largely to better-paid professional women, because of the actually relatively high rents).

The standard and provision of housing increased by the turn of the century. In an article in the *Contemporary Review* of 1900, in response to a paper by a male reformist, Alice Zimmern described a number of options available. Communal blocks such as the 'Ladies' Residential Chambers' in Chenies Street and York Street, and the now established 'Sloane Gardens House' were specifically designed to combine privacy with an overall community atmosphere and were popular alternatives to

---

[34] Leonora Davidoff, *The Best Circles: Society, Etiquette and The Season* (London: Croom Helm, 1973), 67.
[35] *Englishwoman's Review* 19 (15 Mar. 1889), 141, quoted in Vicinus, *Independent Woman*, 295.

lodgings and cheap boarding-houses.[36] The facilities of the former resulted in high rents ranging from £30 to £90 per annum, and tenants were primarily 'ladies of independent means, or such as supplement their professional income from private sources' rather than middle-class working women whose income averaged about £100 per annum.[37] Mary Hughes, for example, part of the formative team of Bedford College, recalling moving from an unsatisfactory tenancy run by an untrustworthy landlady to the Ladies' Residential Chambers, describes them as a 'promised land'. They combined private accommodation (Hughes and a friend occupied a top-floor flat of two rooms and a scullery) for which residents had the important status symbol of their own latch-key, with social interaction at the communal evening dinner with 'a variety of interesting women, all of them at work of some kind—artists, authors, political workers, and so on'.[38] 'Sloane Gardens House', however, which operated a bed-sitting scheme, charging an average 10 shillings per week for an unfurnished, single room, proved more suitable for professional women and included cleaning services and linen change. Other types of accommodation mentioned are lodgings and inexpensive boarding-houses run by respectable and obliging landladies, which, Zimmern asserts, can be found, despite the gloomy picture painted by male urban reformers of the female lodger exposed to a dangerous and morally polluting environment. Shared tenancy of unfurnished rooms was another prospect. Despite Zimmern's rejection of the typecasting of the 'educated working woman' as a homeless, danger-beset urban waif, she does recognize the need for the accommodation developments that social planners propose, noting that the professional woman 'represents a class so large and increasing that there is room for more competition in the attempt to house her comfortably'.[39]

The provision of social clubs for women was another issue, and in 1888 *Woman's World* published Levy's 'Women and Club Life', a defence of the upper-middle-class female clubs that were rapidly arising and being satirically attacked as the environment of the stereotypical 'New Woman'.[40] Levy's aim is to detach the club from the rather confused associations that seem to regard the female club member as both a

---

[36] The Chenies Street housing block consisted of two- or three-room flats and a common dining-room, the York Street block also offering larger quarters for 'co-flatting', significantly less successful.

[37] Alice Zimmern, 'Ladies' Dwellings', *Contemporary Review* 77 (1900), 96–104, p. 99.

[38] Mary V. Hughes, *A London Family 1870–1900* (London: Oxford UP, 1946), 421.

[39] Zimmern, 'Ladies' Dwellings', 100.

[40] Amy Levy, 'Women and Club Life', *Woman's World 1* (1888), 364–67, repr. in *The Complete Novels and Selected Writings of Amy Levy 1861–1889*, ed. New, 532–8.

shabby, feminist spinster and an idle, female version of the complacent clubman. Carefully proclaiming a detached position, to assure her readers of her objectivity, she describes the new clubs in terms of the economics of supply and demand that underlie commercial society, as a response to the needs caused by women's increased involvement in the commercial public life of the city. This is depicted as an inter-city journey, in which '[f]rom the high and dry region of the residential neighbourhood the women come pouring down to those pleasant shores where the great stream of human life is dashing and flowing' (*AL* 532), to converge on the city and take part in the vital rush of city life. She asserts that, despite the existence of a rather vacuous 'smart set', it is the professional woman who most needs and is served by female clubs. The four clubs that she cites, the Somerville (founded 1878), Albermarle (1881), Alexandra (1884) and University (1887), provide a 'haven of refuge' for 'feminine leisure and feminine solitude' (533), enjoyed alike by the 'suburban high-school mistress, in town for a day's shopping', the pastry cook, and the journalist just come from a private viewing.

This is an environment of mental rather than physical indulgence, modelled on the form of the male club but the atmosphere of the female college, with newspapers, tea and cake, debates, organized soirées and, in some, moderately priced rooms.[41] Other clubs, for example the exclusive and artistic Lyceum (1904), offered a more formal environment in which women writers and artists could conduct business with male agents on neutrally gendered territory. Significantly, therefore, the female club had a different mediating function to that of the male; it eased entry into the public city rather than provided a retreat away from it. In answer to the criticism of the single woman for presuming upon club society (which illogically condemned her for indulging 'vices' that constitute 'privileges' for male club members themselves) Levy argues that the style of female club life is not the indulgence and excess that it is for the male counterpart. Obviously aware of the term *flâneur* and associating it in its negative form of the urban idler exclusively with the male, Levy states that '[t]he female club-lounger, the *flâneuse* of St. James' Street, latchkey in pocket and eye-glasses on nose, remains a creature of the imagination' (536). The urban woman Levy supports and imagines is not the *flâneuse* as idle, smart-set lounger, but the *flâneuse* of the streets, enjoying the sustenance of her club in between shopping, working, and going

[41] The similarity of the female clubs to the format of the university college is well illustrated by photographs from women's college archives. See e.g. pictures of resident and common rooms at Bedford College from 1874 to 1917, reprinted in Bedford College, *Educating Women: A Pictorial History of Bedford College, University of London 1849–1985* (Egham, Surrey: Alma 1991).

to a private view. Levy's article is concerned with clubs for upper-class and professional/graduate women, and her own position as a writer possibly made her particularly responsive to their discursive and inter-active opportunities. Martha Vicinus argues that female clubs in general did not continue to be popular after the first decade of the twentieth century, suggesting that, '[c]lubs may have been too public, too filled with those who did not fit anywhere; women's space tended to be more private, more homelike, offering the accoutrements of the domestic even in such public spheres as a college or boarding school. Clubs did not fit readily into such a definition and suffered accordingly.'[42] Yet this is to miss the whole point of the clubs, which was to provide a semi-public space away from the private domestic sphere, precisely for those who did not 'fit' elsewhere—single, professional women.

Miriam Henderson in *Pilgrimage* first moves to central London in 1896, when she starts work at Wimpole Street and lodges at Tansley Street, mirroring Richardson's position at the Harley Street dentists and her lodgings in Endsleigh Street in Bloomsbury. Immediately her life is defined in terms of three distinct urban spaces; her cupboard office, attic room, and the adjoining stretch of the Euston Road. The everyday life of the modern city woman is thus represented as the experience of low-paid work, solitariness, and lots of walking. The office is essentially a place of weariness and grind, a means to economic independence. Miriam's empty room, however, is often harder to face, and Richardson's representation of the atmosphere and meaning of the single woman's private domain contrasts with the hegemonic interpretation of the female room that derives from Woolf's image of the 'room of one's own' as a place of ultimate freedom and support. Miriam's room does give her privacy and repose yet it can also make evident her isolation, and she often feels 'unable to summon courage to turn and face her room' (*P ii.* 327). In fact Miriam is more relaxed when walking, away from both the workplace and the domestic scene, finding that observing the multiplicity of the city streets distracts her from facing the enormity of the ego. Her freedom in walking is increased by her use of the new public spaces catering for women (eating places, evening transport, the female club) and, although these take courage to find, once entered they became favourite haunts.

Despite her isolated walks, Miriam at first fears public spaces, sensing her 'otherness' and lack of place. Her awareness of this transgression is evident in her apprehension at entering the 'Donizetti' restaurant alone in the evening: '[p]erhaps they would even refuse to serve her. Perhaps it

---

[42] Vicinus, *Independent Women*, 299.

was impossible to go into a restaurant late at night alone' (359). Her fear invades the scene as she perceives the proprietor standing over her, separating her from the other diners. Yet Miriam relaxes as she is treated respectfully as a customer and he helps to relieve her isolation by bringing her the *Illustrated London News*. Overcoming her ideologically induced anxiety, Miriam violates the invisible barriers to the 'public' and recognizes the separation of male and female spaces as superficial, inside the 'frightful frosted doors' being a 'home, a bit of her own London home' (360).

A crucial influence in Miriam's growing sense of her identity and ambitions manifest in 'The Trap' is her club, the Belmont, described as 'neutral territory' (*P iii.* 418). Based on Richardson's own experience of the Arachne, which she joined in 1904, the atmosphere of the Belmont indicates the importance of the club for women struggling for freedom and independence in the city yet also faced with its isolation and loneliness. It offers quiet relaxation, and the sense of 'freedom in company, enriched' that results from 'a roomful of independent strangers' (418). Miriam quickly takes her friends, the Broom sisters, to the Belmont when she perceives their kindly covered dismay at the quality of her rented rooms. For despite their long-standing friendship, and Miriam's envy of their suburban self-security, she feels that they are still conventional and not really 'free'. As with Miriam's other friends, she seeks to find in them a model combination of security and freedom, yet, as always, comes to the same conclusion; 'the impossibility of being at once bound and free'. Desperately asking '[i]s there no way of life where the two can meet?', she realizes that the club is 'a small beginning of such a way of life' in which women represent not 'names and families but selves in their own right' (453).

As in Ruscino's, in the club Miriam adopts the encompassing, static perspective of the privileged male spectator. Sitting at a window, she enjoys the panoramic view she gains of the square below, noting that, '[w]alked through, the squares were always a new loveliness, but even at a stroll they passed too quickly. There, at last, was one of the best of them arrested for contemplation' (418). The differences between Miriam's embrace of her modernity and her flat-mate's reserve, however, are evident at the club. Miss Holland is uneasy there and, in complete opposition to Miriam's characteristically acute observation, her eyes are 'turned unseeing [...] upon the prospect beyond the window' (419). They make little connection at the club, and Miriam realizes that their relationship is to be strictly that of fellow lodgers with separate interest. Their friendship deteriorates further when Miriam takes Miss Holland to her favourite haunt, the faithful Donizetti's that has proved to be a restaurant welcoming to the lone woman. Like the female club, Mrs Bailey's boarding-house and Bloomsbury itself, the restaurant is a place for misfits: '[t]he place was not crowded. Every one there was distinctly visible—the lonely intent women in gaudy finery, the old men fêting bored, laughing girls who glanced about; the habitués, solitary figures in elderly bondage to the resources of the place' (427). Although it is a public space in which she is able to relax, Miss Holland's lack of ability to perceive the subtler benefits of the restaurant and its 'little padrone' is obvious to Miriam, who regards her as an 'insulated' ego, who lives and works in the city yet without ever being aware of her surroundings. Miss Holland is no *flâneuse*; constantly described as unseeing and unaware, she can '[s]ee only morally' (427).

The Room and the Street

For Miriam, the 'room of one's own', according to her mood, is sometimes a retreat but often a place of isolation, 'a cell of torturing mocking memories and apprehensions'. By the middle of *Deadlock*, the walls of her room have become 'challenging', 'scornful', 'mocking', and 'indifferent', and regard her as a 'meaningless impermanence', ceasing to be 'the thrilled companions of her freedom' (31). After this she starts reviewing, however, and the atmosphere of the room changes as it becomes a place of creativity. When oppressed by the monotony of her work, and questioning the benefits of her independence, the room had accentuated her loneliness and lack of social relationships, but once she feels that her writing gives her purpose, the rest of her life can take any form. The moments of illumination occasionally experienced by the pools of street-lights in the streets are recalled by and extended into the circle of lamplight that falls onto her desk. Miriam feels part of the urban literary tradition, the old ink-stains she finds on the desk giving evidence of a past writer;

[s]he remembered drawing the cover from the table by the window and finding the ink-stains. They were there in the warm bright circle of midmorning lamplight, showing between the scattered papers. [...] Nothing would matter now that the paper-scattered lamplit circle was established as the centre of life. [...] Held up by this secret place, drawing her energy from it, any sort of life would do that left this room and its little table free and untouched. (133–4)

Mary Datchet's flat in *Night and Day* is represented in a similar way, emphasizing her single state whilst she struggles to come to terms with Ralph's indifference but eventually becoming a haven that gives her identity as a writer. The flat is more comfortable than Miriam's room, as Mary has a private income, and in Woolf's first description is a vibrant social place, crammed with people to hear William Rodney's talk. Yet it becomes increasingly a place where she is alone, and, by the time Katharine visits her towards the end of the novel, it is merely a place of ghosts; '[t]here were ghosts in the room, and one, strangely and sadly was the ghost of herself' (*ND* 469).

Rooms in *Night and Day* are highly symbolic and suggestive of the ideas and position of Edwardian men and women in relation to the city and to each other. The essential contrast of Mary's flat and Katharine's family home is that Katharine has no real place of private freedom. She is connected, first and foremost, with the domestic/social drawing-room rather than any place of her own. Ralph too can only obtain privacy by a churlish 'OUT' notice pinned to his door, and regards the best feature of his adolescent room to be its encompassing view of London, 'the city which lay, hazily luminous, beneath him' (23). Katharine and Ralph live in residential or suburban areas of the city and, although they walk in its streets, are not really at home there, preferring the countryside and its urban substitute of Kew Gardens. By contrast, Mary and William Rodney are more iconographic urban characters. Rodney is an ironic caricature of the urban writers of the past and out of place in modern times and the modern city. Yet he is very much a spiritual Londoner and, perceiving it with traditionalist eyes as 'a town cut out of grey-blue cardboard, and pasted flat against the sky' (71), admits that he cannot live away from it. Indeed, the flat that marks Mary's independence is largely modelled on the rooms of the traditional male bachelor such as Rodney, her knitting basket, coffee, and pink biscuits replacing his male accessories of dressing-gown and slippers, whisky and cake.

Mary Datchet is a thorough and poignant portrait of a woman seeking her own independence and, through her character, Woolf investigates the possibility for the independent woman to enjoy both 'books and stockings', her shorthand for profession and home life. Mary's liberalist feminism does not desire radical independence but personal freedom for both love and a career, which, Woolf comes to decide, seem destined to be incompatible. Again like Miriam Henderson, Mary's daily spaces of office and flat are connected by streets (this time the east side of Blooms-bury; Lincoln's Inn Fields, Kingsway, Southampton Row, into Russell Square) and again the walk provides a paradoxically suspended time period in the consciousness, in which Mary enjoys a special experience of privacy, freedom, and oneness with her surroundings before gathering herself for work. During the walk, she consciously constructs herself as an urban dweller, and in the six months of her residence in London has positioned herself within the genderless crowd as 'worker' rather than 'woman'. Mary's view of the crowd is not the Eliotian image of a mindless, surging mass, from which male writers were so often concerned to distinguish themselves. On the contrary, Mary seeks to be part of the crowd, thus denying the role of woman as spectacle. However, Woolf's narrative punctuates Mary's thoughts in ironic commentary, noting that Mary '*liked to think herself* one of the workers who, at this hour, take their way along in rapid single file along all the broad pavements of the city' and '*liked to pretend* that she was indistinguishable from the rest', as if both she and Woolf know the futility of such idealism (76, my emphasis). And although Mary values the mechanicalism of the crowd and wants to be part of its 'serious business of winding the world up to tick for another four-and-twenty-hours' (76), Woolf's dry humour notes that an unpaid suffrage worker would hardly be regarded as contributing to the interests of the daily masculine world! Yet, at the same time, Mary is part of the routine of that world, with a degree of its freedom. After a morning's work, for example, she reads the city evening newspaper and lunches with a friend (herself a working woman) in a cheap and 'gaudy' restaurant amidst the streets of offices, 'parting on the strip of pavement among the different lines of traffic with a pleasant feeling that they were stepping once more into their separate places in the great and eternally moving pattern of human life' (80). Her modernity is illustrated by ease in such public establishments, and can perhaps be contrasted with the older generation suffrage worker Sally Seal, who lunches on sandwiches in Russell Square, the fresh air of the plane-trees (Levy's female urban symbol) suggesting her idealism but not offering the practical sustenance of Mary's meal.

The importance of the crowd to Mary is emphasized during the crises she undergoes in Chapter 20, when she realizes that her love for Ralph is hopeless but also admits that he had always been more important to her than the suffrage, therefore doubting the strength of her political convictions. The hegemonic perspective of struggle against the crowd is again contrasted with Mary's struggle to be a part of it. She does not feel herself an ego crushed and engulfed by the crowd but rather a non-ego, lacking in identity and therefore needing the crowd's ballast of giving her a purpose. In her disillusionment she feels alien and outside what she sees as a vital crowd of people connecting with the world around them (women looking in shop windows, men buying books). It is by walking in the streets that Mary aims to be part of this crowd, as in walking she finds both physical and mental action and can attempt to gather the threads of self; '[w]ith a brain working and a body working one could keep step with the crowd and never be found out for the hollow machine, lacking the essential thing, that one was conscious of being' (270).

The daytime walks that Mary and Katharine take are determined by their different lifestyles and illustrate their consequent variations in perspective, giving alternative versions of female urban freedom. Mary walks to work along with the early morning crowd of 'clerks and typists and commercial men' and she sees the city preparing for business, aligning herself with it 'for at this hour of the morning she ranged herself entirely on the side of the shopkeepers and bank clerks' (76). Her independence surfaces in her purposiveness and assumption of her justified place in the male city. Katharine's walks in the same area take place in the afternoon and express her sense of freedom in terms of exhilaration and sensual excitement. Woolf's comparison of these options is emphasized by her constant practice of juxtaposing the acts of Mary and Katharine before bringing the two girls together in a focusing scene. That Katharine, as an upper-class woman, is subject to greater practical restrictions than Mary is indicated by the fact that, whilst shopping in Kingsway at four o'clock, she finds herself stranded when desiring tea. The 'gaudy establishment' where Mary lunches would presumably be out of bounds to Katharine as it is not even considered, and as a shop offers no company yet she does not want to return home Katharine has to think of 'some neighbourhood drawing-room' (82) and ends up by finding Mary in her office. For Katharine, however, the suffrage workers are 'enchanted people in a bewitched tower' who have very little connection with the personal freedom she values, being detached from 'the crowded street, with its pendant necklace of lamps, its lighted windows, and its throng of men and women which exhilarated her' (92–3). Although made dizzy by the speed and crush of Tottenham Court Road, this is the result of excitement rather than disorientation and she remains in control, 'an alert, commanding figure' in the city streets. In comparison, Woolf depicts her male protagonist, Ralph, as often more bewildered in the city, frequently pacing and wandering the streets after news of Katharine's engagement, having lost any sense of order or direction '[f]or the substantial world, with its prospect of avenues leading on and on to the invisible distance, had slipped from him' (161).

Mary finds walking conducive to gathering and composing ideas and identity, and takes a walk to the Strand in a mental and physical journey of self-assessment, to find that the two words 'not happiness' make up the conclusion 'which composed itself as she walked down the Charing Cross Road' (271). Registering a change of direction in her life, the walk through her consciousness continues as she stares out of the office window later in the afternoon, 'her mind pursu[ing] its own journey among the sun-blazoned windows and the drifts of purplish smoke which formed her view' (273). Her path now turns from an individualist to a collective feminist impulse, subordinating her own desires to those of others. Woolf seems to imply, however, in accordance with Katharine, that this detachment that Mary develops to protect herself from the pain of her solitary state results in an impersonality and emotional sterility. Through the figure of Mary she attacks the dualistic forces that seem to define the modern woman's options as either marriage or career, yet she cannot offer alternatives that seem satisfactory, only recording with sympathy the irony that Mary's modern independence should result in the loss of her individual identity; '[s]he must check this desire to be an individual again, whose wishes were in conflict with those of other people' (284). Rose in *The Years* also turns to the city as an alternative to lost love. Standing on a bridge over the Thames in 1910, Rose, now a suffragette, recalls standing there years before, crying over an engagement: 'her tears had fallen, her happiness, it seemed to her had fallen. Then she had turned—here she turned—and had seen the churches, the masts and roofs of the city. There's *that*, she had said to herself' (*Y* 154). The iconographical images of the river as a site for the reverie of the male poet or the tears of the fallen woman are here combined. Woolf repeats the refrain 'had fallen', as if reinforcing the traditional connection of the city woman with the prostitute figure of the past, yet now the city is presented as an alternative for women, a sort of surrogate lover that can offer support and independence. By 1910 Rose is a suffragette, and asserting her own presence and her own image onto the urban scene.

Through Katharine Hilbery, Woolf expresses her refusal to be limited by opposing choices. In a walk of self-analysis that parallels that of Mary, Katharine refuses to come to conclusions or make decisions. At a crossroads of streets, for example, she tries to decide on a direction—'should she walk on by the Strand or by the Embankment? It was not a simple question, for it concerned not different streets so much as different streams of thought' (*ND* 282)—but finally avoids making a choice, just as in life, and ends up visiting Mary instead as if seeking an example to follow or reject. Katharine certainly envies the individual freedom she finds manifest in Mary's room, which has become that of the urban writer; '[t]he green-shaded lamp burnt in the corner, and illumined books and pens and blotting-paper. The whole aspect of the place [...] struck her as enviably free; in such a room one could work—one could have a life of one's own' (284). The sudden decision to visit Mary is repeated later in the novel, when Katharine feels detached and isolated from the social world of her family. 'Outside the community in some way', both mentally and physically withdrawn to the margins of the window, she experiences the strange sensation of observing them from a kaleidoscopic distance and longs to be 'driving rapidly through the streets' (371). Her feeling of loneliness prompts her to visit Mary and, walking together along the road, they are connected by the dilemma of their common womanhood—marriage or profession—'upon both of them a cloud of difficulty and darkness rested, obscuring the future, in which they had both to find a way' (379). But, by the time they part, they seem to be set on different paths.

In a vivid, spiralling image, Woolf portrays Mary mounting the stairs to her flat whilst Katharine stays behind in the street. The stairs are a space of separation between them, between the high detachment of the flat and the vitality of the street, and between isolated industry and the possibility of love. Mary pauses before starting the ascent, climbs the first few steps slowly and then stops and looks down, as if painfully giving up her own claim to such a possibility. Going higher, she turns again to see Katharine getting into a cab and disappearing into the streets. It costs Mary immense psychological effort to mount the rest of the staircase, metaphorical of the sacrifice of her love for independence, and it is only the prospect of her work that offers her support for her loneliness;

> Mary mounted the stairs step by step, as if she had to lift her body up an extremely steep ascent. She had had to wrench herself forcibly away from Katharine, and every step vanquished her desire. She held on grimly, encouraging herself as though she were actually making some great physical effort in climbing a height. She was conscious that Mr Basnett, sitting at the top of the stairs with his documents, offered her solid footing if she were capable of reaching it. The knowledge gave her a faint sense of exaltation. (380)

She reaches the top and the hard won security, but at a cost, and she is later described as having relinquished her youth and bloom for a self-possessed maturity that yet brings with it 'hollower cheeks' and eyes that are narrowed and weary rather than 'spontaneously observing' (468). Woolf seems unable to resolve the dualistic position of the woman in the city; Katharine finds a free equality in her love with Ralph but they intend to move to the country on their marriage, whereas Mary remains in London but faces a barren future, as, it is implied, do all city women: '[w]here should I be now if I hadn't got to go to my office every day? Thousands of people would tell you the same thing—*thousands of women*' (412, my emphasis).

In this chapter I have described the growth of urban spaces available to women at the turn of the century, and suggested that these provide a spatial map of female urban experience. In *Pilgrimage, Night and Day,* and *The Years*, Richardson and Woolf use this cityscape of the past to register the personal and imaginative journeys of the female consciousness. They displace the traditional masculine *Bildungsroman* and *Kunstlerroman* onto female journeys around the city and over time. So often, though, the female walker encounters a crossroads, upon which she must choose her direction. Katherine Hilberry and Mary Datchet consider the two pathways, each finally deciding on a different option. Miriam Henderson idiosyncratically refuses the choice, her dominant negotiation of the streets occurring as she walks through Piccadilly Circus, a roundabout rather than a crossroads, in which Eros stands in the middle island. Amy Levy, however, stands caught between the paths of her Jewish and feminist identities, and the tension of this position perhaps contributed to her innate melancholia. Her *flânerie*, unlike that of the English middle-class women, carries the connotations of race, which she aimed to control in her self-identification of her Jewishness and her urbanism in her writing. The role of the crossroad for Virginia Woolf's imaginary Judith Shakespeare, who enjoyed none of the opportunities of the New Woman, is as a gravestone. Levy saw the Jewish women as also denied these opportunities, and the lines from Heine that preface her poem 'A Cross-Road Epitaph'—'Am kreuzweg wird begraben | Wer selber brachte sich um'—anticipate her own eventual decision to take her own life.[43]

[43] 'At the cross-roads they bury those who took their own lives'.

4 | On the Margins of the City

THE modernist literary climate of the 1920s has customarily been defined as both urban and dislocated, influentially described by Raymond Williams as 'the practices and ideas of the avant-garde movements of the twentieth century and the specific conditions and relationships of the twentieth-century metropolis'.[1] Nineteenth-century and pre-war period 'modernity' was linked to the increased urbanism of the industrializing West, and can be characterized by the new experiences, psychologies, and social groups that resulted. By contrast, 'modernism', despite its seemingly indeterminate expansiveness, is, in its original form, far more historically, socially, and geographically specific—defined retrospectively by its own (predominantly male) proponents into a self-perpetuating myth of an Anglo-American expatriate, avant-garde community, rootlessly wandering the cities of Europe in the wake of the First World War. The myth of the 'lost generation' is premised on the conditions and experiences of these expatriate writers and artists; immigrants to foreign cities who have only a visual language in common, that of the city around them. It is with this expatriate existence that deracination and cosmopolitanism became universalized conditions and concerns within dominant culture.

Descriptions of the urban geography of modernism have tended to follow this basic premiss, identifying a series of 'culture-capitals' with particular environmental, social, and political conditions: London, Paris, Berlin, Vienna, St Petersburg, Chicago, and New York.[2] The literary coteries in these cities are marked onto a spatio-temporal map, as groups of American artists and writers migrated to pre-war London, post-war Paris, and back to New York during the Depression. The emblematic modernist artist—Eliot, Hemingway, Joyce, Lawrence, Pound—is thus conceived in a similar way to the emblematic 'Jew as

---

[1] Raymond Williams, 'The Politics of Modernism', in Tony Pinkney (ed.), *The Politics of Modernism: Against the New Conformists* (London: Verso, 1989).

[2] Malcolm Bradbury and James McFarlane (eds.), *Modernism: A Guide to European Literature, 1890–1930* (London: Penguin, 1991).

wandering exile', whose urban environment is made up of a conglomeration of cities perceived through the perspective of the rootless expatriate, and the modernist protagonist is interpreted in terms of a lack of social, spatial, and historical continuity. The writers introduced in this chapter depict disorientating spatial movement in their texts, as they present the struggle of the woman as not so much to enter but to survive in the urban environment.

Richardson's *Pilgrimage* is the paradigmatic female journey or *Bildungsroman*, an extensive 'walk' through and across city, continent, social identities, belief systems, and texts. In this respect it provides a model for the sort of politically active yet aesthetically resonant text that Rita Felski, in *Beyond Feminist Aesthetics*, requires of feminist literature. Felski defines two interpretative categories of female *Bildungsroman*; the liberal socialist, which is realist in style and depicts emancipation as a progression outward into the public social world, and the romantic individualist which represents self-discovery in terms of a move inwards to an awareness of a mythic inner identity, arguing that these should not be taken as mutually exclusive, and that, in fact, the development of a subjective and symbolic self-identity is crucially supportive for social autonomy and agency.[3] To a certain extent, however, this warning should be directed at the assumptions of literary theory rather than at texts themselves, for *Pilgrimage* at least fulfils Felski's demand that '[f]eminism and feminist fiction point outward and forward, into social activity and political emancipation, but also backward and inward, into myth, spirituality, and the transformation of subjective consciousness'.[4] It portrays Miriam Henderson's development of personal and social identity through a combination of textual aesthetic experimentation and thematic social and political debate.

Discussion of the turn-of-the-century woman writer has so far concentrated on the value of the 'pilgrimage', following the feminist practice of '[m]oving away from "home" to deconstruct the terms of social privilege and power' which always 'favors the process of the move over the ultimate goal'.[5] In women's urban literature in the late 1920s and 1930s, however, the pilgrimage seems to reach an impasse and the dominant metaphor changes to that of being lost in a labyrinth, constantly retracing one's steps over the same sterile ground. The desire to experience the open space of the street is countered in the inter-war

---

[3] Rita Felski, *Beyond Feminist Aesthetics: Literature and Social Change* (Cambridge, Mass.: Harvard UP, 1989), 217.

[4] Ibid. 128.

[5] Kaplan, 'Deterritorializations', 193.

period by a desperate attempt to retreat from it. With the examples of
Richardson and Woolf, I have suggested that the turn-of-the-century
female *Bildungsroman* investigated the possibilities of women's identification with urban figures who seemed to accord with their own
experience of alienation yet were not limited by class or gender in their
exploration of city space. Writing in the post-war period of the late 1920s
and 1930s, however, the urban-based novels of Jean Rhys cut through
such metaphorical flirtation with penetrative cynicism as to the realities
of women's actual position in the economic and consumer world of
the city.

Despite the increased independence and public visibility of women
that was gained in the first decades of the twentieth century, the end of
the war brought with it a backlash against female emancipation. As
Mary Lou Emery describes, speaking of Rhys's *After Leaving Mr Mackenzie* (1930), '[w]omen were punished for their earlier adventures, forced
back into a life they thought they had left behind, or abandoned, like
Julia, to their fate on the streets'.[6] Indeed women in public were again
associated with the fallen woman. Such disillusionment was not particular to Rhys and appears in other specifically urban novels by women,
such as Elizabeth Bowen's *To the North* (1927) and Rosamond Lehmann's
The Weather in the Streets (1936). For all three writers, women's posture
of urban knowledge and independence has become futile, sterile, and
rather sordid. The trajectories of their urban wanderings no longer map
engaged pilgrimages but instead confusion, bewilderment, and constant
attempts at retreat. Whereas Richardson and Woolf's characters used the
urban street and room to manifest independence and assert a place on
the urban map, those of Lehmann and Rhys choose to inhabit streets and
rooms that allow them hiding-places; that conceal them from the urban
map. The purpose of their walks is largely retreat, anonymity from
others and themselves. As Anna Morgan in Rhys's *Voyage in the Dark*
(1934) states when she is dropped by her admirer Jefferies, 'Anywhere will
do, so long as it's somewhere that nobody knows' (100).

Adrift in Foggy Labyrinths

A lack of satisfaction with female identification with the cosmopolitan
surfaces in Elizabeth Bowen's inter-war novel *To the North*, in which the
manipulative yet perceptive relic of the gracious Edwardian era, Lady

---

[6] Mary Lou Emery, *Jean Rhys at 'World's End': Novels of Colonial and Sexual Exile*
(Austin: University of Texas Press, 1990), 142.

Waters, voices the central argument that 'this age is far more than restless: it is decentralised. From week to week there is no knowing where anyone is' (*TN* 170). The protagonists Cecilia and Emmeline belong to this decentralized younger generation and are each independent modern women. They live together in St John's Wood, and their lifestyle of 'faint impropriety' is evoked by Bowen's description of the area; 'garden walls are mysterious, laburnums falling between the windows and walls have their own streets. Acacias whisper at nights round airy, ornate little houses in which pretty women lived singly but were not always alone' (13). Cecilia, a natural yet masculine cosmopolitan, is introduced in a train travelling back from Milan alone. '[S]he love[s] strangers, strangeness' (8) and is rarely in one country for long before wishing she is somewhere else. She is most satisfied when actually in the act of travelling, in a state of limbo between places. Emmeline runs a travel agency, the archetypal modern business, through which she would seem to control the 'cosmopolis' of Europe, having the times of trains, the addresses of hotels, and the maps of tourist sights at her fingertips. Taking lunch 'not far from Woburn Place at a shop called "The Coffee Pot", with Peter Lewis, her partner . . . [s]he read a book about Poland, he blue-pencilled manuscript; they ate poached egg on spinach, each paid for their lunches and did not speak to each other' (47). All very modern and professional. Ironically however, just as Cecilia's feminine society image covers her modern indifference and love of speed and strangeness, Emmeline's public identity as a business woman hides a fundamentally emotional and dependent subjectivity. In fact, her placing and orientating of others through her maps and itineraries of Europe can be interpreted as an attempt to vicariously situate herself within space and time. Significantly, she gradually loses control of the business, and spends more and more time out of the office, wandering aimlessly in the streets.

To the North is a novel structured by speed and movement, Bowen portraying the disparity between the mechanical pace of the modern world and the natural rhythms of the inner self. Cecilia at first succeeds in reconciling the two, thanks to her ability to observe life with clear and authoritative detachment, yet ultimately she gives up any radicalism and takes the conventional path of a respectable and comfortable marriage. Emmeline, by contrast, is a far more schizophrenic character. As her poor eyesight suggests, she perceives the world around her through a subjective blur, and she survives only by firmly dividing and keeping separate her public and personal identities. She withdraws her personal self into a cocoon that is yet eventually invaded by modernity in the presence of Markie, who brings with him a speed and tension that entirely overwhelms her. She finally manages to reassert detachment but, unlike Cecilia whose detachment is based in a surety of selfhood, Emmeline's is a detachment from self as she becomes 'lost to her own identity' and able 'to look down unmoved at the shadowy map of her pain'. She eventually decides to make a journey herself rather than just co-ordinate those of others: '[a]n immense idea of departure—expresses getting steam up and crashing from termini, liners clearing the docks, the shadows of planes rising, caravans winding out into the first dip of the desert—possessed her spirit' (244). This journey, however, is both metaphorical and literal—a car ride that turns into a Nietzchean/Lawrentian 'death-drive'.

Occupations and single dwellings were tolerated for young women in the early twentieth century but still only for a brief period before marriage—eventually they were expected to conform to convention. Female characters in women's urban fiction of the 1920s and 1930s frequently have in common the threat of spinsterhood and, although protective of their independence, are yet disillusioned with the single life. They are youngish women, often in monotonous and/or poorly paid employment, who dwell in a rootless bohemia, unsure of their place or position in society. Cecilia and Emmeline are both women past their first youth whose lives of independence prove to be different from what they had envisioned. Olivia Curtis, in Rosamond Lehmann's *The Weather in the Streets*, is another such figure; the fresh young girl from the earlier novel *Invitation to the Waltz* (1932), who held the prospect of Cambridge and an exciting future before her, is now a divorced woman in her late twenties, with no profession or suitor, watching her youth and looks ebb away in a round of wild parties and an affair with a married man.

In *The Weather in the Streets*, Lehmann depicts the female independent life with little romanticized enthusiasm as a superficial and empty freedom, emphasizing the struggle of women to create a fulfilling existence in the city. London, and the urban motifs that spoke freedom to Miriam Henderson, 'getting on a bus [...] bed-sitting-rooms and studios of that sort [...] drifting about for inexpensive meals [...] always the cheapest seats in movies' (*WS* 77), now signify loneliness, drudgery, and sterility for Olivia. Her glimpse of the opposing lifestyles of the rural domesticity of her sister Kate, and the comfortable aristocracy of the Spencers, invokes her perception of the barrenness of her own experience in a rush of interior monologue:

the book taken up, the book laid down, aghast, because of the traffic's sadness, which was time, lamenting and pouring away down all the street for ever; because of the lives passing up and down outside with steps and voices of futile purpose and forlorn commotion: draining out my life, out of the window, in their echoing wake, leaving me dry, stranded, sterile, bound solitary to the room's minute respectability, the gas-fire, the cigarette, the awaited bell, the gramophone's idiot companionship, the unyielding arm-chair, the narrow bed. (77)

The description goes on and on, capturing the endless repetition of the days and the sense of disappearing time. Olivia lodges with her older cousin Etty, and although she pities her socialite, floating lifestyle to a certain extent, describing her as 'shrunken' (79) and exhausted-looking, like a fragile doll with 'brittle white legs and bony little knees' who is 'pale, extinct, ludicrously diminished without her make-up' (8), she becomes increasingly like her. Utterly absorbed in her affair with Rollo Spencer, she rarely works (partying with Anna and her bohemian friends and then lying in bed until late), loses weight, gets pregnant, and tries various quack remedies before having an underhand abortion. Olivia's story is not pleasant and it provides a sober conclusion to the more hopeful accounts of female independence in the rather idealistic *Dusty Answer* and *Invitation to the Waltz*.

Involving a greater use of interior monologue, the novel expresses the dejection of its heroine in a manner that pervades her surrounding environment. London is perceived through Olivia's subjectivity, in winter as a dirty and engulfing fog, in summer as a cloud of nauseating fumes, both ironically reflecting the 'fog' of illusion or later wilful ignorance with which Olivia surrounds herself. The city is never depicted externally by the author, being 'an extension of the mind's loathing and oppression' (230). It is a claustrophobic and confined space rather than a site for exploration and expansion. There is no air in Olivia's London. She is first introduced waking up to fog so thick that the morning seems like night. Etty's house is cramped, 'dense with the fog's penetration, with yesterday's cigarettes; strangled with cherry-coloured curtains, with parrot-greens and silver cushions, with Etty's little chairs, tables, stools, glass and shagreen and cloisonné boxes, bowls, ornaments' (5). This description not only establishes the girls' single state and bohemian taste, but also the strained tone of their existence; the room is like a fragile and unreal 'dolls'-house', 'strangled' by the curtains, crammed with objects that '[shrill] a peevish reproach', stale with cigarette-smoke, and pervaded by the London fog. Setting off to catch a train from Paddington, Olivia steps from house, to taxi, to train, keeping herself immersed in the protection of interior spaces and avoiding the 'smarting draught' (10) of the 'weather in the streets', where she senses time being marked out by the daily tide of traffic and commuters.

Olivia's affair with Rollo Spencer is another attempt to avoid the passage of time, in which she can give herself up to oblivious passivity:

'Beyond the glass casing I was in, was the weather, were the winter streets in rain, wind, fog, in the fine frosty days and nights, the mild, damp grey ones. Pictures of London winter the other side of the glass—not reaching the body' (145). She no longer experiences 'wet ankles, muddy stockings, blown hair, cold-aching cheeks, fog-smarting eyes, throat nose', the evidence of senses heightened by walking in the streets, nor even her 'usual bus-taking winter'. Rather, the relationship is conducted in a sheltered atmosphere that dulls awareness; '[i]t was always indoors or in taxis or in his warm car; it was mostly in the safe dark, or in half-light' (145). Significantly it only successfully takes place in enclosed spaces, needing to be hidden from the public world of city streets. The early days of the liaison occur in what seems to Olivia to be an eternal present: '[i]t was then the time began when there wasn't any time.' She submits to utter engulfment, rather like Rhys's heroines do in their desperate attempts to find oblivion in affairs with men, and loses all sense of her life's direction: '[t]he journey was in the dark, going on without end or beginning, without landmarks, bearings lost.' Yet this experience is forebodingly nightmarelike, and Lehmann evokes it through the metaphor of the amorphous but also fragmented and shock-ridden urban life of modernity:

Time whirled, throwing up in paradoxical slow motion a sign, a scene, sharp, startling, lingering as a blow over the heart. A look flared, urgently meaning something, stamping itself for ever, ever, ever.... Gone, flashed away, a face in a train passing, not ever to be recovered. A voice called out, saying words—going on, on, on, eternally reverberating... fading out, a voice of tin, a hollow voice, the plain meaning lost, the echo meaningless. A voice calling out at night in a foreign station where the night train draws through, not stopping.... (144).

The *flâneur*'s experience of disjointed faces looming out of the darkness of the street and passing by into obscurity is now translated into the experience of the traveller in the train, without feet on the ground, whirled at speed through an unknown landscape of which he catches only momentary glimpses. The rhythm of the train can be heard behind Lehmann's description, in the repetition of 'ever, ever, ever', 'on, on, on'. It is Olivia's own voice that she hears but cannot heed, its meaning lost because it is thin-sounding and fading out. For although she has mentally cocooned herself away from the time and weather in the streets in the artificial space of her passion for Rollo, both still beat in the background. If anything, Olivia is being hurled away by time into a situation that she has no control over, and her external voice calls to her from this place, metaphorically described as a foreign country which she is rushed through without any chance of stopping.

As for Bowen in *To the North*, for Lehmann the train is a meaningful motif of modernity, in which the geographical journey or metaphorical *Bildungsroman* is taken out of the control of the protagonist, whose autonomy is lost to the mechanical speed of the modern vehicle. Just as Markie, Emmeline's satanic suitor in *To the North*, is first presented on the train from Milan, Olivia meets Rollo Spencer on a train to the country. The second train journey in the novel follows the idyllic but indiscreet trip they take to Vienna which marks the limit of Rollo's depth of feeling and leaves Olivia, making her way back to England alone. Ironically, this second journey is exactly that predestined earlier, with Olivia journeying alone through foreign cities at which the train doesn't stop, travelling at night and therefore seeing nothing of the landscape beyond the window, unable to understand the snatches of languages that she overhears: 'Through a station, lights on the blind, under it, sharp flashes; rumble and clank; a man's voice calling out, what does the French voice say?... Cut off.... On again, faster now, gathering speed....' (229). Already pregnant, Olivia is indeed being whirled further out of autonomous control.

The pregnancy is an actual state that Olivia cannot be indifferent to and, symbolically in Lehmann's text, coincides with Rollo's return to his wife and Olivia's return to her single life. She is forced by loneliness and boredom into the streets of a 'scorched irritable airless' (230) London in summer. The railway motif now emphasizes her static, rejected state; '[t]o be alone, sick, in London in this dry, sterile, burnt-out end of summer, was to be abandoned in a pestilence-stricken town; was to live in a third-class waiting-room at a disused terminus among stains and smells, odds and ends of refuse and decay' (263). Her position is ambiguous, however. Essentially, the claustrophobic atmosphere does not seem to have lessened. Winter fog has merely been swapped for summer traffic fumes, and Olivia drags herself through a fortnight of London in a blur of fatigue and sickness. Yet a newly detailed depiction of the external spaces of London also invades the text, as Olivia spends more time out of doors and walking in the London streets. Perhaps as a 'fallen woman', Olivia now has a more legitimately defined place in the urban environment. Carefully making herself up with '[r]ouge, lipstick, powder', she wanders in the urban habitat common to single women, outsiders 'derelicts and eccentrics' (265); the cheap ladies' restaurant the Bird Cage, to which a motley assortment of 'fowls' are confined in order to eat; the park, where Olivia plays the part of daughter, friend, and mother to various outcasts that she meets. Ultimately, however, she is simply biding time, waiting in the airless city for the thunder and rain to arrive. When it does so it coincides with a visit from Lady Spencer, and Olivia's awareness of the futility of her situation and the necessity to terminate both baby and affair.

Yet with this decision, which seems a resolution of the situation, Olivia merely seems to sink back into her original stale state. Before Rollo, Olivia's social life in London revolves around the Fitzroy Square/Mayfair-bohemia of Simon, the artist-lover of her employer Anna, and his acolytes. Resembling the experience of a fragmentary modernity pictured in the metaphors of the murky urban street and the high-speed train, their drunken parties are places of dangerous blindness and then sudden collision; 'a background of more or less amorphous entities' upon which the odd face flashes 'frantic [...] with dilated eyes' (363). The close of her affair with Rollo, which by the end of the novel is ambiguous, however, is simultaneous with the death of Simon who, as Olivia recognized, possessed the 'unconscious power' of principle that held the otherwise amorphous group together. Without him, as his patroness Mrs Cunningham's party indicates, they fade and a younger generation takes over.

The social historian E. J. Hobsbawm has suggested that one new environment that indicated the greater freedom of women in urban public space in the early decades of the century, were cosmopolitan cafés, where '[b]y 1914 the more unshackled youth in the western big cities was already familiar with sexually provocative rhythmic dances of dubious but exotic origin'.[7] In Pilgrimage, Miriam Henderson considered bohemian cosmopolitanism as an alternative to the restrictive Victorian codes and an opening into the public social life of the urban world. Olivia Curtis flirts with the London avant-garde of the early 1930s in an adolescently ostentatious attempt to flout convention. Both however, eventually turn away from a lifestyle that they perceive is emotionally sterile and mentally frantic. Jean Rhys also hints at a lack of fulfilment in urban modernist bohemia. Marya Zelli's involvement with literary bohemia in Quartet (1929) provides her with an illusion of liberation yet ultimately still leaves her as a financially and emotionally dependant woman. The fate of Marya and Anna Morgan in Voyage in the Dark would appear to be the aimless, alcohol-numbed lives of Rhys's older female protagonists, fading women haunting the spaces of a fading bohemia. An important characteristic of Rhys's heroines is that they are natural wanderers—as is constantly proved by their instability in employment and represented by their aimless walks—who collude in their own destinies. They are strays in the city, wanderers who have no

[7] E. J. Hobsbawm, The Age of Empire 1875–1914 (London: Weidenfeld and Nicolson, 1987), 204.

direction and are going nowhere. The omniscient narrator that Rhys employs in *Quartet* states, 'Marya, you must understand, had not been suddenly and ruthlessly transplanted from solid comfort to the hazards of Montmartre. Nothing like that. Truth to say, she was used to a lack of solidity and fixed backgrounds' (*Q* 15). It is this aspect of Rhys's female characters, the 'vagabond by nature', that accounts for the seemingly fatalistic acquiescence they display in the face of the tawdry monotony of their lives.

Through Sasha Jensen in *Good Morning, Midnight* (1939) Rhys also expresses a perception of the city and the urban milieu, however, that develops into a modern aesthetic, in the tradition of Richardson, Woolf, and later Lessing. Although women are relatively impotent figures for Rhys, whose lives are controlled by what she portrays as the determining forces of the city, in Sasha she creates a heroine who realizes that, even if her life is inevitable and unchangeable, she can assert some identity by being aware of her situation, and mocking it. The women alone in the city in the earlier novels are on a naturalistic, Zolaesque degenerative slide into poverty, drunkenness, and inept prostitution, with neither the determination nor the resoluteness to prevent it. In *Good Morning, Midnight* Rhys is attempting to do something different, observing rather than reflecting the state of wandering and using it to plot a female psycho-geographic map.

Jean Rhys and Neglected Maps

In Jean Rhys's fiction, London is as much a city of greyness and gloom as it is in *The Weather in the Streets*. Anna Morgan, in *Voyage in the Dark*, is appalled by what she sees as a dehumanizing labyrinth: 'this is London— hundreds thousands of white people white people rushing along and the dark houses all alike frowning down one after the other all alike all stuck together—the streets like smooth shut-in ravines and the dark houses frowning down—oh I'm not going to like this place I'm not going to like this place I'm not going to like this place' (*VD* 17). Rhys's antipathy, however, is perhaps imbued with a sense of being particularly inferior and 'other', as a colonial and a woman, to the imperial and patriarchal might of England's capital city. It is a place where the inhabitants and the customs and conventions are most antithetical to those of the warmth of the Antilles. Rhys, as a female, colonial expatriate, is a primary example of the modern writer as urban stranger. Arriving in England from Dominica in 1907, when she was 17 (her father was a doctor from Wales and had married a third-generation Creole woman) she studied at the Academy of Dramatic Art in Gower Street for two terms, before her talent was deemed insufficient to justify the expense of fees. Disappointed by her first sight of London, which seemed grey, crowded, and full of poverty, she soon saw England as oppressive and its social structures and rules as incomprehensible. Regarding herself a failure, Rhys opted not to return to the Antilles however, and began several years of a marginal existence, working as a chorus-girl in a touring company and as a part-time model. Living in disreputable boarding-houses in Bloomsbury, along with other marginals such as students and foreign exiles, Rhys was inhabiting the same area, although in even less secure financial circumstances as Richardson a decade before. She moved to Paris on her first marriage, becoming Ford Madox Ford's mistress and literary protégée, and, finding the city far more sympathetic than London, returned there intermittently after settling back in England after 1929.

Rhys's first four novels, *Quartet* (1929), *After Leaving Mr Mackenzie* (1930), *Voyage in the Dark*, and *Good Morning, Midnight*, deriving from the circumstances and events of her life in London and Paris, are frequently interpreted autobiographically. Yet in them Rhys carefully combines fact and fiction to create for herself a faltering *Bildungsroman*. The hegemonic but rather limited interpretation of the novels in early criticism was that they portrayed one heroine: woman as a marginal, incompetent victim, wearily grasping at the illusions of youth and beauty. More recently a degree of progression has been noted through the four books, particularly when one considers that *Voyage in the Dark* was written before *Quartet,* and they have come to reflect Rhys's own early life journey: her work as a model and on the stage in England, her relationship with Ford, her loneliness and disillusionment afterwards, and finally a new self-awareness and mockery at the pathos of her position. The heroine of the novels is still a composite one but she is now accorded a certain trajectory or purpose compared to her previous state of aimless and ineffectual wanderings. Pierette Frickey, for example, describes *Voyage in the Dark* as beginning the 'saga which will take the heroine of *Quartet, After Leaving Mr Mackenzie,* and *Good Morning, Midnight* through England and France, in quest of something better in life before the final return home in Rhys' last novel *Wide Sargasso Sea*'.[8] Yet this 'prodigal daughter' narrative is only conceivable with hindsight and I think it is questionable whether the first novels themselves are so smoothly linear in conception.

---

[8] Pierrette Frickey (ed.), *Critical Perspectives on Jean Rhys* (Washington: Three Continents Press, 1990), 6.

As with Richardson, Rhys's work involves a constant retracing of steps and memory in the urban streets. London and Paris are walked by young girls in their late teens and women in their early thirties, just as they were by Rhys herself. For Julia Martin, called back to England because of her mother's illness, returning to London, to both the body of her mother and the streets of the imperial city, is a return to the past, or rather a layering of past and present when two periods seem to become diachronous, skipping over the intervening period; '[s]he felt that her life had moved in a circle. Predestined, she had returned to her starting-point, in this little Bloomsbury bedroom that was so exactly like the little Bloomsbury bedroom she had left nearly ten years before' (*ALMM* 67). At first Julia is inspired by this vision of her younger and idealistic self. Meeting her ghost in the street she appropriates her old exultancy and recklessness. Yet her pretensions are soon dispersed when she loses her way in Soho and, fearing 'walking about aimlessly' (68), retreats back to the safety of commercial Oxford Street and the company of a Lyons tea house. The London streets are submerged in fog, both physical and temporal, in which shadows and ghosts walk side by side and both buildings and houses are 'withdrawn, nebulous' (67). The ghosts of her past and present selves mingle and merge with the women in the streets with doomful prophecy as, although 'girls were perky and pretty [...] many of the older women looked drab and hopeless, with timid, hunted expressions' (69). As she walks along Tottenham Court Road she thinks she sees her own ghost coming through the fog, the ghost of a younger self from the past 'thin and eager. It wore a long, very tight check skirt, a short dark-blue coat, and a bunch of violets bought from the old man in Woburn Square' (68). Yet even this ghost of herself is indifferent and does not recognize the living ghost that Julia has become. The Julia Martin who buys violets in 1930 is unrecognizable as the pretty and eager Julia Martin who bought them in 1920.

Sometimes the two cities merge in their hostility to the Rhys character's 'otherness' into a universalized non-place, at others they are differentiated as specific places, their particular qualities serving to emphasize character's placelessness in relation to them. Rhys wanders in and between the two cities and the two time periods, creating her texts from journeys and memories that 'are fragmented, weave backwards and forwards, follow associations, circle back again and again certain events, certain phases'.[9] In so doing she resembles the *flâneur*, notably in the form of the surrealist artist picking over urban debris, taking as the focus of her texts the modern urban psyche that is manifest in the fragments of

[9] Helen Carr, *Jean Rhys* (Plymouth: Northcote House, 1996), 85.

everyday discourse, friendships, communications experienced in the streets of a city. As Carr asserts however, she rewrites the traditional 'metropolitan script', and it is my contention that she does so from the perspective of a *flâneuse*.

The *Bildungsroman* theme *is* present in Rhys's fiction, but it is conducted more as a fictional illusion for both the writer and her characters to cling to than as an autonomous quest. Just as Miriam Henderson both is and is not Dorothy Richardson, Anna Morgan, Marya Zelli, Julia Martin, and Sasha Jensen both are and are not Jean Rhys—and indeed the fact that in later life she constantly invoked her characters to describe her own life, blending the latter with her fictions, implies an attempt to transform not so much life into literature but literature into life, to find in art the 'saving illusion'. It is thus important to recognize the poetic construction as well as the biographical details that lie behind Rhys's fiction, to consider her artistic perception and the distancing of fact and fiction through a developing aesthetic. Notably this aesthetic involves a creation of self in the unfamiliar environment of Europe, a careful construction of identity as a woman and a writer in the cities of London and Paris. Rhys has been too frequently thrust under the label of Parisian 'expat' and it does not suit her. 'Expatriate' connotes definite national origins; it is not that the expatriate has no country but rather that he has left it to explore other freedoms, safely retaining links to his homeland. Rhys is a truly placeless outsider, however; described as an expatriate, she countered 'Expatriate? Expatriate from where?' For Rhys is an expatriate with the already marginal cultural identity of the colonial and, as Mary Lou Emery has noted, her novels thus 'portray an absence rather than loss of identity' and 'the homelessness of one who never had a home'.[10]

Rhys's position on the margins of the expatriate community in Paris afforded her a different and autonomous perspective on the city. Separated from the coteries surrounding male writers and artists, and also the Natalie Barney set, Rhys lived in the impoverished thirteenth *arrondissement*. This neighbourhood collected the relics of the city, and here she 'saw something of the other Paris', the city as an entity in itself rather than a blank environment for the self-imposition of expatriate writers, and she complained that '[t]he "Paris" all these people write about, Henry Miller, even Hemingway etc was not "Paris" at all—it was "America in Paris" or "England in Paris". The real Paris has nothing to do with that lot.'[11] Certainly Rhys's outsider status distanced her from the

---

[10] Emery, *Jean Rhys at 'World's End'*, 14.

[11] Jean Rhys, letter to Diana Antwill 1964 in *Jean Rhys: Letters 1931–1966*, ed. Francis Wyndham and Diana Melly (London: Deutsch, 1984), 280.

authoritative view of the Anglo-American hegemony, and she also carefully guarded this difference. Her sentiment is voiced by the female artist
Miss De Solla, in *Quartet*, as 'one ought to make an effort to get away
from the Anglo-Saxons in Paris, or what on earth is the good of being
here at all?' (Q 7).

Rhys is a 'stranger' in the city, rather than a 'cosmopolitan'—the two
terms are weighted and the former is less glamorous, more marginal. In
Good Morning, Midnight, Sasha Jensen revisits a Paris restaurant that she
remembers from her first stay in the city and which she hopes will be a
friendly haunt. As she finishes her meal, however, she overhears a young
girl who has recently entered insult her to her partner and the proprietor,
questioning 'what is she doing here, the stranger, the alien, the old one?'
It is the alien and the unwanted that the term 'stranger' evokes. Helen
Carr has recently situated, or rather desituated, Rhys as a 'migrant' and
connected this state to a particular urban aesthetic, suggesting that if the
flâneur is a metaphor for the modern artist then the migrant or stranger
is a metaphor for the postmodern artist. She cites Virginia Woolf as an
example of the 'modernist flâneuse, who after her street-haunting returns to a welcoming domesticity', comparing her with Rhys, the 'post-
modernist migrant [who] can only go back to her temporary and
friendless lodging'.[12] There is a confusion in this separation of the two
descriptions, however—perhaps accountable to the ambiguity of the
term *flâneur* and Carr's interpretation of it as bourgeois observer-idler
rather than urban walker—and the result is a loss of perception of the
important dynamics between them. Jacqueline Rose warns against assuming marginality as solely an affirmation of reactionary freedom, and
Caren Kaplan cautions 'against a form of theoretical tourism on the part
of the first world critic, where the margin becomes a linguistic or critical
vacation, a new poetics of the exotic'.[13] The decentred migrant is more
usefully a subset of the *flâneur*; he is placeless but still has his feet on the
ground, walking through particular cities. To disassociate the migrant
from the *flâneur* risks conceiving the migrant, in a similar way to the
cosmopolis, as a floating figure, something that Rhys very much does
not do. It is not so much that Rhys's protagonists are not placed within
her texts as that they have no claim on these places for identity. Indeed
the places themselves are paradoxically places of non-place, places of the
dispossessed.

The urban environment is a much more influential feature of Rhys's
fiction than critics have credited. The consensus has been to downplay

[12] Carr, *Jean Rhys*, 51.
[13] Jacqueline Rose, *States of Fantasy*; Kaplan, 'Deterritorializations', 191.

Rhys's metropolitan modernism in favour of concentration on issues of determinism or existential angst. In the preface to *The Left Bank and Other Stories* (1927), for example, Ford Madox Ford explains that his aim is not only to introduce the collection but also to provide a topographical context for the stories, one that he had urged Rhys herself to emphasize but which she had refused to include.[14] V. S. Naipaul agrees that '[e]ven in her early stories, of Left Bank life in Paris, she avoided geographical explicitness'.[15] Naipaul continues that '[t]he Jean Rhys heroine of the first four books is a woman of mystery, inexplicably bohemian, in the toughest sense of that word, appearing to come from no society, having roots in no society, having memories only of places, a woman who has "lost the way to England" and is adrift in the metropolis'.

Yet although Rhys's protagonists may be adrift, it does not follow that her settings are equally amorphous. Indeed she is sensitive to the tones and shades of the different cities that her characters inhabit. They may be reduced to the limited environment in which the women move, 'a few cafés, boarding-houses, and hotels', but these sites are telling. Metropolises are each individual. London has a different meaning from Paris, and the social spaces of the two cities are distinct. Both cities can be contrasted with the cosmopolitanism of the existence led by the characters in the novelette 'Vienne'. What is common to these urban settings is the alienation of the protagonist, for whom the city is full of 'hazy ambiguity [...] "not-quite-there"'.[16]

Guidebook to the Left Bank

Ford's purpose in the Preface to *The Left Bank and Other Stories* is not only to introduce and recommend but also to locate both writer and text within the geographic and aesthetic urban landscape of expatriate modernism. It is interesting that despite the emphasis on uprootedness, placelessness, exile, and alienation that prevails in discussions of modernism, as a movement it has always been located, mapped in terms of groups of artists and the places (usually urban) that they inhabit.

[14] Jean Rhys, *The Left Bank and Other Stories* (1927; New York: Arno Press, 1970).

[15] V. S. Naipaul, 'Without a Dog's Chance', *New York Review of Books* 18 (1972), repr. in Frickey, *Critical Perspectives*, 54–8, p. 54.

[16] Colette Lindroth, 'Whispers Outside the Room: The Haunted Fiction of Jean Rhys', *The Review of Contemporary Fiction* 3/2 (1984), repr. in Frickey, *Critical Perspectives*, 85–90, p. 85. I disagree with the rest of Lindroth's argument, however, in which she asserts that Rhys makes no distinction between the identities of cities in her work.

Perhaps it is exactly the experience of placelessness that leads to a need for self-assertion in locational form in the visible places of the map. Ford therefore argues for the need to place Rhys's fiction, proceeding to locate it within his own socio-psychological urban awareness. Admitting that, despite his suggestion to 'the young author of the *Left Bank* to introduce some sort of topography of that region, bit by bit, into her sketches', she refused and in fact '[w]ith cold deliberation, once her attention was called to the matter [...] eliminated even such two or three words of descriptive matter as had crept into her work' (*LB* 26), Ford blithely ignores Rhys's deliberate reassertion of authority over her fiction and proceeds to add these details through the Preface. In so doing he explicitly counters Rhys's own subject-matter and style, framing the city of Paris that *she* views, along with the aesthetically experimental method through which she portrays it, in terms of the perceptions and aesthetic assumptions of a white, male, establishment expatriate. His discussion is ultimately a manifestation of his own perception of the Left Bank—that place that has always held a mythical identity for him as 'one of the vastest regions of the world' (7). The Left Bank is itself for Ford a cosmopolis. As a child, he regarded it as a continent in itself and even in the present he describes it as an immense place, larger than either Europe or Australia. Moreover, this 'cosmopolis' is an ideal city, it is 'upon the whole, perfection' (11). Ford then lays claim to describing the 'real Latin Quarter' (13), mapping the space of the area of the Sorbonne, the XIIIth *Arondissement* and the Luxembourg Gardens, yet in terms of the personal meanings that result from the memories of his 'hot youth' (14), his imagination of his grandfather's Paris in the mid-nineteenth century, and his stance as an Anglo-Saxon expatriate, an outsider who yet possesses a comfortably secure sense of his own cultural origins. The 'topography' he fills in as the background for Rhys's collection is therefore dubiously objective.

Ford does accord Rhys a cosmopolitan identity, emphasizing the 'profound knowledge of the life of the Left Bank—of many of the Left Banks of the world' (23) that resulted from her life in Bloomsbury, Vienna, and the Quartier Latin. This is ultimately knowledge of a universal urban underworld, with 'its gaols, its studios, its salons, its cafes, its criminals, its midinettes' (24). The result however is to deny Rhys observational authority twice over. First, by defining her subject as cosmopolitan, as the Left Banks of the world, he himself diminishes any particular topographicality Rhys may evoke. Secondly, the cosmopolitanism he ascribes is one of a marginal vagrancy that belongs to the 'mournful' and 'hard up' parts of the city, and it is still down to Ford himself, the authoritative, upper-middle-class cosmopolitan or leisured *flâneur*, to introduce, frame, and situate Rhys's geographical and textual (non-)place.

Because of our complicity with the hegemony that literally, textually, and culturally associates 1920s and 1930s Paris with the Anglo-American expatriate community, a complicity that studies such as Benstock's are invaluably exposing and critiquing, the title of *The Left Bank* immediately arouses certain expectations in the reader—expectations of authoritative topographical vignettes that indeed Rhys fails to supply and that Ford thus apologizes for. In fact the volume does fulfil its promise of portraying the Parisian 'other' place, but in a way that differs from the conventional depictions of the urban scene in which the male observer surveys and describes the urban scene. As a result, Ford ignores Rhys's spatial depictions, describing her focus as 'passion, hardship, emotions', and 'the locality in which these things endured' as 'immaterial' (26), implying an indulgence of the 'feminine' disposition in his suggestion that she is perhaps right to value human interest over topography. Yet this is to misrepresent Rhys's position, in which territory, or rather deterritorialization, is a fundamental factor of the human condition. She may not portray the 'Latin Quarter' of the expatriate community— the social hubs of the Dôme and the boulevard Saint-Germain—but instead she retreats into the Paris that exists on the margins of this society, its back streets and dilapidating small hotels. Moreover, these are essentially depicted through surrealistic atmosphere, conversation, and social encounter rather than naturalistic spatial description. Rhys's urban consciousness differs from the detective or botanist approach of a Dickens or a Zola. The stories vary in theme and focus shifts from the inner urban psyche to depictions of Parisian scenes, and from memories of the Caribbean to snapshot images of cosmopolitan Europe. 'In a Café', 'In the Luxembourg Gardens', and 'In the Rue de l'Arrivée', for example, are fragmentary glimpses of the urban low-life of Paris—street musicians, struggling artists, students, *grues*. 'In a Café' is a perfect example of the tone of the collection, creating expectations in the reader of a spectacle observed by an authoritative male observer that are replaced instead by the brief sideways glance of the marginal female. Like many of the patrons of the café, the reader is a tourist hoping for a glimpse of Parisian bohemia. Instead of the entertainment they expect, however, Rhys provides a pathetic and miserable scene of an old musician singing a song about a fallen *grue* that creates a sense of discomfort in the audience.

London and Paris pervade Rhys's texts with their atmosphere and cultural identities. The walks that her heroines frequently take, microcosms of their life journeys, are largely introspective and rarely involve conscious observation of the surrounding city, but this does not mean that that area is absent from the text. The urban areas that Rhys depicts are in fact quite defined. Place, however, tends to lie behind Rhys's narrative, structuring and framing it just as it provides the setting and context for the heroines' nocturnal wanderings. Rhys's characters drift among the same residential areas of London as Miriam Henderson in *Pilgrimage*, cheap boarding-houses in the poorer side streets of Bloomsbury. Areas and addresses are meticulously listed; Bloomsbury, Notting Hill, Chalk Farm, Golders Green, Judd Street, Brunswick Square, Adelaide Road, Bird Street, Langham Street, Arkwright Gardens, Woburn Square, and Gray's Inn Road. More often than not these place-names refer to the boarding-houses or hotels that characters reside in. In *Voyage in the Dark*, Anna Morgan lives for a while in a 'ten-and-six' room on the second floor of a house in Judd Street, but moves during her relationship with Jefferies to a more commodious establishment in Chalk Farm (presumably paid for by Jefferies) that has its own sitting-room with a piano, sofa, and easy chairs. She finds a certain continuity with the previous occupant of the rooms, a poet, when she finds some scribbled pages left in a drawer that manifest a similar rejection of London. He describes it as '*Loathsome London, vile and stinking hole . . .*', a deterministic and indifferent city with '*grey streets, where old men wail unnoticed | Prayers to an ignoble God*' (*VD* 47). Anna and her friend laugh at the lines but the sentiment is close to Rhys's own.

With *Quartet* Rhys shifts her setting to Paris. The emphasis changes to public cafés and bars, the narrow streets of the north-west hinterland towards Montmartre, and the boulevards of the Left Bank; the Dôme and the Closerie des Lilas, the Avenue d'Orléans and the Place Pigalle, the Boulevards du Montparnasse and Saint-Michel. Rhys's Parisian world is that of the marginal social spaces of society. Although no longer an exclusively male domain, it is an urban landscape in which women are still dubiously respectable figures. Rhys's lack of moral interest in her characters and her concern instead with their status as figures of modernity is also reminiscent of Baudelaire. Post-Freud, however, she is able to depict the destitute urban woman as a psychological as well as a physiological type. In the later novels Rhys registers the female perspective in style as well as theme, using an interior monologue technique that conveys only what Anna or Sasha themselves experience, emphasizing the wandering perceptions of these drifting heroines. Consequently, the feelings of alienation and incomprehension become more immediate and the reader too is left floundering amidst the streets and room of Paris. As Elgin W. Mellown notes, '[i]n the Rhys world there is no superior vantage point for anyone'.[17] The Left Bank and Montmartre are marginal areas with narrow streets and decaying buildings—there are no Haussmann vistas or balconies from which to gain a panoramic perspective.

Quartet opens by placing the protagonist Marya Zelli firmly within a specific locale, 'the Café Lavenue [...] a dignified and comparatively expensive establishment on the Boulevard du Montparnasse', and according her an identity as an emancipated young woman, '[s]he had been sitting there for nearly an hour and a half [...] had drunk two glasses of black coffee, smoked six caporal cigarettes and read the week's *Candide*' (Q 5). They apparently form her common habitat and habits. Almost immediately, however, the carefully defined setting is undercut by being superimposed onto another city, Marya thinking as she crosses into the Rue de Rennes, '[t]his street is very like Tottenham Court Road' (5), thus identifying herself as a traveller, and sensitive to the tones and purposes of different streets and areas. Perhaps Marya finds comparison in the identity of both roads as boundary lines that mark the edges of city districts. Dorothy Richardson repeatedly describes Tottenham Court Road as a major thoroughfare that defines the western edge of Bloomsbury, and the Rue du Rennes plays a similar role for Montparnasse. The merging of the two cities goes little further in *Quartet* as, overall, Montparnasse provides Marya with a 'feeling of melancholy pleasure' that the monotonous rush of London cannot provide. The only time in the novel that London and Paris converge is after her husband is sentenced to a year's imprisonment, and Marya's gloom is incarnated in the environment around her. The 'foggy afternoon, with a cold sharpness in the air' and a sense of Paris as an 'endless labyrinth' where she no longer has any place, again prompts an identification with London. Like the *flâneur*, she finds a haunt in the neglected 'narrow streets full of shabby *parfumeries*, second-hand book-stalls, cheap hatshops', streets that are long and where '[y]ou could walk for hours' (8). Yet this idly wandering existence that she delights in is not that of an authoritative observer, for '[i]t lacked, as it were, solidity; it lacked the necessary fixed background. A bedroom, balcony and *cabinet de toilette* in a cheap Montmartre hotel cannot possibly be called a solid background' (8). And indeed the implied warning in this statement indicates the thin line that separates the cosmopolitan *flâneur* from the immigrant wanderer. Marya, and Rhys's older heroines, later realize just how lacking in fixity and solidity their urban lives are.

---

[17] Elgin W. Mellown, 'Character and Themes in the Novels of Jean Rhys', *Contemporary Literature* 1/3 (1972), 103–17, p. 115.

The dominant street in *Quartet*, significantly recurring in *Good Morning, Midnight*, is the Avenue de l'Observatoire, where the Heidlers live in a high building with a panoramic view of the city, 'observing' with cruel indifference the lives of the people around them. Marya is married to a Polish black marketeer, himself a 'stranger and alien' (17), and the Zellis have lived in London and Brussels before moving to Montmartre and a flat overlooking the Place Blanche. Between them, the Place Blanche and the Avenue de l'Observatoire signify opposing aspects of Marya's urban life. The former is 'Paris, Life itself', where '[o]ne realised all sorts of things. The value of an illusion, for instance, and that the shadow can be more important than the substance' (23). This, for Rhys, is the ultimate appeal of Paris, its belief in the indulgence of illusion.[18] The Avenue de l'Observatoire is the domain of the hard and indifferent Heidlers, ruled by Lois with her intelligent and clear eyes. Painting in her studio, Lois makes definitive observations on her limited Parisian milieu, like a penetrating social-scientist, 'explaining, classifying, fitting the inhabitants (that is to say, of course, the Anglo-Saxon inhabitants) into their proper places in the scheme of things. The Beautiful Young Men, the Dazzlers, the Middle Westerners, the Down-and-Outs, the Freaks who never would do anything, the Freaks who possibly might' (60). Marya attempts to resist this classification into types, 'to assert her own point of view' and her enjoyment of 'vagabond nights' that do not fit into Lois's conceptual categories. Yet she is increasingly imprisoned in the detachment of the flat, by Lois's use of her as a model and Heidler's jealousy of her friendships, and can only assuage her 'longing for liberty' (67) in solitary walks in the boulevards of Montparnasse.

The text of *After Leaving Mr Mackenzie* is split into headed parts and sections that firmly establish the whereabouts of Julia Martin's movements in and between Paris and London. Part One is set in Paris and begins with 'The Hotel on the Quay', immediately locating Julia in the position of the rejected fallen woman, living in a cheap and out of the way hotel. It closes with the prospect of a journey, 'The First Unknown', and a train journey to London, where her mother is dying. The second section is also geographically specific and the milieu of 'Return to London' is automatically set with the description that '[t]he taxi stopped at Arkwright Gardens, WC. The street was dark and deserted as if it had been midnight instead of eight o-clock' (*ALMM* 65). A dreary London is evoked by the taxi, the Bloomsbury slum address and the dark emptiness

---

[18] This point is reiterated in *Good Morning, Midnight*, in the comparison of the London, Florentine, and Parisian lavatories, for example, the last of which offers drugs, 'something to heal a wounded heart' (10).

of the street at the beginning of the day. As Julia books into a shabby London hotel the contrast with the opening of the first section is implicit—the cheerful idiosyncratic individuality of her Parisian room, with its large and comfortable bed, has been substituted by a small, tawdry room with basic furniture. She cannot even endow the room with the excitement of a first assertion of independence, as Anna Morgan could, for she is a decade older, has lived in such a place before and seemingly has never progressed beyond it.

The London districts that Julia moves through are explicitly labelled; she visits her mother in 'Acton', attends the funeral in 'Golders Green', and is installed in a new boarding-house in 'Notting Hill'. This move is announced by 'Change of Address', as if Rhys is attempting to reassure both herself and the reader that Julia is progressing along a trajectory in which her locational movements become metaphors for personal learning. Julia takes up a similar practice in her walks, getting confused in the streets and appealing to signs in order to reassure herself that '[t]hat's all right; I'm not walking in a circle' (117). The irony of this situation is that, even if she does not actually double back on herself, Julia still feels that she does, walking a monotonous 'labyrinth of streets, all exactly alike' (117) and disorientatedly wandering in a circle with no sense of direction. Boarding a bus at Oxford Circus she mounts to the top deck but closes her eyes to the panoramic view it offers. Ultimately, Julia feels placeless in the London landscape, the two places she asserts a preference for being the Café Monico and an unfashionable dance bar, both social haunts for impoverished marginals and cosmopolitans. Ordered to leave the boarding-house after an altercation with Horsfield on the staircase to her room, she returns to Paris, the setting for the third section of the novel. It is a second journey 'home' that proves as illusory as the first—neither city provides a place of origin or identity for Julia. Significantly, the two 'returns' are respectively heralded as 'The First Unknown' and 'The Second Unknown'.

'Île de la Cité' locates Part Three and refers to the location of Julia's new hotel, on the detached and ancient section of the city bordering the Seine. Her status and loneliness has hardly changed but her walks, along the Pont Neuf and the Quais and in the warmth and light of the sun have a new buoyancy. The Parisian milieu seems more indulgent of her illusions and supports her clinging to the hope that new clothes, wine, and cigarettes will accord her an identity and bravado that she does not possess. Carefully dressed in a new dress and hat, she spends the evening lingering in the streets and cafés of Montparnasse, only to be mistaken for a prostitute by a young man who turns away in disgust when he sees her face and age. Her walk now becomes a nightmare, and the branches of the trees resemble claws rather than the uplifted arms of people struggling in torment. For Julia suddenly loses her sympathy and becomes hard and indifferent, feeling nothing and only able to acknowledge that she has 'gone too far' in her 'life' walk.

The Street with No Name

It is from the standpoint of *Good Morning, Midnight*, however, Rhys's final commentary on the single woman in the city, that the act of rewalking past trajectories, 'street-haunting' as it were, is made clear. In this novel Rhys most fully engages with the dynamics of the female walker's relation to the urban features of street and room, and employs a stream of consciousness narrative style that reflects the subjectivity and fragmentation of metropolitan experience. Ultimately, as this text is less a pilgrimage than a constant rewalking of the past—of Rhys's own life, and the subjects and motifs of her earlier novels—it is also peculiarly static. Both Sasha's street and her life are at '[w]hat they call an impasse' (*GMM* 9). To negotiate it, and to deny the resurgence of the past from her subconscious, she is careful not to wander aimlessly and plans an urban route that involves the 'avoidance of certain cafés, of certain streets, of certain spots' (14). She returns to only one place that she remembers from her previous life in Paris, a café on the Avenue de l'Observatoire. Whereas for Marya in *Quartet* the street stood for detachment from the vital life of Paris, for Sasha ten years later it provides a place from which to observe and be anonymous, to remove to a safe distance from memories of the active urban world. For Sasha always seems to walk around Paris with the shadow of her younger self, perceiving it simultaneously with both past and present eyes. In a reversal of Julia Martin's visit to London, where she watches her youthful ghost buy violets in Woburn Place, Sasha's visit to Paris confronts her with her own ghost, coming out of the metro on her way to work.

Rhys's exploration of the physical and psychological experiences of the single woman in the city thus takes a different view from that of the writers I have looked at so far, as her heroines occupy a different social class and position to Miriam Henderson, Mary Datchet, or Olivia Curtis, for example. The latter were all born into the English upper-middle class, are financially solvent, determined in their desire for independence and part of supportive social groups, whether family, like-minded friends, or work colleagues. They stand at a crossroads between the benefits and demands of independence or conformation to lives of traditional domesticity. Rhys's female protagonists, who abandon or are complicit in their rejection from reasonably well-off families, have no such option and have travelled down the path of independence to the point that they are weary of it. They are not independent working girls—Rhys portraying the counterparts to the university-educated and professional women entering the city in the first decades of the twentieth-century city: mannequins, models, showgirls, and prostitutes—and are problematically uncertain realizations of the urban woman as model for emancipated identity. They follow the vagaries of determinism rather than the principle of determination.

The contrast to familial relations in Rhys's novels is a life of isolation, physical and emotional instability, and sexual unrespectability. Whereas Miriam and Mary make homes of their solitary rooms which eventually become sanctuary retreats for their writing, Anna, Julia, and Sasha stay in numerous cheap hotels and boarding-houses for short periods, often not even going back there at night. In London they are far less nervous than Miriam Henderson on entering restaurants or coffee shops, and in the more liberal Paris they sit over Pernods and *fines* for long hours in bars, indifferent to the other patrons. This detachment is the result of a careful mapping of public spaces and the selection of certain places where they can feel comfortable. Sasha Jensen, for example, designates the two cafés on her street as 'one where the proprietor is hostile' and 'one where the proprietor is neutral', a practice of differentiation which she acknowledges extends to all aspects of her daily life: 'My life, which seems so simple and monotonous, is really a complicated affair of cafés where they like me and cafés where they don't, streets that are friendly, streets that aren't, rooms where I might be happy, rooms where I never shall be, looking-glasses I look nice in, looking-glasses I don't, dresses that will be lucky, dresses that wont, and so on' (40). She possesses an instinctive knowledge of the marginal and in-between areas she inhabits, and is sensitive to the tone of acceptance, rejection, or indifference that they exude.

With Rhys, the setting for the pilgrimage of the woman in the urban landscape becomes the city of surrealism, the phantasmagoric Paris that provided the context for Benjamin's writing. Moreover, the streets of the city and the pilgrimage through them become internalized, as city and psyche become one in the surrealistic imagination and are then in turn translated into the pages of the text. The characters of *Good Morning, Midnight* are the *détraqués* of urban life. Resembling a vagrant animal, who makes her way by instinct to places she senses are sympathetic and avoids those that are not, Sasha is far from being a knowledgeable urbanite. Ironically, considering her constant assertions of her placelessness and poor sense of direction, one of Sasha's previous jobs was as a guide to American tourists in Paris, for which she had to venture into the unfamiliar Haussmann Paris of the Place de l'Opéra, the Madeleine, and the Rue de la Paix. Able to negotiate the habitat of the placeless and dispossessed around Montmartre and Montparnasse, she is entirely out of her depth on the Right Bank and cannot follow its ordered street plan; '[n]orth, south, east, west—they have no meaning for me' (26). She is thus complicit in her state of impasse, as she is only able to return again and again to places that are familiar and understandable. Her existence depends on '[a]lways the same hotel. [...] Always the same stairs, always the same room' (28). And these are always the non-spaces of the dis-possessed, the hotels and rooms being only places for pause in an ongoing wandering journey and therefore blurring with the streets themselves;

[t]o the Hotel of Arrival, the Hotel of Departure, the Hotel of the Future, the Hotel of Martinique and the Universe.... Back to the hotel without a name in the street without a name. [...] This is the Hotel Without-a-Name in the Street Without-a-Name, and the clients have no names, no faces. You go up the stairs. Always the same stairs, always the same room. (120)

All hotels without names become embraced within a conceptual Hotel Without-a-Name. The question that opens the novel, and Sasha's at-tempt at a new life, is answered at the close—'The room says: "Quite like old times. Yes?... No?... Yes"'—and Sasha resorts to the only option she knows for finding security in the city, the arms of any man.

Rhys and Lehmann's characters tread a thin line between the status of friend, mistress, and prostitute in their dealings with men, and thus offer a twentieth-century commentary on the nineteenth-century implication of the term 'streetwalker'. To a certain extent the urban women in their novels are still 'public women' in the Victorian sense; walking a night-time city, sitting in public spaces and picking up unknown men. Yet the connotations of these acts have now altered and, although the putative authoritative male continues to view all women as 'Encore une grue', the value boundaries of notions of independence, respectability, and public visibility have collapsed confusingly into each other for the middle-class single woman in the city. Despite greater liberalism and tolerance, however, society still imposes limits and, as the overwhelmingly empty sterility of Rhys and Lehmann's texts imply, one of these is the repro-ductivity of the urban female.

Rhys's tales of impoverished women struggling for acceptance in the public spaces of the city thus directly address and undercut the signi-ficance of the woman as moral in the world of the urban streets. This issue tends to lie somewhat dormant in the novels of James, Richardson,

Woolf, and Bowen, whose middle-class subjects and interest in aesthetic form invoke the question of prostitution as a metaphor rather than reality of female transgression. In Rhys's urban novels the motif of the fallen woman in the city, like Sasha herself, is afforded an alternative fate, is '[s]aved, rescued, fished-up, half-drowned, out of the deep, dark river,' and with 'dry clothes, hair shampooed and set' is given the opportunity to recreate her respectable identity. Rhys's opinion, however, seems to be that fate cannot be avoided, and that one can drown oneself in the street and in alcohol as much as in the river. For in her deterministic philosophy the urban woman cannot be separated from the claim of the street, however much she disguises herself with money, clothes, and cosmetics. Carefully dressed and sitting in a respectable café, Sasha imagines that 'the street walks in. It is one of those streets—dark, powerful, magical. . . . "Oh, there you are," it says, walking in at the door, "there you are. Where have you been all this long time?"' (89).

An interesting progression can be noted in the response of the single woman to the male figure in women's urban texts. The 'New Women' that Richardson and Woolf portray commonly gain an independent relationship with London through a rejection of men as partners. They turn from claustrophobic patriarchal demands and find recompense in the social, professional, and vocational opportunities of the city. Later protagonists reject London and attempt to escape from it in the arms of men on whom they become dependent. In the 1920s and 1930s, for example, Emmeline, Olivia, and Sasha find the male figure a numbing drug (equal to alcohol or nicotine) who will temporarily obscure the equally claustrophobic atmosphere of the monotonous and isolating city itself. The myth of urbanism has consistently involved the preclusion of women enjoying both peripatetic and visual freedom and motherhood; Miriam Henderson suffers a miscarriage, Olivia Curtis and Anna Morgan have abortions, and all three pregnancies are the result of illicit relationships. What I will suggest follows in the late 1930s and the war years is that a new female mobilization results in an alternative attempt to interrelate city and reproductivity, in which women writers and their characters use men to create their own imagined cities.

In Rhys's eyes, Paris is the city for women, or at least the city that grants them the comforts of imagination and the illusion of place. It is a city of consumption, where Sasha is sent for a holiday, to buy new clothes and visit the 1937 world exhibition, to invent herself anew. In this respect it makes allowances for the female gaze that the disciplining, patriarchal air of London does not. Sasha remembers a walk she took in London, for example, before leaving for Paris; 'I had looked at this, I had looked at that, I had looked at the people passing in the street and at a shop-window full of artificial limbs. I came in to somebody who said: "I can't bear to see you looking like this"' (11). Ostensibly the comment refers to Sasha's appearance, yet by juxtaposing it with Sasha's own *act* of looking, Rhys ironically switches the meaning to imply constraint to Sasha's urban freedom. The freedom of the gaze in Paris is itself immediately undercut, however, by the allusion to the Exhibition Internationale des Arts et des Techniques Appliqués à la Vie Moderne, the dominating feature of which was the buildings of Soviet Russia and Nazi Germany that faced each other across the aptly named Champs de Mars. The claustrophobia and lack of space that Sasha senses in the urban environment forms into a nightmare in her drug-induced sleep, in which the prospect of war, the London underground, signs to the exhibition, and a hallucination in which her father (figure of patriarchal authority) is murdered, blur into a labyrinth with no way out. When Sasha tries to give up her pretensions to urban independence—'I don't want the way to the exhibition—I want the way out' (12)—she finds that it is impossible.

At the end of the novel Sasha *does* actually visit the exposition, indeed is adamant that she must go. Perhaps Rhys has finally accorded her heroine a degree of progress in her urban journey; Sasha has at least eventually discovered the 'Way to the Exhibition'. It is significant that the exhibit she goes to see is not the two masculine aggressors to war but rather the 'Star of Peace'. This building was slim, fragile-looking and impotent in reality, but in the text presides over the exhibition at night with an illusory promise. Again Paris can give the Rhys heroine a 'saving illusion', to use Elizabeth Bowen's term, and the pre-war magical city at night resembles that of the blitzed dream-city Bowen herself was to create in her wartime fiction: '[t]here aren't many people about. Cold, empty, beautiful—this is what I want I imagined, this is what I wanted. [...] the cold fountains, the cold rainbow lights on the water' (137). Rhys finds something of a 'saving illusion' in Paris, but her uncompromisingly deterministic perception of the urban condition prevents her from being able to accept it.

5 | The Cosmopolitan and the Rag-Picker in Expatriate Paris

SHARI BENSTOCK has pioneered the assertion of the significance for women's modernist literature of the forgotten 'left bank', universalized by Ford Madox Ford in his 'Preface' to Jean Rhys's *The Left Bank and Other Stories* as the marginal area of a city, remaking 1920s and 1930s Paris according to a female literary community. The problem with the 'anticanonical' approach is that it can lead to an equally oppositional and reductive analysis.[1] Benstock focuses on the sapphitic female modernism of the largely expatriate community centred around the lesbian world of Natalie Barney, and the 'female modernism' she reconstructs is thus one of aesthetic and sexual experimentation within a mutually supportive group drawn together in the interior space of the salon. Rarely questioning the dynamics of place, her study thus seems to fix women into asserting urban independence and the rootlessness of exile, but from within the limits of certain social places in a confined part of the city. This spatial definition is confirmed by the street plan Benstock plots, upon which the domestic and communal centres of the women writers are marked. This street map serves to tie them to the particular place of their domestic home rather than represent their movements in the urban text of the street or the novel. Jean Rhys, whose novels are characterized by peripatetic and dislocated figures wandering the contemporary cities of 1920s London and Paris, cannot be placed on Benstock's map, being on the borders of the expatriate social group of the salon. The map therefore serves actually to localize and confine the writers it places, ignoring those outside its boundaries, and neglecting representation of the dynamics between, and movement within, city

---

[1] Benstock's map of expatriate Paris is itself a political construction, in which the gendered ideology of modernism is merely inverted; male writers and publishers, equally present in the same map-space, are referred to only in so far as they relate to their female counterparts.

space. Benstock's 'Left Bank', which evokes a sense of an insular female community, is thus curiously artificial. Her model and her map are essentially static and deny the woman subject in modernism, and the woman writer of modernism, the freedom of the city.

There are multiple versions of Paris in the literature of the 1920s and 1930s, created by the perceptions of expatriate writers in a foreign city. Significantly, these writers are largely expatriates from a particular country, the United States, itself a nation with a weak sense of rooted identity. In a move that manifests the mutual self-definition of opposite entities, by characterizing themselves out of place as expats, these writers defined themselves more firmly as coming from a place, the United States. As J. Gerald Kennedy has noted, Paris offers these writers the 'symbolic material for the construction of an expatriate self' and 'clarifies the emergent identity made possible by the conditions of exile', the image of the city that these writers create 'inescapably reflects the creation of an exilic self'.[2] Crucial to the connotations of the expatriate perspective, however, is that it is a legitimated form of outsiderness. Part of the freedom of the literary expatriates in Paris resulted from the fact that they were for the most part comfortably well-off, restricted by few of the demands of family or workplace. As writers, artists, and/or journalists, it was their profession to observe the social environment around them. The expatriate exists relatively comfortably in an exile that he has chosen himself, and, as Kaplan notes, to choose expatriation is to 'go into literary/linguistic exile with all [...] cultural baggage intact'.[3]

Despite the history of critical emphasis afforded the male figures of this group—not only in memoirs such as Cowley's *Exile's Return* (1951) and Hemingway's *A Moveable Feast* (1964), but also criticism such as Eagleton's *Exiles and Emigrés*—numerous women writers also participated in this experience, as made evident by Benstock's pioneering *Women of the Left Bank* (1987).[4] The female expatriate would therefore seem to participate in a position that entitles freedom of movement and the gaze in the city. Expatriation becomes a form of the *Bildungsroman* or pilgrimage, in which women undertake a displacement and reterritorialization in order to construct personal and creative identities. What is interesting in the Parisian context is that, whereas male writers pre-

[2] J. Gerald Kennedy, *Imagining Paris: Exile, Writing, and American Identity* (New Haven: Yale UP, 1993), pp. xiv, 4.

[3] Kaplan, 'Deterritorializations', 191.

[4] Malcolm Cowley, *Exile's Return: A Literary Odyssey of the 1920s* (New York: Viking, 1951); Ernest Hemingway, *A Moveable Feast* (New York: Scribners, 1964); Terry Eagleton, *Exiles and Emigrés* (London: Chatto and Windus, 1970); Shari Benstock, *Women of the Left Bank: Paris 1900–1940* (London: Virago, 1987).

dominantly retain their American identity, returning to the States once economic consideration reduced the possibilities of Paris, large numbers of women writers came to identify Paris rather than New York as their defining 'place', indeed the imaginary, 'sapphic', 1920s Paris that Benstock evokes is largely derived from the myths through which these women viewed and constructed themselves. Certainly Paris was the city in which their social, emotional, and creative energies developed and were nurtured. Describing Paris as her home for half her life, Gertrude Stein stated that it was 'not the half that made me but the half in which I made what I made'.[5]

With regard to my earlier differentiation between the international and the cosmopolitan themes in the literature of Henry James, the male expatriate could perhaps therefore be described as more of an 'international' figure (the American in Europe), in contrast to the 'cosmopolitan' female expatriate (who merges the qualities of the European identity with those of the American). Yet at the same time, as Dorothy Richardson sensed, there is something problematic for women writers in the cosmopolitan viewpoint, and Janet Flanner and Anaïs Nin, like Jean Rhys, engage uneasily with the issue of the cosmopolitan identity. There are ultimately two icons of cosmopolitanism; the alien Jew who has no national identity (therefore retaining the connotations of racial degeneracy prevalent in discussions of cosmopolitanism at the end of the nineteenth century) and the leisured, bourgeois resort dweller (an idle observer, reminiscent of the dandy-*flâneur*). Neither of these offer positive role-models for the female outsider. The former is rejected on the grounds of class difference and the restrictiveness of religion, the latter for his dilettantism and retreat into a mythical 'cosmopolis'. The uneasiness that seems to persist in accounts of the urban cosmopolitan by women writers is perhaps the result of their awareness that the cosmopolitan identity will enable them to masquerade with the privileges of a masculine possessive and all-encompassing gaze, yet at the same time require them to negate their femaleness in doing so. Examples are Miriam Henderson in the bohemian café in *Pilgrimage*, and Janet Flanner in her professional position as transatlantic reporter of the Parisian social scene.

Janet Flanner as Dandy Artist of Modern Life

Negotiating the urban identity, notably in the arena of 1920s and 1930s Paris, thus involved women writers in an investigation of types of

[5] Gertrude Stein, 'An American and France', 1936 lecture at Oxford, quoted in Kennedy, *Imagining Paris*, 40.

cosmopolitanism and the generic styles these embodied. Janet Flanner, as a successful expatriate journalist, occupied the role of the society dandy-*flâneur*. Anaïs Nin at first uses her cosmopolitan birth to construct for herself a new identity as a female writer within her diaries. After her association with the psychological explorations of surrealism, however, the cosmopolitan wanderer takes on for her the significance of the urban *détraqué*. For surrealism provides women writers with a mythic, irrational perception of the urban environment that suggests a possible alternative to the rationalizing order of masculine mapping, and in engaging with the surrealist project they thus take up its iconography of refuse and dereliction. In pre-war Paris, therefore, Rhys, Nin and their compatriot Djuna Barnes, analyse and/or identify with the marginal, vagrant, or itinerant figure as metaphor for the pilgrimages in psyche, city, and text. As for Benjamin, the essence of the nineteenth-century *flâneur* is inherited in degenerate form in the twentieth-century interwar years by the archetypal *détraqué* or lover of decrepitude, the rag-picker.

One experience of the expatriate outsider is that his sense of himself within space is grounded in two points on the geographical map; the place of origin and the place of destination. What is important, however, is that these two places inflect each other in the psychological map. Therefore, for the American expatriate, for example, New York takes on a new identity once the New Yorker is in Paris, just as the Paris he has moved to will be different from that he imagined in New York. Such an experience was recorded by the French-born writer Anaïs Nin. Having moved to New York in 1914 at the outbreak of the First World War, Nin recorded in a diary entry just before her return to Paris in 1924 that, '[t]he New Yorker dreams of Paris while the Parisian wonders about New York. And we go through life without definitely realising any place. They all remain unreal for us.'[6] Janet Flanner, who arrived in Paris a year after Nin, also discovered that her identity hovered indeterminately between the American and the Parisian. Her description of Walter Berry, a 'Parisian figure to Americans, American figure to Parisians' is equally applicable to Flanner herself (*PY* 36). As such she is cosmopolitan, her identity defined by her non-place. Interestingly, both women in their later years denied any sense of biography or identity in childhood, Nin asserting that she had no voice until it was developed through the writing of her diary, Flanner that she actually did not exist until moving to Paris and starting to write.

[6] Anaïs Nin, *The Early Diaries of Anaïs Nin*, 4 vols. (San Diego: Harcourt Brace Jovanovich, 1985), iv. 42.

Born in 1892, Flanner hides a bourgeois, midwest upbringing in Indianapolis behind her reticence, and the New York identity that she gives up to Paris is itself only self-acclaimed.[7] Her father, an undertaker, committed suicide in 1912, after which Flanner became something of a geographic wanderer, spending a year at the University of Chicago before a short-lived marriage during which she moved to Greenwich Village. The Village became her home for three years, a stimulating society in which she became friends with Djuna Barnes and Solita Solano, and the site of inspiration for her only novel *The Cubical City* (1926). It was on leaving America for Paris with Solano in 1922, however, that Flanner discovered her literary vocation. Writing regular newsy letters to her friend Janet Grant, by 1925 she was offered the post of Paris correspondent by Grant's husband on his newly formed magazine the *New Yorker*.[8] The fortnightly column, 'Paris Letter', a round-up of the social, fashionable, and political climate in the French capital, continued until her death in 1976. At first the impressions of a New Yorker, presenting Paris to her audience across the channel, the tone of the column gradually shifts to that of a Parisian imagining the interests of a foreign readership. Flanner's letters from the 1920s and early 1930s were written from the eye of the dallying, cosmopolitan *flâneur*, and were 'chatty and instructive, angled for the prospective tourist', offering a spectacle of Parisian types through physiological description for her readers in the States. In these letters Flanner occupies the role of the dilettante *flâneur* as a professional position, and indeed she lived amidst an affluent international society, staying for most of her time in Paris in either the Hotel Continental or the Ritz. She lunches in fashionable street cafés, visits couturiers as well as department stores such as the Galeries Lafayette, attends art previews, and takes trips to the races, with the express purpose of recreating these in journalistic vignettes. Flanner later described her early *New Yorker* essays as 'nothing but the ephemeral politics of the fleeting scene'. But although it is possible to draw a comparison between the superficial concerns of the early letters and

[7] Brenda Wineapple, *Genêt: A Biography of Janet Flanner* (New York: Tickner and Fields, 1989).

[8] The features and regular columns of the early editions of the *New Yorker*—such as the society pages of 'On and Off the Avenue', the recommendations for dining in 'Tables for Two', Hollywood updates in 'The Current Cinema', and the physiologies of 'Metropolitan Monotypes'—were joined by those with an international focus—'Letter from London' and Flanner's 'Letter from Paris', along with advertisements by French and English manufacturers and couturiers that accompanied them. From its beginnings as a metropolitan journal, therefore, the *New Yorker* quickly transformed into a cosmopolitan magazine that linked three world cities.

the political and historical interests of those written in the climate of European Fascism—the former as slice-of-life snapshots of the social life of a city, the latter as analyses of a cultural identity—even the brief social sketches are valuable for more than their information on the latest society fashions.[9] Flanner's 'Paris Letter' is a penetrative account of social, political, and cultural life in Paris and, as the title suggests, one that is not merely documentary but involves 'a certain personal aspect or slant of the writer's mind' (*PY*, p. xix). What Flanner offers her readers is not a catalogued, Baedecker account of Paris, however, but what Benstock calls 'the city of the French'.[10] She portrays 'the mind and muses *of* a city' (my emphasis), of the city itself rather than the objectifying writer.[11] Just as the content of a snapshot is controlled by the direction and focus of the camera, so Flanner's sketches are framed by her particular angle of vision—one that goes against what she recognized as a particular style of 'American male fiction-writing', the prominence of 'outsized masculinity' epitomized in Hemingway's texts (although in every other way she admired his writing and looked to him as a role-model), that became a dominant and overpowering mode of expatriate fiction during the period.

Shari Benstock recognizes the emphasis on women in Flanner's 'Letter from Paris', noting that 'there is a perceptible space between the language of the letters and their subject matter, a space in which Parisians and Americans move about a mythical city constructed by a woman who continually places herself midway between expatriates and Europeans' (101). Within this space, women are accorded a rare visibility and status. Paris has consistently been identified as a city that is more conducive to the public spectacle of women than London and, although this can result in women being positioned firmly as objects of the gaze, it also implies the greater freedom of women in public spaces. Moreover, in Flanner's letter, Paris seems dominated by an influx of women, notably mobs of American tourists who themselves make of Paris an object for their gaze. American female artists also converge on the city, among them the writers Edith Wharton and Djuna Barnes, and the cabaret singer Josephine Baker. She accords a great deal of attention to female artists, particularly dancers. The American dancers Isadora Duncan and Loie Fuller were both resident in Paris during their last years, the former all but overlooked by the press, the second its darling. Flanner's obituary for Duncan in 1927 was followed by that for Fuller a year later. These

[9] Janet Flanner, letter to William Shawn, 31 Apr. 1964.
[10] Benstock, *Women of the Left Bank*, 100.
[11] Flanner, 'Letter from Paris, October 13', *New Yorker*, 23 Oct. (1937), p. 61.

international women are met by the women of a fading Second Empire aristocracy, and the struggling artists working in the French theatre and cinema.

Flanner did identify herself as an expatriate writer, one of a group that 'had settled in the small hotels on the Paris Left Bank near the Place Saint-Germain-des-Prés, itself perfectly equipped with a large corner café called Les Deux Magots' (p. vii). Indeed she was attracted to Paris because it made her feel that she 'was living both at home and abroad', exploring freedom away from home but still surrounded by her American friends and acquaintances; Hemingway, Pound, Archibald Mac-Leish, John Dos Passos, e. e. cummings, F. Scott Fitzgerald, and Djuna Barnes. Yet she implicitly counters the masculinist perspective of expatriation, carefully placing herself somewhat apart from Paris as a city constructed through the eyes of the male expatriate: 'Paris then seemed immutably French. The quasi-American atmosphere which we had tentatively established around Saint-Germain had not yet infringed onto the rest of the city. In the early twenties, when I was new there, Paris was still yesterday' (p. xxiv).

The Paris Flanner arrived in was not a cosmopolis, and for her '[i]ts charm lay in its being in no way international'. Unlike New York '[t]here were no skyscrapers. The charm still came from the *démodé* eighteenth- and nineteenth-century architecture that marked the façades of the private dwellings and the old-fashioned apartment houses' (p. xxi). Therefore, although the early letters are still written by an outsider, albeit a knowledgeable one (the tourist guide rather than the tourist), as the letters progress Flanner's own viewpoint becomes more pervasive and increasingly distanced from that of the American community she writes for. For, if Flanner left New York to escape from both American puritanism and philistinism, she yet had little regard for the American expatriate investors who exploited the weakness of the franc and flaunted their leisured lifestyles. As Benstock notes, Flanner's sympathies are consistently for the French and '[w]hatever sense of Americanism Flanner might have felt, she had become a European during these years in Paris' (118).

Flanner's Paris is one observed from ground level, from a position of participation within rather than detachment above the life of the city. She does not attempt to give order or design to the city that she relays through her letters, instead simply presenting what she observes going on around her at any given moment of time; thus celebrities emerge, disappear, and re-emerge in her reports just like people on a street, and she switches from arts to café gossip to commercial enterprise within the space of a letter just as different experiences juxtapose in the modern city. Rather than being laid out statically beneath a panoptic gaze, Flanner's Paris thus moves around and with her. It is a city of movement and internal as well as external migration. She is particularly sensitive to the seasonal Paris; the fluctuations of population with the arrival and departure of tourists, the annual exodus of the fashion set of 'rotogravures', the fortnight 'hegira' of the Parisian artisan-class at the end of August, the migrations of expatriates and the avant-garde across the city as one café and then another gains popularity. This changing social milieu is reflected in the letters, which change both in subject and tone during the quiet summer months in between the social 'seasons'.

Whereas, for much of the year, Flanner's concern is with reporting the latest first night openings, the current singers and dancers (American or in vogue with the American audience), society parties, and automobile fairs, in the summer months it is the streets and stone of Paris itself that becomes her focal subject. Satisfying her audience with social anecdote during the 'season', she is free to observe the physical Paris landscape, empty of characters of interest to the *New Yorker* audience, during the silence and spaciousness of the summer. Predominantly, Flanner describes the Left Bank of the middle class; the world of the *bals musettes*, respectable dance halls patronized by students from the Sorbonne and the better-off skilled young workmen, rather than the *boîtes*, which she notes were 'brazen, gay, and licentious in their atmosphere' (p. xxiii).[12] Another social group that she generally depicts are not Parisians but wealthy cosmopolitans, who she affectionately but rather sarcastically describes as 'those dear, familiar, fashionable faces seen, as the season demands at Antibes, Biarritz, Beauville, Longchamp, or the Bœuf sur le Toit'.[13] Yet she is ambiguous in her response to both, and the letters betray a certain relief when they flee to the Riviera in the summer. During the months of July, August, and September, the largely emptied boulevards and side-streets of Paris can again become spaces that accommodate the *flâneur*, and Flanner strolls and observes them at length. Her attitude recalls that of Miriam Henderson in *Pilgrimage*, who also revels in urban life in summer, feeling part of the community of 'true' Londoners who remain at work when the social set leave for the cooler air of the coast. On 11 September 1929, for example, Flanner writes that for two weeks Paris has been 'deader than a doornail', its theatres,

---

[12] Jean Rhys was familiar with both aspects of Left Bank bohemia. In 1926, for example, Flanner mentions that Ford Madox Ford held dancing parties in 'the *bal musette*, behind the Panthéon' (12), events that Rhys frequented. Yet the female characters in her texts inhabit the less respectable, smaller *boîtes*.

[13] Flanner, 'Letter from Paris, March 25', *New Yorker*, 4 Apr. (1931), p. 50.

shops, and restaurants having been closed and its shutters drawn during the hegira. Yet this is not a negative opinion, as she goes on to state that,

[w]ith taxis and taxpayers absent, Paris becomes dead and divine. By day there is opportunity for sidewalk dawdling and gazing; there is peace for reinvestigating the fine eighteenth-century fenestration along the emptied streets of the Marais, and for appreciating the city's cornices and its ripe dahlia garden alone in the dusk. For fourteen days and nights Paris was an elegant deserted village, all its boulevards lacked under their spreading chestnuts was the blacksmith.[14]

This is Flanner the Parisian *flâneur*, rather than the American reporter, 'dawdling and gazing' in a city free from crowds and speed (certainly her summertime reports are also less frantically inclusive in narrative terms than usual), contemplating the architecture of its elegant eighteenth-century past when dawdling was the common and available order of the day. The only thing missing is the blacksmith to resole her shoes *en route*.

While the social set is away the city takes the opportunity to renovate and change, with the result that Flanner walks amidst streets of rubble that resemble those walked by Baudelaire at the beginning of the Second Empire, describing the constant demolition of the Paris of the past in order to replace it with new rebuilding.[15] Again in 1932 she records that '[t]he usual democratic summer activities are now in full swing: crowded railway stations; half the public buildings scaffolded for vacation repairs; perfectly good streets torn up and laid down again, not so good'.[16] Flanner's act as *flâneur* is thus as short-lived as that of Baudelaire himself, and she mourns the derelict landscape as the nineteenth-century poet did in 'Le Cygne'. The rubble of 1850s Paris, creating the grand boulevards, signalled a modern society that offered no space for the *flâneur*; the rubble of 1930s Paris, making ready for the return of its populace, reasserts the transitory nature of any opportunity for leisured *flânerie*. Le Corbusier recalls writing *The City of Tomorrow* 'during the emptiness of a Paris summer', his architextural blueprint paralleling the actual rebuilding of the city that Flanner observes. His response to the crowded rush of autumn begins as a rather nostalgic mourning for the privileges of the leisured *flâneur*: '[t]o leave your house meant that once you had crossed your threshold you were a possible sacrifice to death in the shape of innumerable motors. I think back twenty years, when I was a student; the road belonged to us then; we sang in it, while the horse-'bus swept calmly along.'[17] Yet this impressionistic *flânerie*

[14] Flanner, 'Letter from Paris, Sept 11', *New Yorker*, 21 Sept. (1929), 96–8, p. 98.
[15] Flanner, 'Letter from Paris, May 10', *New Yorker*, 17 May (1930).
[16] Flanner, 'Letter from Paris, July 20', *New Yorker*, 30 July (1932), p. 28.
[17] Le Corbusier, *The City of Tomorrow*, 3.

swiftly turns into a futurist celebration of the motor machine, the symbol of modern society and 'a magnificent expression of its power'. In the next paragraph, however, he returns to a scare-mongering assertion of the collapse of the city under this modern 'torrent', which destroys 'the joy of being alive, the everyday happiness of walking peacefully on one's legs'.[18] Unpacking the ambiguities of this response and the city seems to divide into several layers of significance for Le Corbusier; a seemingly conservative regret for the city of the past is combined with an awareness of the vitality of modern technology, and a recognition of the need for a new urban form to accommodate the new urban existence that results. Flanner's attitude is similarly characterized by a simultaneous regret for the past yet awareness of the (possible) progresses of the modern. Unlike Le Corbusier, however, she does not advocate sweeping away the present city to make way for a new one entirely developed from a blueprint plan. To Le Corbusier's anti-surrealist eye, the city, 'like a charnel-house, is strewn with the detritus of dead epochs. The great task incumbent on us is that of making a proper environment for our existence, and clearing away from our cities the dead bones that putrefy in them.'[19] For Flanner, however, the past, the derelict, and the unwanted retain value.

As a self-acclaimed Parisian, Flanner possessed something of the rag-picker spirit of Baudelaire and the surrealists. Interspersed with her social commentaries, the elegies on Parisian sites that were being destroyed imply a resistance against the pressure of modernization. Mourning the loss of the Flea Market at Clignancourt, for example, threatened by destruction for the creation of skyscraper blocks of flats and finally shut down by the Sunday selling law, she notes the fascination of this 'superb rubbish-vending agglomeration' where, '[a]mong its fields of black mud was always to be found the choicest rubbish—the better cracked-ivory miniatures, the daintiest slightly broken Venetian glass pitchers' (PY 44). Moreover, one of the female dancers that drew Flanner's prolonged attention was La Goulue, cabaret dancer and model for Toulouse-Lautrec in the 1890s. A coveted courtesan in her heyday, she turns up in Flanner's Paris as 'fat, old, and dancing drunkenly in a few feet of a remarkable documentary film about the rag-pickers of Paris' (PY 49), herself now both a rag-picker and an example of the once valued objects, now discarded as unwanted refuse, that only the rag-picker finds worthy of desire.

Flanner is not a nostalgic, however, trying to recover for herself the social position of the nineteenth-century *flâneur*. Dallying in his

---

[18] Le Corbusier, *The City of Tomorrow*, 4. [19] Ibid. 144.

footsteps during the quiet summer months, she is yet aware that this leisured lifestyle is one that is not only past but also inappropriate for the 'artist of [current 1920s/1930s] modern life'. In an interview in the *Little Review* in May 1929, Flanner stated that she

should like to be a traveller proper to this century: a knapsack and diary no longer enough. A voyage suitable to the 20th century is like no exploration into visible space ever taken before, must be conducted with elaborate knowledge, scientific data, vaccinations and most particularly, the superb modern mechanics which only a millionaire can rent. Poor people should not travel now. The day of pilgrims is over.

Flanner thus distinguishes herself from the wandering pilgrim set on a journey or *Bildungsroman* of self-discovery. Unlike Dorothy Richardson, who seems to choose the structuring narrative of the pilgrimage over that of cosmopolitanism, Flanner gestures towards the well-equipped and wealthy cosmopolitan as the model for modern exploration. A background of pre-learned knowledge is required, along with the convenience and speed of modern transport and instruments. Flanner's letters themselves, however, hardly epitomize this new study of visible space. The information they contain is not gained from elaborate science or dependent on the possibilities of modern transport. Rather, it is picked up from the everyday, from what Flanner observes with her senses as she *walks* through the city, literally through its streets and metaphorically through his society pages. Indeed, recognizing the ironic and sardonic tone that often invades Flanner's letters, it is worth reading her statement with circumspection; that the 'poor' should not travel and that the knapsack and diary are obsolete is perhaps more of a caustic social observation than a personal opinion.

Flanner's relationship with Paris noticeably altered over the years from that of an amused observer or outsider to that of a concerned participant. Gradually the letters of the 1930s become less concerned with social frippery and more with the unpropitious social and political climate, which pervades Flanner's perceptions. Her dallying glance at the latest fashions in art and dress give way to a prolonged gaze at the question of nationality and a European identity threatened by Fascism, and how these political concerns informed or effected the literature of the period. As early as 1931 the city is marked by a threatening atmosphere and, in August, Flanner senses that 'to the normal vacancy of the streets deserted in the annual summer hegira were added November weather, a December lack of tourists, and an even more wintry psychological climate, condensed by national strain, expectancy, and fear'.[20]

---

[20] Flanner, 'Letter from Paris, Aug 26', *New Yorker*, 5 Sept. (1931), p. 46.

The summer streets no longer offer an agreeable leisure space, instead taking on the grey appearance of the winter months, and their emptiness signifies fear rather than pleasure. Partly this was the result of the changed cultural climate of Paris in the 1930s, as many of the American expatriates had returned to the States after the financial débâcle of 1929, leaving Flanner with less of an international theme as subject. Yet it also reflects a more evidently political aesthetic consciousness, aroused by the Spanish Civil War and the increasing surge in political inflexion to art and spectacle manifest in exhibitions of Soviet collective art, the 1937 exposition, and the anti-Semitic reaction in Germany against the Jewish avant-garde.

Flanner does retain the *flâneur*'s innate pleasure in the visual and experiential qualities of the city, accentuated by the Paris Exhibition preparations. One letter, for example, provides a tourist-style guide detailing clubs, bars, and restaurants in the different central Parisian districts.[21] In contrast to this objectifying list, Flanner also comments on her enjoyment of the metro's new technologies, in which 'colored lights trace your journey, and illuminated letters give the names of the stations where you must change', making 'getting lost in the Paris subway a real literate pleasure'.[22] Flanner's impressionistic experience of the metro is thus very different to the surreal labyrinth experienced by Sasha in Jean Rhys's *Good Morning, Midnight*. Yet the politically tense city that provides the implicitly present, if unspoken, urban setting for Rhys's novel, is also ultimately the background for Flanner's observations, as her descriptions of consumer throng and artistic coteries are increasingly replaced by those of 'dense, anxious crowds gathered around the newspaper kiosks'.[23] The 1937 exhibition, which is a repressed, haunting influence on Sasha, is also recognized as a degenerate phantasmagoria by Flanner's journalistic eye. Just as Rhys's description of the luminous fountains in the Seine seems eerily premonitory, Flanner's 'fountains in the centre of the river, playing like geysers of liquid electric color while superb fireworks spiral and bang in the sky overhead' anticipate the oncoming scenes of war.[24] Caustically noting the exhibition's chaotic and delayed opening, Flanner's aesthetic perspective is socially and politically grounded, however, and her assessment gives evidence of the change from the social descriptions of the early letters to the more personally assured and liberalist political stance of the later ones.

[21] Flanner, 'Letter from Paris, March 17', *New Yorker*, 27 Mar. (1937), p. 56.

[22] Flanner, 'Letter from Paris, April 14', *New Yorker*, 24 Apr. (1937), p. 69.

[23] Flanner, 'Letter from Paris, n.d.', *New Yorker*, 28 Mar. (1936), p. 41.

[24] Flanner, 'Letter from Paris, August 18', *New Yorker*, 28 Aug. (1937), p. 36.

Structurally, the layout of the exhibition resembles that of the argument of Flanner's late 1930s letters. The 'first perspective of the Exposition, as one enters the Trocadéro Gate' is of 'the gigantic statue of a marching man and woman, sickle and hammer in hand, high in the air; facing them on the left is the great gold German eagle, crouched on the Nazi's stern Doric skyscraper', and, lying peacefully and naïvely between them, 'the pretty, part-coloured buildings representing many lands and commerces'.[25] The opposing Russian and German pavilions reflect her constant description of the opposing and equally destructive political options being forced on the European, and immediately French, population; Communism or Fascism. Finally fleeing Paris days before occupation in October 1939, Flanner's last letter before the war years describes a mass migration in ironic contrast to that which brought herself and others to Paris in the 1920s, '[t]his period has brought about the greatest, most terrible, and most destructive migration of modern times, a movement of men, women, and children trekking across Europe in flight from other men, women, and children.'[26]

Janet Flanner's 'Letter from Paris' is very much a *social* female perception of the city, at first offered for public consumption and later used to stimulate a more earnest political awareness. Depicting a recognizable, public world, it is a social travelogue by a selective yet perceptive and informed Paris 'insider'. For other women writers of the time, however, Paris became the landscape for a more subjective writing, exploring the terrain of the inner female psyche in relation to the external world of the city. Gertrude Stein, in her discussion of place in *Paris, France*, notes that often 'writers have two countries, the one where they belong and the one in which they live really. The second one is romantic, it is separate from themselves, it is not real but it is really there.'[27] This impulse, one that we shall see that Elizabeth Bowen and Doris Lessing also follow, is equally applicable to the city, particularly in its significance for women writers. Within the female imagination rises an eroticized and dreamlike urban landscape. Anaïs Nin, for example, an expatriate contemporary of Flanner, describes in her diaries a private and more symbolic city, an urban labyrinth that was to become the underlying metaphor for her work. In diaries, novelettes, and short stories, and the collected novels of *Cities of the Interior* (1959), Nin rejects one Paris but turns to another, an imagined city of words. She creates a dream city over which she has omnipotent knowledge. This experience is collected on a metaphorical

[25] Flanner, 'Letter from Paris, June 9', *New Yorker*, 19 June (1937), p. 53.
[26] Flanner, 'Letter from Paris, September 24', *New Yorker*, 4 Oct. (1939), p. 46.
[27] Gertrude Stein, *Paris, France* (New York: Scribner's, 1940), 2.

journey, pilgrimage, or act of dream *flânerie*. The central figure in her writing is always 'an instrument of awareness, the centre of conscious-ness and experience [...] a mirror for many other personalities', all qualities of the perceptive *flâneur*, which Nin innately was.[28]

Anaïs Nin's Cities of the Mind

Nin's relation to Paris was particularly complex as a result of her widely cosmopolitan parentage and upbringing, and her relationship to 'place' as described in her diaries is often uncertain and changeable.[29] When she arrived in 1929 she was essentially returning to a city that she had been expatriated *from*. The Paris she records in her diaries of the 1920s is a palimpsestic city, in which childhood memories, and the imagination of the expatriate combine with her perceptions in the present. These con-verge in an uneasy alliance to form Nin's ambiguous view of the city. Born in Paris in 1903, she spoke fluent French and retained a certain familiarity with the city, enjoying walking in its streets and parks. Yet her teenage years were spent in New York, and she returned for brief sojourns in 1935 and 1936 as both patient and analyst under Otto Rank, before settling finally in 1939. Her diaries manifest a constant interplay between the two cities; the city of residence being frequently ignored as monotonous and sordid, a repository for her dissatisfaction rather like the urban dumping ground, whilst the other is portrayed and discussed, mythicized into an ideal. Nin's urban environments are thus always to a certain extent 'cities of the interior'. It is ultimately Paris, the city of her physical and literary birth, that provides Nin with some roots however, in comparison to New York, in which she feels she is 'travelling in a country with no landmarks'.[30] Sometimes a 'magic city', Paris more often seemed 'hell on earth'.[31] It was a place of beautiful façades, but Nin feared that behind them lay a mono-tony and oppression that would leave her creatively impotent. In an act of self-preservation she thus took the cosmopolitan perspective of the de-tached outsider, literally sequestering herself from the city streets into a top-floor workroom that she rented at 11 rue Schoelcher and which afforded her a panoramic view of the surface of the city. From this height she was able to observe the city as a Haussmanian/Le Corbusian planned

[28] Nin, *The Early Diaries of Anaïs Nin*, v. 280.
[29] Of Catalan-Cuban parentage, Nin lived in Paris and Barcelona until the age of 11, when her mother moved the family to New York after desertion by Nin's father. See Deidre Bair, *Anaïs Nin: A Biography* (London: Bloomsbury, 1995).
[30] Nin, *The Early Diaries of Anaïs Nin*, i. 251–2.
[31] Ibid. iv. 89, 198.

and controllable map of arterial boulevards and landmarks. It would take the translation of the city into something like a surrealistic dream land-scape before Nin could feel comfortable as a presence within it.

Paradoxically, however, Nin's beginnings as a writer seem to have been dependent on the aesthetic climate of Paris, and after her disillusion-ment with psychoanalytic therapy in New York, she returned to Paris to attempt her own form of writing therapy, producing her first volume of prose fiction, *House of Incest* (1936). Nin's *œuvre* is characterized by its preoccupation with dream, visions, and mythic realities, and journeys within them. Her work constantly conducts a female protagonist through a psychological *Bildungsroman* (the autobiographical tone im-plying that the journey undertaken is also the professional one of the *Kunstlerroman*) in which the landscape of the mind is imaged as a dream city. As her protagonists turn from external experience to the refuge of life within the city of their imagination, Nin repeatedly investigates and evaluates the relation of female self and society. That she is making a gender comparison between the city of reality and that of the mind—in that in creating the latter, women can provide a place for themselves much harder to achieve in the real city—is manifest in the subject, poetic style, and generic indistinction that she employs. The opening aphorism of the *House of Incest*, for example, reads:

ALL THAT I KNOW IS CONTAINED
IN THIS BOOK WRITTEN WITHOUT
WITNESS, AN EDIFICE WITHOUT
DIMENSION, A CITY HANGING IN
THE SKY.

Nin's urban fiction is thus advertised as an alternative to conventional panoramic urban sketches. That *House of Incest* represents 'all' its author's knowledge seems to be a claim for insight rather than an assertion of omniscient authority; 'written without witness' it does not claim to be the observations of a detached urban observer; as a structure divorced from the causal laws of dimension in time or space, an unreal or half-real city in the sky, it is therefore unlimited by the boundaries of physical geography and extends into the world of the unconscious. This dream world remains as a dominant motif in the majority of her work, as she continually attempts to negotiate the desire to escape the threats of the external city (Paris or New York) with the damaging solipsism of retreat exclusively into the mind.[32]

[32] The motif of the imaginary city, and a preoccupation with a quasi-spiritual journey to it away from the world of present reality, is also taken up in Doris Lessing's series *The Four-Gated City* (1969).

In her diaries Nin explicitly links the reality of life in Paris as a catalyst to the imaginative life of her writing, but because the former is ultimately so unfulfilling. In October 1935, for example, she writes:

Yesterday I began to think of my writing—life seeming insufficient, doors closed to fantasy and creation. I had written a few pages now and then. This morning I awoke serious, sober, determined, austere. I worked all morning on my Father book. Walked along the Seine after lunch, so happy to be near the river. Errands. Blind to cafés, to glamor, to all this stir and hum and color of life, which arouses such great yearnings and answers nothing. It was like a fever, a drug spell. The avenue des Champs-Elysées, which stirs me. Men waiting. Men's eyes. Men following. But I was austere, sad, withdrawn, writing my book as I walked.[33]

The response to the city in this passage is ambiguous and changeable; she loves walking along the Seine, and is stimulated by the Champs-Élysées, yet resists the life of the city for fear of addiction to an environment that she believes cannot ultimately deliver pleasure. That this is the result of her gender position in the city streets is implicit in the awareness of physical intimidation from men waiting, watching, and following. The city proffers possibilities towards which the woman yearns, but such freedom and possibility is curtailed by her remaining an objectified and threatened figure. Nin thus withdraws inside herself, walking the external city but observing and writing an interior landscape. This inner 'city', that was to emerge in various guises as the psychic shelter of many of her female protagonists, Nin privately terms 'Fez'.

She visited the actual city with Miller in April 1936, recalling its imaginative effect in her diary when she was back in Paris, and transforming the Moroccan city into the map of her own psyche:

Fez. I have just left the balcony where I stood listening to the evening prayer rising over the city. Overwhelmed by all I have seen.

Mystery and Labyrinth. Complex streets. Anonymous walls. Secrecy of the houses without windows on the streets.

Fez is the image of my inner self. This explains its fascination for me. Wearing a veil. Full and inexhaustible. Labyrinthian. So rich and variable I myself get lost.

Fez is a drug. It enmeshes you.

The layers of the city of Fez are like the layers and secrecies inside of me. One needs a guide. Traveling, I add everything I see to myself. I am not merely a spectator. It is not merely observation. It is experience. It is expansion. It is forgetting the Self and discovering the self of affinities, the infinite, limitless worlds within the self.[34]

---

[33] Nin, 'October 30, 1935', *Fire: The Unexpurgated Diary of Anaïs Nin, 1934–1937* (New York: Harcourt Brace, 1995), 159.

[34] Nin, 'April 5, 1936', *Fire*, 159.

The experience of Fez is one of overwhelming sensory stimulation. As Dorothy Richardson exhibited through Miriam Henderson's response to the more tangible London of *Pilgrimage*, and Nin now implies through her imaginative recreations of Fez, the relation of the woman writer to the city is less one of detached spectatorship than involved and mutual development. Moreover, again like Richardson, Nin held to a belief that women perceive and write differently from men, aiming through her work to express the female psyche through a 'female' sentence. Using the imagery of spatial observation, Nin describes that women write from 'deduction' and through their 'core' being, in comparison to men who observe disinterestedly from the 'periphery'.[35] She defines herself through the city rather than the city through her self; indeed it is in interaction with the city that she can 'walk', explore, and discover this identity. The labyrinth of Fez translates for Nin into the labyrinth of her diary, and both are places where she is not disorientated but finds identity. In two essays that compare the diary writing to walking in a maze, Nin, again like Richardson, describes the development of her writing as a woman with the metaphor of a walk, the manner of this walk, that of 'the little donkey—my diary burdened with my past—with small faltering steps', recalling Le Corbusier's abhorred 'pack-horse'.[36] Nin asserts however that the labyrinth she wanders is not threatening but rather accords with the natural arrangement of the psyche that she explores, and she does not fear that she will lose her way as, '[t]he beginning and the end were different, and why should the coming to an end annihilate the beginning. And why should the beginning be retained.'[37] In the diaries, then, the urban and textual labyrinths merge: 'the city lay like a carpet under contemplative feet. I was awakened by the sound of paper unrolling. My feet were treading paper. They were the streets of my own diary, crossed with bars of black notes.'[38] Nin writes on the rags that make up her notebook as she walks through the fragments that make up the cities she inhabits.

[35] Nin, unpublished diary entry quoted by Bair, *Anaïs Nin: A Biography*, 240. Nin's 'female' style is formally different to that of Richardson, involving the manipulation of genre definitions rather than the stream of consciousness sentence, but there are definite similarities in terms of the multiple volumes and autobiographical nature of their novels. Nin herself recognized her affinities with Richardson, noting, '[h]ad a terrible fright reading a eulogy of Dorothy Richardson, thinking someone had usurped my place, or rather, preceded me in literature', Nin, *The Early Diaries of Anaïs Nin*, iv. 432.
[36] Nin, 'Through the Streets of My Own Labyrinth', *Under a Glass Bell* (1948; Penguin, 1979), 72.
[37] Ibid. 66.
[38] Ibid. 70.

This heterotopic 'Fez' remained a touchstone to identity for Nin, and its exploration paralleled her private self-exploration in writing in her diaries. It became a place that she could imaginatively appropriate for female discourse, seeming to deliver the fullness and possibility unanswered by Paris, and she wrote about it in her fiction, diaries, and essays again and again throughout her life. In the August after her return she records: 'Making more notes on Fez. In the intricate streets of Fez I no longer tried to glimpse those parts of me which had died in order to prevent them from dying. I left no shreds of myself in Fez. Each moment being lived completely. [...] here was Fez, shaped like the pages of my journal [...] I can uncover my face to the world.'[39]

This note is particularly illuminating with regards to the motif of urban rubbish and the fascination with the inclinations of the rag-picker that reappears throughout Nin's writing. Nin is intrigued by the positive philosophy that accords value to fragments and waste and preaches the possibility of phoenix-like regeneration out of the old. It was an impulse that she experienced around her in the surrealist works of her contemporaries. Yet she also distinguishes herself from the surrealist aesthetic, disconcerted by the idea of attempting to recover and reassemble herself from past unwanted fragments.[40] In the stories of Paris, as we shall see, women characters *do* identify themselves with the broken and abandoned, but attempts at regeneration are ultimately futile. In Fez Nin has no need of this practice, as the city allows her to live to the full, to use up everything and therefore leave no superfluous bits of herself behind. It is this belief that is more positive for Nin as it implies complete satisfaction from life as it is lived in the present.

In the imaginative space of 'Fez', 'human imagination could draw its own inferences, its own architecture from its private myths, its streets and personages from a private world'.[41] The interior cities that Nin constructs in her fiction continue this role for a specifically female imagination. They provide an architextural structure for walking and exploring the female mind. The experience of the 'city' in Nin's texts is thus of a multiple map with varying degrees of relation to the real or the imaginary. In some cases the city merely acts as a metaphor for psychological states, but predominantly the exterior and interior cities become one, as the urban landscape acts as both a thematic and structural model.

[39] Nin, 'August 10, 1936', *Fire*, 279.

[40] In the diary entry for 30 October 1935, Nin comments on the differences between her art and that of Miller, noting that '[i]t is also clear that surrealism is for him and not for me', *Fire*, 159. On 6 December she states, '[m]ore and more I'm against surrealism, the belief that the dream is reached through absurdity and negation of all values', p. 177.

[41] Anaïs Nin, *Seduction of the Minotaur* (Chicago: Swallow, 1961), 61.

Fragments of Cities and Bodies

In Nin's *House of Incest*, the female narrator lives almost entirely within a surrealistic dreamworld of her own making, in order to escape the fragmentation and facelessness threatened by the city outside and even within the relative security of her own room, 'a room with a ceiling threatening me like a pair of open scissors'. Nin's second collection, *Winter of Artifice* (1939), also registers the desire to escape from reality into a soothing etheric dream but creates a more tangible actual world in opposition to it. The last story, 'The Voice', set in New York, describes the instabilities of the modern urban psyche of a group of patients being counselled by the 'modern priest', the psychiatrist (*WA* 121). Djuna, one of Nin's cast of reappearing fictional characters, lives in the Hotel Chaotica, the tallest hotel in the city, 'a building shooting upward like a railroad track set for the moon' (120).[42] Djuna is not only detached from the city streets, therefore, in a building that aims at transcendence of the city but results only in the confusing layers of a tower of Babel, but also caught within it on a careering journey. The inhabitants ride up and down the building in the elevator, which merely repetitively moves from the ground floor to the sun terraces and back again, never allowing them to break free from this limbo into the realms outside, which Djuna envisions as a world of ascension and a pit of 'hysteria and darkness, wells, prisons, tombs' (120). Yet the crowd outside the hotel seems equally out of control to her, swept along by a mindless force that undercuts their autonomy:

I have the fear that everyone is leaving, moving away, that love dies in an instant. I look at the people walking in the street, just walking, and I feel this: they are walking, *but* they are also being *carried away.* They are part of a current. [...] I confuse the moods which change and pass with the people themselves. I see them carried into eddies, always moving out of some state they will never return to. I see them lost. They do not walk in circles, back to where they started, but they walk out and beyond in some irretrievable way—too fast—towards the end. (123)

Djuna separates herself from this flow of the street, and to her immobile perspective its movement appears rootless and undirected. She is an instinctive surrealist, fascinated by the detritus of real life, the dead objects from the past that indeed promise to take one back to the past,

---

[42] Nin is another writer, therefore, who constructs a 'pilgrimage' narrative through her *œuvre*. Rather like Jean Rhys's characters, Djuna is a familiar character in a number of thematically related but separate texts.

to where he/she 'started'. Obsessed by broken dolls, decaying vegetation and flowers, empty bottles and dead cats floating in the river, the significance of this rubbish for her is only the futility and impotence of human struggle in the modern world, however. In fact, 'the end' which the people in the street seem to be walking so fast towards is just the waste landscape of rubbish, the realm of the rag-picker, but one in which objects have no value. Djuna identifies herself with this useless and unwanted waste, largely as a result of her inability to communicate with others in her urban environment. She thus shuts herself up in her cell-like room in a frantic act of self-preservation reminiscent of the narrator in *House of Incest*.

Rather than support this retreat, however, Nin counters it with a revaluation of the real city that Djuna fears; the fragments and waste only seem symbols of death from Djuna's detached standpoint and indicate her lack of involvement with the vitality of the city itself. 'The Voice' again manifests Nin's resistance to the surrealist stance; her practical suspicion of aestheticizing rubbish into the valuable, her belief that unwanted fragments only testify to unfulfilled experience, and her eventual disillusionment with the extent of experience offered by the surrealist preoccupation with living within soporific states. Omnipresent in Nin's 1934–7 diary, appropriately titled *Fire*, is her celebration of Fez, city of imagination where nobody leaves shreds of themselves behind, being all-consumed by the fire of life. Repeating this doctrine, the Voice proclaims that '[w]hat is burned, used, is not regretted by anyone who *is* the fire consuming all this. If you were on fire you would enjoy throwing out what was dead. You would fight for the lightness of your movements. It is not living too fast and abandoning oneself that carries one towards death, but not moving' (124). Upturning conventional modernist representations of the metropolis, Nin suggests that the continual flow of the city is not a directionless death-drive, and that it only looks that way to the static observer who cannot grasp the multiplicity around him. The moving rhythms of the city are rather the life-blood in the arteries of its streets, and the detached and still observer is a figure of death in trying to impose static order onto this flow: '[w]hat refuses to live in you will become like cells through which the blood does not pass. The blood must pass. There must be change. When you are living you seek the change; it is only when you stop that you become aware of death' (124).

The role of the psychiatrist (the Voice) is to reinstate Djuna within the urban world from which she is detached, and to voice Nin's suggestion that '[i]f you were in the current, in love, in ecstasy, the motion would not show just its death aspect. You see what life throws out because you stand outside, shut out from the ferment itself' (124). In this sense, those who detach themselves from the actuality of city life in an attempt to transcend what they perceive as its chaos and waste, only confine themselves to never-ending disjunction from and incomprehension of the urban environment. As Amy Levy described, in the streets, as one of the crowd, the burden of self-awareness lessens. Nin also recognized the necessity of connection with the 'real' world in order to avoid the solipsism of self-analysis:

My head is empty now, it is full of streets. One may have nothing when one has the name of a street, but one possesses a street in place of a thought; and slowly the earth, the street, the rivers, gain ground, fill the mind with noise, odors, pictures, and the inner life recedes, shrinks. This advance of life, this recession of meditation, was my salvation. Every street displaced a futile yearning, a regret, a brooding, a self-devouring meal. (322)

As Djuna forces herself into the collective world of the street and tentatively becomes part of the urban crowd she finds that the moving city is an image of life rather than death: 'She was moving faster than the slowly flowing rivers carrying detritus. Moving, moving. Flowing, flowing, flowing. When she was watching, everything that moved seemed to be moving away, but when moving, this was only a tide, and the self turning, rotating, was feeding the rotation of desire' (124). This passage draws a distinction between the moving and the static individual in the city, between the *flâneur* and the spectator. I have argued that the *flâneur* has been distorted as a metaphor for urban observation into the spectator, and that a transition can be noted in Benjamin's analysis in which the walking male observer retreats to a static, panoramic position as the urban environment becomes increasingly modern and fast-moving, to be replaced in the city streets by the rag-picker. At the beginning of 'The Voice', Djuna struggles in confusion with her fragmented, split identity; as a woman in the city she conforms to neither male or female gender stereotypes. Rather than attempt to assert her presence as a female urban dweller, she chooses to retreat to high-placed solitude, as if taking on a masculine perspective of the city. Yet this option is ultimately to deny her female identity and her access to a multivalent understanding of her urban environment. By placing Djuna amidst the life of the city streets, the 'Voice' therefore prompts a sense of connection with both self and city.

On returning to the hotel Djuna is in a state of ecstasy and effusing life, reaching a sense of fullness and coherent identity that is described metaphorically through the harmonies of music. After this moment, Djuna becomes something of a touchstone for the fragmentary psychological states of the other patients, as well as the underlying insecurities and impotence of the Voice himself. For despite his advice to her, the Voice remains contained within his room, living vicariously by listening to the confessions of his patients, his flesh 'dark and sad and muddied like the very ancient flesh exiled from joy and faith to the kingdom of thought' (165). Djuna, by contrast, develops a burgeoning connection with city and self; '[s]he felt the multiple footsteps of those walking along with her, not like a march, but like a symphony. In the shock of feet against the pavement she felt the whole collision and impact of human being against human being. They resounded in her' (155). Djuna, the crowd, and the city thus merge and become one in the harmonies of footsteps on the pavement. This sense of oneness with the surrounding city recalls the experience of the narrator in Virginia Woolf's 'Street-Haunting', who similarly overflows the boundaries of her detachment from the city streets. Catherine Broderick, in her excellent essay 'Cities of Her Own Invention: Urban Iconology in *Cities of the Interior*', has contrasted Nin's 'postmodern' connection and physical interplay of self and city with the (masculine) modernist archetype of the 'singular antagonist against the city, an isolated individual consciousness observing the urban scene'.[43] Nin and Woolf's relation to the city is less one of solitude than of merger as people in the crowd mingle, become anonymous, and lose defined identity. In 'Street Haunting' Woolf recognizes that this experience of dispersion through others can turn onto itself to finally destroy self-identity, however, and Nin also represents Djuna's new self-awareness as fragile and likely to be overcome: 'Djuna stopped walking. Everything had come too near, too near. The cells were full to overflowing with the warm invasion. [...] Djuna lost her face, her name' (156).

This dispersion of self, however, seems to lead to a bonding with a universal identity of Woman, described by Nin in Lawrentian terms as a powerful, malignant, and orgiastic moon.[44] As Djuna explains to another patient, Lilith, '[w]e are the same woman. There is always the moment when all the outlines, the differences between women disappear [...] We lose our separate identities' (161). The combination of the experience of urban involvement with the consequent effect of self-dispersal thus results in a psychic oneness. It is a spiritual state achieved through connection with the real city, 'entered from the dissonances of the street, from the separate, hard fragments walking without legs or

---

[43] Catherine Broderick, 'Cities of Her Own Invention: Urban Iconology in *Cities of the Interior*' in Suzanne Nalbantian (ed.), *Anaïs Nin: Literary Perspectives* (Basingstoke: Macmillan, 1997), 33–51, p. 45.

[44] Nin consistently identifies herself with the moon in her diaries, the name Anaïs meaning moon goddess.

head or arms, always mutilated, into the immense vault of an organ chant' (162). Yet, according to Nin, this is also a predominantly feminine state, and in her diary she compares this relation to the city with that of Miller: 'He symbolizes and represents the disease of the modern man. He is one with the chaos of the world, of cities, of streets. His anonymity gives me the greatest anguish because it is collective, the loss of self. I do not lose myself. His dispersion seems more deadly to me than mine. [. . .] that is a circuit, an expanded life, but not dissolution.'[45] Yet although Nin consistently explores the relative advantages and disadvantages of urban detachment and involvement for women in her literature, she ultimately lacks conviction in the ability of women to find consistently homogenous self-identities in the city. Djuna is 'a child of the cities' but she retreats increasingly into a dreamlike, abstract identity: '[a]wareness hurts. Relationships hurt. Life hurts. But to float, to drift, to live in the dream does not hurt' (169).

'The Voice' closes with a section of interior monologue in which Djuna describes her nightly retreat into a dream place and her daily attempt to recreate or find this place in the everyday world. Her dream is ambiguous in portent, transporting her to a paradoxically spacious labyrinth where she possesses a penetrating awareness of the illusions of life, a nightmarish state that she yet becomes completely absorbed by. It is 'no crowded city' but rather a place of overwhelming space, where she walks 'among symbols and silence' (173). The self is entirely dissipated in this dream world into 'a mercury which ran in all directions' (172). Gradually, Djuna's connection with the actual city is lost beneath her obsession with the city of her dream: '[b]y day I followed the dream step by step. I felt lost and bewildered if the day did not bring its replica' (174). Each day, however, a fragment (a window in a house that she remembers living in) is missing and Djuna becomes again the surrealist, 'walking through the city at night, looking for the window' of memory that will make the dream whole (174). The point is that the window overlooks two avenues, offers the onlooker 'the dual aspect of existence', two choices that Djuna can never choose between (174). Nin here, in the image of the window, in Djuna's very practice of trying to find the replica of her dream in reality, and in the symbolic imagery of the passage itself, attempts to combine the worlds of dream and reality, and to indicate that this is as a starting point for connecting with reality. Her own ambiguous response to the urban environment seems manifest in this exercise, perhaps partly an apology for her own tendency towards detachment, and the effusive rapture that attends Djuna's attempt to

---

[45] Nin, 'August 20, 1936', *Fire*, 283.

unite dream and reality remains unconvincing as a satisfactory outcome, turning to abstract aestheticism rather than the more social involvement with urban life that the Voice (although hypocritically) had preached.

Following Richardson and Bowen and prefiguring Lessing, Nin ultimately suggests that a heightened awareness can result from certain spatial conditions in which urban walking can lead to an introspective enlightenment. In the later *Children of the Albatross* (1959), for example, Djuna is still walking 'into her labyrinthine cities of the interior [. . .] but knew that at this surrender of the self began a sinking into deeper layers of awareness deeper and deeper starting at the topsoil of gaiety and descending through the geological stairways'.[46] Again in relation to the other writers in this study, Nin's imagery in this passage forefronts the landscapes of city and psyche as palimpsests; layers of personality and urban terrain that are each different but together form the foundations of a surface identity. These lower layers, impenetrable to the superficial eye, are at times retainable, however; when torn open by emotional/ physical abuse, and when probed by perceptive sensory instruments.[47]

Both *House of Incest* and *Winter of Artifice* were published in Paris before Nin returned to New York at the beginning of the Second World War. The original short stories of *Under a Glass Darkly* (1944), however, were also written whilst Nin was still in Paris, and continue the preoccupation with the relation of dream and reality as imaged through the city. Significantly, Nin's description of writing in the new genre of the short story during the troubled period of the Spanish Civil War prefigures similar remarks by Elizabeth Bowen concerning writing during the war years in London: 'These stories represent the moment when many like myself had found only one answer to the suffering of the world: to dream, to tell fairytales, to elaborate and follow the labyrinth of fantasy.' This fantasy world, which Bowen was to find in her mythic city of Kôr (a London equivalent of Nin's Moroccan Fez), was ultimately an opiate against torment, yet Nin was constantly aware of the dangers of succumbing to addiction, and her texts manifest an increasing tension between the value of dream and reality. This tension surfaces explicitly in her questioning of the doctrine and themes of surrealism.[48]

[46] Anaïs Nin, *Children of the Albatross* (Chicago: Swallow, 1959), 173.

[47] Broderick offers a different view, arguing that Nin's urban iconography is architectural rather than palimpsestic. I suggest that the two are actually compatible, with the architext of the novel/ego-identity being built upon the palimpsest of the cityscape/psyche.

[48] Nin consistently admitted the influence of surrealism on her writing, yet argued that she was selective with its techniques, using them 'to describe subtle reveries, dreams, states of feeling; in other words, when not describing action', 'The Artist as Magician', in Anaïs Nin, *A Woman Speaks* (London: Penguin, 1975), 195. It was the tendency of surrealism never

Valorizing the wastelands of the city, the surrealists, in common with many women writers, would seem to have a concern with the forgotten objects and sites of the past that form the urban palimpsest. The city wasteland is a crucial factor of Nin's aesthetic technique. Appropriately described as 'a ragpicker of experience', she questions the implications of what she regarded as an abstract and confiningly subjective surrealist doctrine, however.[49] For although Nin may have developed her own erotically charged spiritual aesthetics of the urban landscape, the dreamscapes and landscapes of her fiction interact, peopled by women characters who actively mediate them rather than remain separated within the abstract realm. Her attitude towards male surrealism is an ongoing theme in her writing, and although her position against it is never clearly delineated, her ambivalence is obvious. As Margaret Cohen notes, although surrealism exalted women as 'embodiments of socially disruptive libidinal energy, this embodiment [was] too often inseparable from an exploitation and misogyny all the more objectionable given women's marginalization within the actual workings of the movement', and Nin was aware that adoption of the surrealist approach by women required careful negotiation.[50]

André Breton's *Nadja* (1928) exemplifies the surrealist representation of Paris, to which Benjamin's 1930s analysis of the urban encounters and landscapes of modernity corresponds as much as it does to those of Baudelaire. The Breton persona is an idling *flâneur* who wanders the streets without purpose, stating: 'I prefer, once again, walking by night to believing myself a man who walks by daylight' (*Na* 60). Nadja, a twentieth-century version of Baudelaire's *passante*, personifies in her dissolutionary effect Benjamin's description of meeting an unknown woman in the streets. Breton first encounters Nadja on an October twilight, surrounded by people pouring onto the street as offices and shops close. He immediately identifies her as disrespectable—describing her smile as 'knowing' and her claim to purpose in the streets as a fabrication—and approaches her without qualm. Yet, the prolonged narrative of the story,

to go beyond these dream states into the world of action that disturbed her, as it did Benjamin, who complained that 'Aragon [for example] persistently remains in the realm of dreams, but we want here to find the constellation of waking', quoted in Gary Smith (ed.), *Benjamin: Philosophy, Aesthetics, History* (Chicago: University of Chicago Press, 1989), 44. In the story 'Je suis le plus malade des surréalistes', she describes the male protagonist's dream as a 'crystal cell', Nin, *Under a Glass Bell*, 50.

[49] Sharon Spender, *Collage of Dreams: The Writings of Anaïs Nin* (New York: Harcourt Brace, 1981), 1.

[50] Margaret Cohen, *Profane Illumination: Walter Benjamin and the Paris of Surrealist Revolution* (Berkeley: University of Los Angeles Press, 1993). Of all the surrealists, Nin found Breton particularly antipathetic.

in which the neurotic yet visionary Nadja leads the protagonist through a maze of multiple encounters, streets, and selves, creates a sense of an urban labyrinth in which the artist cannot retain scopic authority. A natural urbanite who belongs to the streets rather than the domestic interior, and in fact depends on them for existence, Nadja is a bewildering if liberating feature in Breton's urban landscape. His valorization of Nadja is ambiguous as he is increasingly unable to pin her down to a place or an identity. He thus resorts to defining her according to the traditional images of the young urban female as muse or fallen woman, classifying and containing her as either ephemeral non-identity or morally reprehensible degenerate: 'is the real Nadja this always inspired and inspiring creature who enjoyed being nowhere but in the streets, the only region of valid experience for her [...] or (why not admit it) the one who sometimes *fell*, since, after all, others had felt authorised to speak to her, had been able to see in her only the most wretched of women [...]? (113). Breton's celebration of the urban woman is ultimately only at the level of a poetic principle; his *passante* is the typical urban muse, completing the creative identity of the male observer rather than possessing tangible autonomy in her own right. Indeed Nadja herself seems to have imbibed the cultural stereotypes for urban women. Wandering urban space in which she is not accorded a place, she thus defines herself as 'a soul in limbo' (71).

Adrian Rifkin has described the narrative of the *flâneur* as a classification of the urban sites of visually or literally available female sexuality, and that likewise, through verbal maps and visual photographs, the surrealist writer condenses woman and city into one as a feminized environment which he can walk, observe, and inscribe.[51] Although the surrealists deny the monumental perception of a city's history and identity, for example, and *Nadja* portrays Paris through daily life and debris rather than a map of royal palaces and imperial buildings, the places that Breton's haunted steps continually return to (the Place Maubert, the Porte Saint-Denis, the Passage de l'Opéra, Montmartre, the *marché aux puces* at Saint-Ouen) are differentiated and designated according to their effect. Often accompanied by a photograph, they produce a 'guidebook' plan of the city, albeit that of places of bohemian decline rather than monumental history. Indeed in a postscript Breton describes the novel as a subjective yet authoritative capturing of the city within 'a photographic image of [people, places and objects] taken at the special angle from which I myself had looked at them' (152). For all the wandering that Breton undertakes in *Nadja*, predominantly under

---

[51] Rifkin, *Street Noises*.

the guidance or influence of the girl herself, his city is, as Victor Burgin states, 'a space whose co-ordinates are fundamentally Cartesian, whose geometries are Euclidean [...] different from that of Nadja's' so that therefore 'they are never in the same place, and never meet'.[52] Breton's stance *vis-à-vis* urban understanding is perhaps best illustrated by Gillian Rose's distinction between 'social-scientific' and 'aesthetic' masculine geography. He does not claim 'complete access to a transparent and knowable world' like the former, instead celebrating the subjectivity and reflexivity of his perceptions but only to claim a new authority, 'complete sensitivity to a mysterious yet crucial world'.[53] Still the male *flâneur* assuming control of his city space, Breton is aware of an alternative landscape as observed by Nadja but he remains detached, observing, and classificatory of it. It does not influence the form of his perception and can only act as his theme; perhaps suggesting that the surrealist city, although the subject of male writers, is only inhabited by their unapproachable female muses.

One of the sites visited by Breton in his wanderings with Nadja in 'the worst wastelands in Paris' (80) is the flea-market of Clignancourt at Saint-Ouen. He roams, 'searching for objects that can be found nowhere else: old-fashioned, broken, useless, almost incomprehensible, even perverse' (52), a collection of the otherwise unwanted in which Nadja becomes another object. Indeed, if the metatexts of surrealism such as *Paysan de Paris* and *Nadja* revere the woman as erotic object, it is moreover because she personifies for their authors 'the most dreamed-of of their objects', Paris itself, and is therefore regarded as equally as fragmented and collectable as the city itself.[54] As Benjamin describes, Breton seems 'closer to the things that Nadja is close to than to her'.[55] The flea-market at Saint-Ouen was both a collection point for city refuse and itself a neglected area, threatened with destruction in 1926 by urban growth. Describing the expulsion of the market from the Porte Clignancourt, a reporter stated that '[o]nce more, the marginal ragpickers disperse, seeking new locations on the sidewalks'.[56] Marginalized *flâneurs*, they are constantly on the move as their habitat itself changes sites. Nin's short story, 'Ragtime', takes place in the surrealist world of the Parisian flea-market and again engages with the question of the value of

[52] Victor Burgin, 'Chance Encounters: *Flâneur* and *Détraquée* in Breton's *Nadja*', *Qui Parle* 4/1 (1990), 47–61, p. 58.
[53] Gillian Rose, *Feminism and Geography*, 61.
[54] Benjamin, 'Surrealism', in *One Way Street*, 229.
[55] Ibid.
[56] Jean, *Les puces ont cent ans* (Cany-Barville: La Côte des Antiquités, 1985), 85, quoted in Cohen, *Profane Illumination*, 98.

refuse in the city.[57] Nin visited the rag-pickers at the Porte de Montreuil, on the outskirts of Paris, with Gonzalo Moré in September 1936, noting 'the leftovers of the city, the odds and ends, the rags [...] detritus, broken objects without name, lying on the mud; and men bending over, bargaining and sorting' (*UGB* 60). Through the philosophy of the rag-picker, Nin again re-evaluates the relation of the individual to the modern city. Fragmentation may be the experience of urban modernity, but this is only terrifying if what is valued is homogeneity and wholeness. Paris itself is personified in the story as an old tramp, 'asleep on its right side and shaking with violent nightmares', unable to cover itself with a blanket of clouds (60). The central figure of the rag-picker wanders across this landscape of rubbish which is yet not barren to him but covered with value: 'His eyes sought the broken, the worn, the faded, the fragmented. A complete object made him sad. What could one do with a complete object? Put it in a museum. Not touch it' (60). To the rag-picker a whole object is useless as it cannot be put to a new purpose—it is thus inert and dead. It is rather waste, the broken, that is valuable and alive because it can undergo constant transformation or renewal. What pleases him are '[f]ragments, incompleted worlds, rags, detritus, the end of objects, and the beginning of transmutations' (61). Thus he sings that 'Nothing is lost but it changes' (63).

Interestingly, the dominant figure in Breton's flea-market is a female junk seller, Fanny Beznos, a cultured bohemian with a taste for 'Shelley, Nietzsche and Rimbaud' (*Na* 55) who is aware of the surrealist movement but averse to what she regards as its negativity, the underlying point being that the objects Breton observes take on a quality that subverts the order of everyday urban life and possesses revolutionary potential only by remaining useless, not by being transformed into objects with a new use. Breton's surrealist doctrine and depiction of the female rag-picker draw an interesting contrast with Nin's mistrust of surrealism and her representation of the male rag-picker. For Nin does not go so far as Baudelaire or Benjamin and Breton and romanticize the rag-picker, equating his position with the artist.[58] Following the rag-picker as he makes his way home, the female protagonist is led to the wasteland of shacks on the edge of the city. Breton glamorizes the realities of the rag-picker and his environment, and the figure of Fanny is an aestheticization of the poverty and sordidness of this marginal

---

[57] Nin, 'Ragtime', *Under a Glass Bell*, 60–4.

[58] Like the literary surrealists, Benjamin fails to acknowledge the destitution of marginal figures in the city. Their interest remains at the level of their position as allegories of urban modernity.

existence. Nin, however, remains well aware of the degraded living conditions of the market-place and the urban landscape that she depicts is less an abstract ideal than an interrelation of the actual environment with its significance for the psyche. For every discovered item of some value there is much that is merely trash and the landscape of the flea-market remains a place of impoverished squalor: 'Rags for beds. Rags for chairs. Rags for tables. On the rags men, women, brats. Inside the women more brats. Fleas' (*UGB* 59).

This classed self-distinction from the community, however, is under-cut when the rag-picker begins to exhibit old objects from the narrator's past, repressed in her memory. Pushed to the borders of the city there-fore, along with the unwanted objects of the past, exist unwanted memories. If the rag-picker is right in asserting that the old can always be transformed into the new, then the implication is that the memories of the past can be recalled and reformed in a positive combination with the present. Again, however, Nin is ambiguous in her convictions, for the female body, to the surrealist and hence the rag-picker in her story, is a broken and fragmented one. The woman narrator anxiously checks her identity: '[t]ouch myself. Am I complete? Arms? Legs? Hair? Eyes?' (62) and, significantly, what she seems to have lost is the sole of her foot, the power to walk. The first item that the rag-picker reveals to her is a blue dance dress that had been torn and ruined when she was 17. The implicit sexual narrative underlying the symbol of the dress is reinforced by the dream that to create a new dress from this old one will be to allow her to dance again, implying that she has not danced in the intervening years. The dream dress disintegrates however when she attempts to dance; the past cannot be returned to, its objects cannot be transformed into the completely new, and the narrator cannot regain her lost innocence. In fact the positive dream rapidly turns into a nightmare, as the rag-picker produces increasingly grotesque objects that cannot be regained or transformed yet instead remain to haunt; a wisdom tooth, a coil of cut hair. The narrator seems to turn into an old hag before her own eyes, experiencing that premonitory vision of urban age and destitution that is a common preoccupation of so many women urban writers. For this is the wasteland as place of the abject, that which, as Julia Kristeva describes, 'disturbs identity, system, order'.[59] By the end of the story the narrator has indeed become just another fragment, picked up by the rag-picker and stowed into his bag of broken objects.

[59] Julia Kristeva, *Powers of Horror: An Essay on Abjection*, trans. Leon S. Roudiez (New York: Columbia UP, 1982), 4.

Djuna Barnes and Landscapes of Urban Detritus

Similar to Jean Rhys, Nin was on the outskirts of the female literary community in Paris, living and developing her 'woman's' aesthetic amongst male rather than female influences. One writer whom she profoundly respected, however, was Djuna Barnes, recognizing in her novel *Nightwood* (1936) a surrealistic awareness of 'the unconscious or emotional or irrational life' combined with a female point of view.[60] Arriving in Paris from Greenwich Village in 1920, Barnes, like her friend Janet Flanner, played the part of the literary dandy *par excellence*, making the cafés of the Boulevard du Montparnasse her habitat and dressing in Whistlerian style. Paris pervades her early writings, from the bohemian characters captured in cruelly witty sketches to the netherworld of the satiric, mythic, and mysterious *Nightwood*, although, as Benstock warns, her *œuvre* and biography have been taken up and blurred by conventional expatriate memoirs in their invention of a sleazy night city occupied by a drunken lesbian community. The landscape of *Nightwood* is at once geographic and psychological, a mythic perception translated onto the streets and spaces of bohemian Berlin, Paris, Vienna, and New York in the 1920s. Unlike Nin, however, for whom the dream landscape was a site of sanctuary and self-identity, where she could wander and find herself, Barnes portrays the woman in the squalid city wasteland as a victim, less helpless than Rhys's protagonists but still degraded in the urban landscape.

The urban landscape of *Nightwood* is a site of carnivalesque modernity, where the city becomes one with the image of a chaotic circus. The characters are all displaced outsiders of one form or another. Jews, inverts, and neurotics practise not a sexuality that moral society defines in terms of debauchery and bestiality. The quack doctor Matthew O'Connor (himself a transvestite) describes them as suffering from the disease of modernity, as 'those who turn day into night' (*Ni* 94). They are the vagrants of the city, 'the young, the drug addict, the profligate, the drunken and that most miserable, the lover who watches all night long in fear and anguish' (94), who scavenge around the streets of Paris at night. Nora Flood, the American protagonist and a reporter publicizing the circus, is thus not only a bewildered observer but also an implicit

---

[60] Nin, 'The Unveiling of Woman', in *A Woman Speaks*, 86, 93. Nin wrote several times to Barnes requesting a meeting, and named her regular protagonist after her. Barnes was reportedly furious and refused to answer Nin's correspondence. See Bair, *Anaïs Nin: A Biography*, 582.

inhabitant of this landscape, into which she is led by the literal and sexual peregrinations of her faithless and alcoholic lover Robin Vote. For, rejecting her aristocratic identity, Robin is drawn instinctively to the city wasteland and its itinerant inhabitants, a figure who embodies the surrealist eroticization of urban degradation and detritus. As Dianne Chisholm describes, 'Robin sleep(walk)s her way through the streets and slums of Europe's great commercial cities', an international, lesbian *flâneur*.[61] She is a 'somnambule' (34), a Nadjaesque female urban sleep-walker. Nora follows her as Breton does Nadja, and like Breton as much fascinated by Robin's depravity and its reflection of her own unadmitted desires as she is concerned with retaining their relationship itself.

Nora is not entirely alien to Robin's world, and manifests natural leanings towards it. She is the hostess of the 'strangest "salon" in America [...] the "paupers" salon for poets, radicals, beggars, artists, and people in love; for Catholics, Protestants, Brahmins, dabblers in black magic and medicine' (50), a conglomeracy of characters that prefigure those she meets in Europe—Robin, O'Connor and others suffering from 'the disease of modernity'. Yet Nora remains within the boundaries of conventional ideology however, constantly struggling to reconcile her American puritanism with the 'primitive' instincts retained from the old continent. Her salon takes place in her country home in upstate New York, her *flânerie* is more bourgeois then surrealist, and she wanders Europe in the acceptable form of the expatriate journalist and through the acceptable spaces of affluent bohemia. It is only her desire for Robin that leads her into conflict with the internalized views of her society, and into the geographic spaces of the rag-picker.

Walking through the spaces of the seedy world of Paris at night, Nora herself becomes implicated within its values, yet cannot see outside the preconceptions that designate these values as depraved. For Barnes, the underworld of cosmopolitan Europe is an urban jungle that rejects the rational ideal of the city as product of the enlightenment mind and becomes one with the primitive wild. Robin is a native animal of the modern labyrinth, yet trapped within the mentality of a society that turns her into a curious spectacle. Nora, for example, meeting Robin at the circus, is at first fascinated by the 'primitive innocence' and instinctivism of this wild creature, and then moved to attempt to tame and possess her.[62] Robin responds by identifying more strongly with the marginal women of the streets, singing 'like a practiced whore' (57)

---

[61] Chisholm, 'Obscene Modernism', 181.

[62] An engagement with Darwinism and questions of heredity, degeneration, and sexual selection runs throughout *Nightwood*.

and later aligning herself with 'a poor wretched beggar of a whore' against Nora, who she describes to the beggarwoman as a puritanical philanthropist with a mission 'to save us!' (144). Whereas Robin experiences the city streets as the place of freedom, therefore, where she can roam and wander, Nora traps herself within self-alienation and repression, denigrating her desires. Yet, as Chisholm notes, Robin is 'less a free spirit than a haunted soul' and her night walks are not autonomous but rather conducted in an absent-minded trance.[63] The spiritual illumination of the streets is curtailed by the bourgeois values internalized in Nora, and which Robin struggles to resist. Her streetwalking thus becomes instead a frenzied attempt to escape from these limitations and leads to self-hatred and destructiveness. Nadja too, we must recognize (the influence of Breton's inaugural surrealist text on Barnes as well as Nin becomes increasingly clear), is not only the icon of revolutionary freedom that Breton's esoteric love interest perceives, but, more tangibly, a maddened and tortured figure.

Nora's attempt to orientate herself in Robin's environment leads to her appeal for help in the chapter 'Watchman, What of the Night?' to O'Connor who, similar to Nin's character the Voice, is not only philosopher ('watchman') of this world but also exemplar of its processes. His advice at once describes both Robin's way of life and the surrealist techniques Barnes employs in her text. He incites her to conceive of a 'night life' through the medium of dream, in particular a life of 'French nights' (82) that attract the European modern *détraqué* because 'he can trace himself back by his sediment, vegetable and animal, and so finds himself in the odour of wine in its two travels, in and out' (84). *Nightwood* explores a particular night world, and the instinctual identity one has at night, when dreaming or sleepwalking for example, compared to the conscious and controlled identity one has during the day. Matthew O'Connor is the 'watchman of the night' who describes its norms and values, constructing a night world that parallels but differs from the conventions of day. This doubled reality is perhaps best explained with the example of the map. The street-plan of a city is definitive, but the urban map changes its meaning according to day or night; the night city is of a different reality to that of the day. Thus, for Robin, who finds it her natural habitat, the night world does not have the degraded connotations it does for Nora. To Robin the night-time, homosexual café society is lively and undemanding, whereas for Nora it is sordid and abnormal. O'Connor explains the night in terms of primitive evil, evil in a devalued, pre-Christian form. The tragedy of the novel is that the

---

[63] Chisholm, 'Obscene Modernism', 182.

primitive conduct of the night world is defined as debased by the codes of the day, which are so pervasive that they become internalized by the night figures themselves, who come to conceive of themselves as the degenerate of society.

Nora is not a native of this world as the other characters of the book are. She is a tourist, disorientated and constantly trying to interpret the place she finds herself in from the context of her own society. Much as she attempts literally and emotionally to follow Robin into the night world of dream, it is finally impossible for her as she belongs to the daylight world of waking, and instead she can only communicate with the girl by slapping her into consciousness and the day. It is this act that awakens Robin to the value judgements of society and forces her into guilt and shame. As Nora recounts in horror to O'Connor, '[n]o rot had touched her until then, and there before my eyes I saw her corrupt all at once and withering, because I had struck her sleep away' (131). Robin is so mysterious because for a long time she manages to avoid such realization—she seems will-less, somnambulant and detached because the moral values of the human world are irrelevant to her. She exists in a pre-moral world that tastes fruit without the accompanying knowledge of evil. It is as impossible for us to conceive of Robin's sense of existence (a sort of Nietzschean pre- good and evil) as it is for Nora, and it is partly this that makes her character so mythical. Yet, although Nora can neither join Robin in her innocent dream nor pull her into her own rational consciousness, she does end up joining her in the frantic nightmare that the night becomes for those aware of the profane. As O'Connor says to her when she is sunk in despair and self-torture after Robin's desertion, 'Robin is not in your life, you are in her dream' (132). For in her desperate desire for Robin, Nora becomes one of those women 'who turn day into night', 'the lover who watches all night long in fear and anguish' (84).

Nightwood is a study of displacement and estrangement—from place and identity. Even chronology is blurred, as the time-scale and temporal location of action seem subordinate to the intensity of spatial and psychological atmosphere that Barnes creates. Dates appear occasionally, but suddenly and randomly, as if attempting to reassert some tangible framework to 'the life of the night' in which the characters become immersed. Just as in the dream or nightmare whilst sleeping, time is irrelevant or discordant and people's place within time is discontinuous. The textual narrative in this way resembles the conditions of the modern city noted by Simmel. It is fragmentary in terms of place, time, and commentator, made from blocks of narrative spoken by different voices who do not necessarily refer to events chronologically. The text will move swiftly over a period that the speaker knows little about, only to return to that time in a flashback when details are discovered later. Consequently, the reader too can only fill in the plot and time schemes gradually and disparately. The effect is disorientating—the novel seems to proceed, take short cuts, turn onto a side street, return to the main thoroughfare, retrace its steps, and be bombarded with various shock experiences, much like Simmel's walker in the city street. The reader's orientation of events in the text depends on familiarity with these events by the speaker at the time, just as orientation in the city street is determined by the walker's familiarity with the urban map. In *Nightwood* only two characters are really cognisant of the nocturnal map of cafés and bars and what happens within them; Robin Vote and Matthew O'Connor. The reader learns nothing from Robin. She is a character that, although at the centre of the text, rarely speaks and certainly never recounts information. Perhaps this silence suggests the inability of language to express Robin's experience of life, its lack of significance for her completely alternative conception of the relation of value to action. That Robin's instinctual sense is inexpressible means that the only other way of voicing the night world is through the daylight judgements that define it as evil. O'Connor knows the night and is its interpreter, but can only describe it in terms of bitter connotation.

As the rag-picker symbolizes, the waste products of the city contain its past within them. Nin and Barnes translate this perspective into the surrealist aesthetic of their texts, using the forgotten memories and refuse objects of the past, that they relocate as they travel the inner streets of the mind and the outer streets of the city, to trace a self and write a text. The poetry of Mina Loy is underlined by a similar rejection of the authoritatively objectifying observation of the urban landscape and a similar obsession with urban detritus. In the ironic allusion in the title of her third poetry collection *Lunar Baedecker*, the name of the male Baedecker is prefaced by the female symbol of the moon (also personally associated by Loy with the retrograde artist), and the tour-guide-style depiction of the city is replaced by surrealistic evocation of the urban landscape most evident in the series of poems on social outcasts in hostile city streets. Loy is still a walker-observer of the city, but, turning to Baudelaire's identification of artist and rag-picker, as a vagrant rather than leisured *flâneur*. The Baudelairian influence extends to the prominence of the symbolist/surrealist impulse in Loy's work, her valuing of artificial objects and the city, her depiction of the artist as an outcast figure elegaically mourning a beloved urban wasteland, and a belief in the role of the artist to create a vision of 'everyday life'.

Like Nin and Barnes, Loy was a natural cosmopolitan fascinated by the underworld. Born in London in 1882, she spent the early 1900s at the centre of its bohemian art student set, moving to Paris, Italy, New York, back to Italy, Germany, Paris, and finally New York again. As Gillian Hanscombe and Virginia Smyers note, these travels over a period of forty years introduced Loy to different aesthetic movements and their representations of the city environment, 'from Victorian England to impressionist Paris, to futurist Florence, to bohemian Greenwich Village and back to expatriate Paris'.[64] Arriving in Paris in 1923 and remaining until 1936, Loy was quickly absorbed into the female expatriate community flourishing there, renewing contact with Barnes who was a fellow ex-Greenwich Villageite. From 1928 she shared not only the same building as Barnes (in 9, rue Saint-Romain) but also emotional, social, and aesthetic understanding. The urban poems of her collection of verse, *Lunar Baedecker* (1923) profess a fascination with modern detritus in their presentation of the refuse of the city, both human and inanimate, that is also omnipresent in Barnes's work. As with the other writers in this study, both Loy and Barnes 'focused on the predicament of the modern woman adrift in the urban wasteland' that in the 1920s and 1930s was, as the works of Rhys and Nin also testify, an environment in which '[women's] new freedoms (which proved to be only relative) culminated in psychic disillusionment, spiritual lassitude, or [...] in real or imagined suicide'.[65]

The poet of *Lunar Baedecker* is an observer in an urban environment constructed from the cities of Loy's inhabitance; London, Munich, Paris, and New York. This landscape is a place that advertises freedom and exhilaration, the opportunity of self-development, yet that is ultimately indifferent or malevolent. If Paris was a place in which women writers found an encouraging environment for personal and aesthetic self-discovery, Loy is ambivalent about it and her poetic city is a place that continually opposes such attempts at self-awareness. Already, in 'To You', an early poem written in 1916, 'The city | Wedged between impulse and unfolding | [is] Bridged | by diurnal splintering | Of egos'. By the *Lunar Baedecker* poems of the 1920s, the urban figures Loy depicts retreat from the disappointments and opaqueness of the external world into their own personal landscapes created from alcohol and delusion. In the poetic 'montage', 'Three Moments in Paris', she seemingly accedes to the dominant cultural stereotypes of Parisian women—the café-dweller,

[64] Gillian Hanscombe and Virginia L. Smyers, *Writing for Their Lives: The Modernist Women 1910–1940* (London: The Women's Press, 1987), 112.

[65] Carolyn G. Burke, '"Accidental Aloofness": Barnes, Loy and modernism', in Mary Lynn Broe (ed.), *Silence and Power: Djuna Barnes, a Revaluation* (Carbondale, Ill.: Southern Illinois UP, 1986), 67–79, p. 69.

the mannequin, the streetwalker, and the shop-girl—but does in order to indicate the self-perpetuation of these images by the weakness of women themselves who assume masculine eyes in the city. The poet-speaker is female but the detached perspective with which she observes the urban scenes implies an adoption of a masculine mode of vision, reiterated by her realization that she has separated herself from and classified the women that she watches. It is in one of Loy's late poems, 'Chiffon Velours' (1947), that she confronts the stereotype of the old woman, that urban figure also daunting for Richardson and Rhys. A degraded figure in the filth of the gutter, this woman, like the bag lady Miriam Henderson encounters in 'Revolving Lights' and the image evoked for Nin by the old tooth and hair, yet has a visionary effect. Loy puns that 'She is sere', both old and predicting the future, and immediately the poet's response is one of fright and horror at the woman's haggard appearance; 'Her features | verging on a shriek | reviling age, | flee from death in odd directions | somehow retained by a web of wrinkles.' In her essay on Barnes and Loy, Carolyn Burke notes that in Barnes's works 'the anonymity of urban life simultaneously provides her nameless female subjects with the freedom of movement and the solitude that lead them to spiritual death'.[66] It is the tension between these two aspects of urban experience that women writers constantly attempt to negotiate, fighting for a place in the city against the cultural attribution of sterility that accompanies that place. For Dorothy Richardson the fight was ultimately fairly successful, for Virginia Woolf the outcome remained ambiguous, but for the modernists of the 1930s, disillusionment was the predominant result.

Loy's experimental narrative of urban modernity took the form of an idiosyncratic and highly ocular poetry, perhaps comparable in its visual intensity to the Imagism of H.D. Through a decorticated vocabulary, she both imaged the objects and material of everyday life with crystalline clarity and endowed them with a (less clear) spiritual significance that she termed 'the radium of the word', a quality that she specifically associated with women's writing.[67] After returning to New York in 1936, and living near the slum area of Bowery, Loy's interest in the marginal figures of the urban environment became more explicit, and she sought new ways of representing in art the experience of the Bowery tramps or 'bums'. Her poem 'Hot Cross Bum' was accompanied by a new foray into 'constructions', in which a montage of street and alley

[66] Burke, '"Accidental Aloofness"' pp. 67–79.
[67] Mina Loy, 'Gertrude Stein', *Transatlantic Review* 2 (1924), 305.

sights were created out of arrangements of collected rubbish. Having always valued the visual and the object, these 'constructions' are a culmination of her experimentation in expressing the observed city. No longer in a position of public recognition, Loy's works of this time were yet significant, despite overlooked, contributions to the surrealist impulse in New York during the 1940s.[68]

The landscape of rubble, detritus, and later bomb damage that informs the urban settings of so many of the women writers of my study, testifies to the pervasive iconography of T. S. Eliot's *The Waste Land* on modernist representations of the city. *The Waste Land* is itself a pilgrimage by a disembodied, multiple urban persona, a textual journey through a 'city of dreadful night' that is made up of a conglomeracy of cities, peopled by cosmopolitans, Jews, wanderers, voyeurs, and 'odd women', littered with waste objects, lives, and memories. The various urban 'seers' in the poem (Madame Sosotris, the one-eyed merchant, the Cumaen sibyl, Tiresias) together form two perspectives on the city, one masculine and one feminine, as Eliot himself implied.[69] Women inhabit this city more prominently than men, however, and its refuse is notably often female. As Maud Ellmann has described, Eliot's poem 'conflates the city with the body' and therefore '[a]bortions, broken fingernails, carious teeth, and "female smells" signify the culture's decadence, as well as bodily decrepitude'.[70] This female flesh in *The Waste Land* is objectified into the typist's sordid objects, the working-class women's false teeth, the grimy but sexually available bodies of the Thames maidens. Like the rag-picker or the surrealist who perversely venerate unwanted fragments, Eliot is fascinated by the fragments and leftovers of the female body. Barnes and Nin, like Rhys and also Lehmann in *The Weather in the Streets*, relate the city landscape to the waste and sterility of the female body: the city/body map of abortions, synthetic fragrances and desperate attempts at self-preservation. Yet, in so doing, they do not concur with the surrealist perspective, instead engaging with it to point to the misogyny of the male urban surrealist and to counter his version of the city

---

[68] Loy's son-in-law, the art dealer and gallery owner Julien Levy, was a central figure in the promotion of surrealist artists (including women) in the United States.

[69] Eliot states in his notes to *The Waste Land*, in *Collected Poems 1909–1935* (1936; London: Faber and Faber, 1959), 80, that all the men are one man, and all the women are one woman, just as all the cities form one urban landscape: '218. Tiresias, although a mere spectator and not indeed a "character", is yet the most important personage in the poem, uniting all the rest. Just as the one-eyed merchant, seller of currants, *melts into* the Phoenician Sailor, and the latter is *not wholly distinct* from Ferdinand Prince of Naples, so all the women are one woman, and the *two sexes meet* in Tiresias. What Tiresias *sees*, in fact, is the substance of the poem.'

[70] Maud Ellmann, *The Poetics of Impersonality* (Brighton: Harvester, 1987), 93.

as a text to be created from the collection of the fragments of the female body. The urban women in Eliot's poem ultimately remain silent, their words being superficial, occluded because filtered through the all-seeing Tiresias. By addressing images of waste, sterility, and effluvia in relation to female experience as opposed to male fascination, Barnes, Nin, Loy, and Rhys give a voice back to the woman in the city.

The recent feminist revision of the gendered space of artistic 1920s and 1930s Paris by Benstock and others discovered a mutually supportive art community through which women writers, publishers, journalists, and patrons had the opportunity to assert individual social, professional, and sexual identities. This freedom was curtailed with the arrival of Hitler, when the expatriate community was forced to leave Paris, breaking the gender network and uprooting these women from their relation to the city itself. Paris may have been the place of *Bildungs/Kunstlerroman* for a large number of women defining themselves as individuals across a geographical and psychological urban landscape of exile, but it was also to become the city from which they were exiled, as authoritarian might reasserted itself in that urban space. The result in Paris was largely a severing of relations with the city that had formed their individual identities as urban writers and women. Finally exiled to New York with the outbreak of war, for example, Nin condemned its garishness and the destructive assault of light and noise on the senses. Dominated by sky-scrapers, the immediate impression being one of huge size and height, Nin felt disorientated. New York is perhaps the city that most requires De Certeau's conception of the urban observer as 'in flight' and hovering panoramically over the urban landscape. Yet to do so is to be detached from its street life, to be caught in the limbo between dream and reality that Nin always feared. Nin's first impression was of New York as a city of unreality and glitzy fantasy, from which she lived 'externally, superficially', in comparison to the intimacy of Paris: 'The luxury after the tender human scale of Paris is overpowering. Where are the cafés with only three small tables, and tottering chairs? This is Gulliver's country. But I, who love small scale, small objects, small intimate cities, small trains, small cars, small restaurants, small concert halls, do not respond to giant scales.'[71] She mourned that 'I felt every cell and cord which tied me to France snapping in me, the parting from a pattern of life I loved, from an atmosphere rich, creative and human, from intimacy with people and a city.'[72] Lamenting the loss of the literary community of

[71] Anaïs Nin, 'Winter, 1939', *The Journals of Anaïs Nin: 1939–1944*, ed. Gunther Stuhlmann (London: Peter Owen, 1969), 12.
[72] Ibid. 3.

Paris, she found relief in Greenwich Village, which provided a simulation of the European city in its slower and more leisured café life, cosmopolitan shops and streets, and creative atmosphere. Unlike Paris, in unoccupied London, as the next chapter will explore, war strengthened the ties of women to the city and afforded them renewed access to its streets and public spaces both day and night. Notably, the surreal wartime landscape and the social sense of urban community fostered a reawakening of an ardent sensory response to the city by women writers, a renewed determination to find foundation rather than fragmentation in the urban scene, and consequently an outburst of creative activity.

6 | Wandering the London Wasteland

THE literature of the Second World War has been marginalized compared to other periods in the twentieth century; Salman Rushdie bluntly summarized the consensus of opinion that 'America, Germany and Italy all produced extraordinary novels about it; England didn't', going on to suggest that this was the result of the English tendency to live in 'a green world of the past', as the young male characters in Bowen and Macaulay's novels are certainly shown to do.[1] Yet this is to overlook the distinctive representation of the city in wartime, largely created by women writers; the world of Bowen's *Heat of the Day* (1949), H.D.'s *Trilogy* (1942–4), and Macaulay's *The World My Wilderness* (1950). As Phyllis Lassner's metaphor appropriately describes, these writers literally took on the identity of the wandering urban rag-picker both to collect and register their wartime experiences, literally creating 'from the rubble of the Blitz an art that has been largely ignored'.[2] This art reconstructs the city from a female point of view. It is not the city of the authoritative, masculine urban observer; the ordered London of neat squares and panoramic vistas falls into dreamlike ruins, rubble-strewn wastelands, and geographic fragmentation. To mythologize the blitzed city was the 'saving illusion' practised by women artists, and an alternative to nostalgic regression to the past.

In women's representations of wartime London, the city frequently becomes the province of the *flâneuse* rather than the *flâneur*. There are obvious tensions within the idea of *flânerie* during wartime, that again stem from the difference between Janet Wolff's Benjaminian *flâneur*, a powerful figure of surveillance on the Foucauldian model, and the

---

[1] Salman Rushdie, quoted in Michiko Kakutani, 'Novelists Are News Again', *New York Times Book Review* (14 Aug. 1983), 22–3, p. 23.

[2] Phyllis Lassner, 'Reimagining the Arts of War: Language and History in Elizabeth Bowen's *The Heat of the Day* and Rose Macaulay's *The World My Wilderness*', *Perspectives in Contemporary Criticism* 14 (1988), 30–8, p. 30.

Baudelairian *flâneur*, who is always a marginal, melancholic rootless figure. It is a tendency of postmodern and feminist critics to celebrate the nomadic existence of the urban wanderer, acclaiming the non-static perspective as an alternative to what they regard as fixed and limiting traditional and patriarchal standpoints. Of course I too want to use the trope of *flânerie* as a metaphor for the increased freedom of women in wartime urban life and for a consequent peripatetic aesthetic position, but I want to avoid acclaiming these traits to the neglect of the less positive aspects of enforced wartime nomadism. In the example of Virginia Woolf, the wandering spirit loses all sense of base and private identity and, unable to retain any sense of personal continuity, she committed suicide in 1941.

City of Women

The climate of war resulted in an increased visibility and mobility of women in the urban landscape. Alice Coates, an artist at the Slade who served with the Women's Land Army, described London in her poem 'The Monstrous Regiment' as a female world in which mothers, aunts, and wives take over the jobs and roles abandoned by men who have gone to fight. Jobs in every sector and of every status—from the labourer to the doctor, and the milkman to the poet—are fulfilled by women, 'all are shes', and men are only mentioned in parentheses as an afterthought or an embarrassment '([t]he few remaining men are small and pale— | War lends a spurious value to the male)'. It is the woman who is now visible in the city; 'What hosts of women everywhere I see!' Coates does not glorify the war as an occasion to laud female emancipation, however, noting with a weary realism the monotony, dullness, and sterility of a solely female society. '[S]ick to death of them—and they of [her]' (l. 2), she states that all are 'doubtless, worthy to a high degree; | But oh, how boring! Yes, including me' (ll. 25–6). Yet these women cannot be avoided and seem to force themselves into Coates's line of vision:

> Dames, hoydens, wenches, harridans and hussies
> Cram to congestion all the trams and buses;
> Misses and grandmas, mistresses and nieces,
> Infest bombed buildings, picking up the pieces.[3]

Young and old women, the respectable and the promiscuous, all mix in the wartime landscape. Like the Baudelairian rag-picker or the surrealist

---

[3] Alice Coates, 'The Monstrous Regiment', in Catherine W. Reilly (ed.), *Chaos of the Night: Women's Poetry and Verse of the Second World War* (Virago, 1984), 29.

artist, they discover fragments of their histories amidst the ruins. What they then do is to find new identities in the fragments themselves, rather than attempt to piece them back together into a society that they are unsure whether they want to return to. Men returning from the war walk back into a world that is new, unknown, and female.

Elizabeth Bowen's wartime London is at once a place and a non-place; a site of dislocation and displacement, inhabited by wanderers, people who have lost both homes and identities in the disruption of war. Like Coates, her London is also a particularly female world, populated by working girls, widows, and wives whose husbands have gone to the front. The few male figures that do appear are emasculated men, too young, old, or incapacitated to fight. In women's literature from the war the landscape of London becomes a newly female-domin-ated place. Moreover, traditionally feminine *private* spaces are lost as living spaces become no longer homes, but instead are other people's houses, let as flats to people staying in the city yet bombed out of their own buildings. The inhabitants of Bowen's London move between different *public* spaces; parks, cafés, bars, and most notably the city streets. Along with other women writers such as H.D. and Rose Macau-lay, she seems to find in the city of the war years an environment and set of conditions conducive to a new urban spirit, that of the female wanderer or *flâneuse*.

It is profitable to continue the discussion of the *flâneur* into the period of the Second World War as it is at this time that the traditions of English culture essentially broke down and new perceptions arose. For despite the claims of modernist writers and artists that the structure of English life changed with the end of the Edwardian era and the beginning of the First World War, it did not do so to such a degree as with the Second. The two wars were very different experiences and prompted different cultural reactions. In the 1914–18 war, casualties at the front were hor-rifically high but the war was largely confined to the battlefields on the continent, relatively isolated from the English home. The Second World War intruded on civilian life far more drastically and obviously; civilian casualties from the successive bombing campaigns made up a high proportion of the war dead, and the sounds of fighting in France could be heard from the south-east coast. At the same time, however, the global nature of the war meant a sense of disconnection from an understanding of the situation as a whole and any conception of its progress. Bowen writes in *The Heat of the Day*, for example, that '[w]ar's being global meant it ran off the edges of maps; it was uncontainable' (*HD* 308). The effect of this global war was the further disorientation of a society dominated by the traditional mastering gaze of the male observing figure. The war broke into everyday life, fragmenting it both literally and spiritually, but it could not be grasped as a whole.

The most visible and tangible effects of the war were the intense raids of the Blitz, beginning in the summer and autumn of 1940 and continuing until the spring of the following year, in which London was persistently and intensely bombed. The result was over thirty thousand civilian deaths and about two million homeless.[4] A respite of three tense years followed before the repetition of bombing by the V-bombs in 1944, yet this later experience was very different from that of the Blitz. The unsequential flying bombs aroused a new terror and nervousness, yet the community spirit and heroism of the Blitz months had faded into a jaded weariness and staleness produced by six years of war. When victory dawned, relief was the prevalent emotion and celebrations seemed anticlimactic, Bowen describing the fireworks, planes, and sweeping lights as a 'hilarious parody of war'.[5] Bowen's visually impressionistic London scenes come from the surreal atmosphere of the earlier period.

For men away at war, 'London' and 'home' could be sentimentalized as ideals, assuring an essential stability and security amidst the upheaval of war, yet, back in England, the effects of the war were also felt. Confidence in personal identity and the social conventions that supported it was lost, and, as a result, 'the war spiritually exhausted British culture and transformed it into something approaching a theatre of dead mannequins'.[6] As buildings and traditional beliefs crumbled, the ideal of stability was shown to be erroneous. In Bowen's fiction, male characters frantically attempt to surround themselves with objects, traditions, and houses that convey familiarity and continuity. Women, however, no longer fulfil any nurturing role. They have experienced the war in terms of disorientation from the conventions of English life, and therefore have no illusions about the 'London/home' ideal. Losing or giving up homes because of the bombing, and gaining new economic and social freedoms because of the nation's need for women to be involved in war work, women were forced to grow increasingly accustomed to a nomadic rather than a settled lifestyle. The scale of women's increased presence in the public wartime city was limited at first, and in fact an immediate effect of the war was high female unemployment because of cutbacks in the tertiary sector in which women were largely employed.

[4] Peter Lewis, *A People's War* (London: Thames Methuen, 1986), 105.

[5] Victoria Glendinning, *Elizabeth Bowen: Portrait of a Writer* (London: Weidenfeld and Nicolson, 1977), 157.

[6] Adam Piette, *Imagination at War: British Fiction and Poetry 1939–1945* (London: Papermac, 1995), 2.

Yet by 1941, in the particularly dark period of the war, that compulsory registration by women aged 19–40 for 'essential work' was instigated and large numbers of women were classed as 'mobile' for work and conscripted.[7] As an early analysis of the effect of the war on women's social position, Margaret Goldsmith's *Women at War*, recognized, large numbers became 'more self-reliant, and [...] learned to use their own judgement and initiative'.[8] They could also gain greater physical freedom through working as air raid wardens, ambulance drivers, fire-fighters, or in mobile canteens, and, although at the beginning of the war 'women wardens were not allowed to patrol the streets', this restriction soon had to be relinquished as the bombing increased.[9] The traditional urban relationship of the male *flâneur* observing the objectified woman is thus disrupted in the wartime city landscape. Women adjust to the enforced displaced and 'wandering' lifestyle, and come to experience it as a new freedom. Men, on the other hand, cling to, or are entrapped by, symbols of the past and view the uprootedness of the wartime urban condition with nihilistic horror.

Souls Astray

Elizabeth Bowen's stories repeatedly depict male figures returning to the domestic environments they had known before the war, only to find them decaying or destroyed. The opening story of *The Demon Lover*, for example, depicts a man disillusioned by his sense of disorientation within a once familiar place. 'In the Square' describes the altered social relationships of a Georgian terrace, the home before the war of a society hostess, where the protagonist had frequently attended dinner parties and receptions. Now, however, although still standing, it is a shell of its past splendour. Grimy and in disarray, it gives a sense of 'functional anarchy, of loose plumbing, of fittings shocked from their place' (*DL* 10). Reflecting the physical disruption of the house, the inhabitants too are discordant, with Magdela, the hostess, now sharing the house with her husband's secretary-mistress and a caretaker couple. The visitor is at a loss in the new atmosphere of the house, with its lack of identity. He is disorientated and 'had Magdela not sat down where she did sit, he would not have known in which direction to turn' (12). This experience is

---

[7] Between January 1941 and October 1943, registered female unemployment fell from 350,000 to 24,000. See J. Hooks, *British Policies and Methods of Employing Women in Wartime* (Washington: US Government, 1944), 16.

[8] Margaret Goldsmith, *Women at War* (London: Lindsay Brummond, 1943), 126.

[9] Ibid. 129–31.

repeated in *The Heat of the Day*, when Stella's son Roderick visits her on leave. Having giving up her own house at the beginning of the war, Stella now rents a fully furnished flat, in which even the ornaments are not her own and therefore have no personal connection. For Roderick, then, the flat is not home and he looks desperately for some sign of habit or convention that will indicate to him a code for behaviour. Taking the coffee tray into the main room, for example, he is disappointed in his hope for directions on where to place it, proof that he is returning to a steady, routine way of life:

In this flat, rooms had no names; there being only two, whichever you were not in was 'the other room'. Proceeding into what *he* saw as the drawing-room, Roderick, grasping the tray, stood looking round again. Somewhere between these chairs and tables must run the spoon of habit, could one but pick it up. [...] Roderick, for the moment, was confounded by there being no one right place to put down a tray. (*HD* 52)

For Roderick and his army friends 'the authoritarianism of home life' is all important, giving a degree of structure to their displacement. For this displacement is psychological as well as physical, and Roderick has little identity in the civilian city. When on leave, he is always 'at the beginning physically at a loss; until, by an imitation of [Stella's] attitude he supplied himself with some way to behave, look, stand—even you might say, be. [...] He searched in Stella for some identity left by him in her keeping' (48). Yet, although Stella is aware of the fragility of Roderick's sense of self, fearing that 'her son might simply disappear' in terms of thoughts and feelings, to become merely an empty shell, she does not realize, or cannot provide, the controlled stability that he seeks. A similar male reaction to the war is that of Richmond Deniston in Rose Macaulay's *The World My Wilderness* (1950), set just after the war. Richie is in his first year at Cambridge, having served in the army for three years, and grasps at the promised traditionalism of Catholicism and 'the ivory tower of aristo-cratic culture' (*WW* 150). Like Roderick, Richie is 'one of those returned heroes whose hang-over was not toughness, but an ardent and delighted reaction towards the niceties of civilisation' (21). Indeed, despite the apparent naïveté of both men, and their relative impotence in terms of the plot of the novels, there is something of a resigned acknowledgement by Bowen and Macaulay that, ultimately, it is their view of society that will prosper and overcome. Thus Roderick becomes the master of Mount Morris, and Richie takes the final walk of *The World My Wilderness* through a post-war London that is beginning to be cleared and rebuilt, a landscape that his sister Barbary is now restricted from walking in, being confined to her bed with injuries from a fall in the ruins.

In *The Heat of the Day*, Bowen presents two parallel female lives in the city (Stella Rodney and Louie Lewis) that briefly interconnect along their otherwise separate paths, a structure that is similar to that used by Woolf in *Mrs Dalloway* with Clarissa Dalloway and Septimus Smith. As in Woolf's novel, the two characters are shown to be fundamentally similar, despite the apparent differences that result from class and economic circumstances. Stella comes from an upper-middle-class background, works in the War Office, and has a son training in the army. Long since divorced from a now dead husband, she is involved in a steady relationship with Robert Kelway, whom she met at the beginning of the war. Louie Lewis is a young, uneducated girl whose husband is away at war and who works in a factory, regularly going out with other men. Despite the apparent contrasts of their lives, however, there is an underlying connection between the two women that both intuitively recognize. Both are ultimately trying to develop and place their identity in the wartime landscape. Moreover, their responses to the war and the city environment they live in are particularly female, and in contrast to the attitudes of male characters.

Roderick, Robert, and the counter-intelligence agent Harrison, are all figures who ultimately depend on past, traditional means of stability. Roderick clings obsessively to the thought of his inheritance of the Irish family home, and Harrison also desperately desires the conventional secure base of home, hearth, and wife. Even Robert's activities as a Fascist spy are depoliticized by Bowen, his lack of national identity represented as the result of the lack of the support of a stable and continuous personal background. The Kelway family home is only a sham, a fake, and an imitation of the traditions of the past. No older than the turn-of-the-century, and bought rather than inherited, Holme Deane is a place of appearances in which the antiques are reproductions and even the grounds seem impermanent. It also epitomizes deception, as Robert is well aware: '[e]verything can be shifted, lock, stock, and barrel. After all, everything was brought here from somewhere else, with the intention of being moved again—like touring scenery from theatre to theatre. Reassemble it anywhere: you get the same illusion' (*HO* 121). Robert's response is to become disillusioned with the very principles that Holme Deane attempts to simulate. Rather than recalling them with desperate nostalgia, as Roderick does, he works from the premiss that they no longer exist. Robert sees himself as part of an 'unwhole' race, a 'class without a middle, a race without a country' (272), and his spying actually gives him 'a new heredity' (273). Honour and heroism he regards as illusions belonging to the last war, that do not exist for the men fighting in the second.

Women also experience a loss of conventional definitions of identity in the war, yet Bowen's depiction of Stella and Louie suggests a new wartime, urban female existence that is not based around family and home. The stability of these latter features they acknowledge, like Robert, to be illusory, yet, as women, the loss of them offers some compensations. Stella belongs to the 'lost generation' growing up in the 1920s and is a natural spiritual 'wanderer'. With her brothers killed in the First World War, her husband divorced and dead soon after, and Roderick away in the army, she cannot be defined by the feminine roles of sister, wife, or mother. As a result, she gains a new freedom and enjoys a degree of cosmopolitanism—'between the wars she had travelled, had for intervals lived abroad; she now qualified by knowing two or three languages, two or three countries, well'—welcoming the lack of ties brought about by the wartime situation and 'the opportunity to make or break, to free herself of her house, to come to London to work' (25). Louie too places value neither on her married state nor on her married home, which she feels is oppressive and unconnected to her, and from which she spends as much time away as possible. She wanders around streets and parks, sits in cheap cafés, picking up men, and becomes friends with a female ARP warden, Connie, who soon supersedes Tom Lewis's position, advising and influencing Louie, and even sharing her bed. Bowen therefore contrasts a male desire for the stability of the traditions of the country or family home, with a female rejection of that home for the activity and freedom available in the city. Both Stella and Louie conduct the 'solitary Londoner's footloose habits of living' (111), for whom, like the *flâneur*, '[t]he very temper of pleasures lay in their chanciness, in the canvas-like impermanence of their settings, in their being off-time—to and fro between bars and grills, clubs and each other's places' (94). It is in crowded, public spaces that the two women feel a sense of identity and connection, again in contrast to the male characters. Roderick turns away from the city to his mother's hearth or rural Ireland. Harrison and Robert, as spies, are iconographically urban types, yet they are always detached and observing, suspicious of communication. Stella, for example, contrasts her sense of the community spirit of wartime London, evident in its streets and bars, with Robert's rejection of it: '[t]he war-warmed impulse of people to be *a* people had been derisory; he had hated the bloodstream of the crowds, the curious animal psychic oneness, the human lava-flow. [. . .] as for the impatiences, the hopes, the reiteration of unanswerable questions and the spurts of rumour—he must have been measuring them with a calculating eye' (275).

The position of women in *Heat of the Day*, which begins in late summer 1942, is specific to the later war years of female mobilization.

Whereas a large proportion of women in England were reluctant to enter war work at first, particularly if it required leaving home, the three women Bowen portrays are examples of women already away from the family home and anxious for some new experience, whether greater freedom, individual identity, or active war effort.[10] Stella, Louie, and Connie are all wartime working women, conducting non-domestic styles of living. Stella has volunteered for war work, and her class privileges of education and connections have secured her a position of secret importance in civil defence.[11] Louie works in a factory, but her status as a soldier's wife would seem to give her some exemption from compulsory work. By earning a wage, however, which rose considerably during the war to an average of £3 per week, women such as Louie were able to enjoy social activities without being financially dependent on family or husband. Connie, on the other hand, is officially designated a 'Mobile Woman' and is constantly afraid that she may lose her position as an ARP warden if the bombing becomes less frequent. For although she complains of her job as boring and monotonous, to be relocated elsewhere in the country, or into the service of the ATS, would involve a considerable loss of the prestige afforded by employment with the Civil Defence. Connie's pay is poor, as was typical of the services, but her job has the alternative benefits of responsibility and periods of exciting activity.

Significantly, Bowen's London is not feminized by female group collectivity so much as an existential connection of spirit, her concentration being on moments of empathy experienced between otherwise isolated individuals in the wartime city. In *The Heat of the Day*, for example, it is through a contrast from work colleagues that Bowen defines what are particularly female class-transcending bonds. Louie and Connie are anomalies to the stereotypical perceptions of their professions. Factory work, for example, was seen to be undertaken by lower-class, often 'rough', women, and service women were regarded as cheap and with loose morals. Bowen's description of the two girls not only attempts to avoid such class and gender bias, but also serves to emphasize the displacement of wartime urban existence, the fine line between the inadequacy of generalizing definitions and yet the need for supports and ballasts to identity. Louie, for example, no more corresponds to the idea of the rough factory worker as the regimental Connie

---

[10] Gail Braybon and Penny Summerfield, *Out of the Cage: Women's Experiences in Two World Wars* (London: Pandora Press, 1987), 185.

[11] Bowen herself worked for the Ministry of Information, writing reports on the political climate in Ireland. Civil defence was one of the employment areas where middle-class women were particularly prevalent during the war, forming one-quarter of the workforce.

does to that of the sexually available service woman. Yet she regrets her inability to identify with the groups of girls at the factory and belong to a certain 'sort' that would indicate how she should perceive herself and behave, thinking that '[i]t is advantageous being among all sorts if you are some sort, any sort; you gravitate to your type. It is daunting if you discover you are still no sort—the last hope gone' (149). It is this lack of friendship, place, and point of contact with others that results in the spiritual affinity between Stella and Louie and the supportive kinship of Louie and Connie. Stella, Louie, and Connie's employment and work-places are only background elements in the novel, but are thus crucial to their position and freedoms within the urban landscape, as well as their social status.[12]

All three women are variants of the urban streetwalker; Stella through her aesthetic, musing wanderings, Louie through her haunting of cafés and soliciting of men, Connie through her job of patrolling the city streets. All are also directionless, and they tend to walk amidst the streets rather than through them to particular destinations. The urban wander-ing of Stella and Louie corresponds to their wandering search for a sense of identity. Louie, in particular, conforms to the conventional interpre-tation of the city woman as prostitute, walking in the city and develop-ing 'vagrant habits', picking up men in parks and cafés. Louie desperately needs to label herself with an identity, and indeed the appeal of the propaganda of the daily newspapers is their construction of a typical, homogenous reading public that Louie can place herself within: '[w]as she not a worker, a soldier's lonely wife, a war orphan, a pedestrian, a Londoner, a home- and animal-lover, a thinking democrat, a movie-goer, a woman of Britain, a letter writer, a fuel-saver, and a housewife?' (152). Yet, ultimately, the role that is innate to her is that of the female urban 'streetwalker', an instinctive response to her displaced state, like that of a stray animal, to which Louie is frequently compared. There is nothing calculated or intentionally seductive in Louie's manner, and Bowen distinguishes her from the 'good-time' girls of the war period, stating that 'it was a phenomenon of war-time city night that it brought out something provocative in the step of most modest women; Nature tapped out with the heels on the pavement an illicit semaphore. Alone was Louie in being almost never accosted; whatever it *was* was missing from her step' (145). Louie is not a streetwalker on display, indeed '[t]o be seen was for her not to be', and, returning from work at twilight she is almost invisible, one of numerous 'indifferent shadows' (145). She be-longs to the streets less as a sexual object for the male gaze, therefore,

[12] Braybon and Summerfield, *Out of the Cage*, 163.

than as a vagrant, stray figure who seeks attention. In Bowen's female urban landscape even Louie is not a sexualized streetwalker. Women walk the city instead as shadows.

Under the surveillance and control of Connie (whose role as an ARP warden is significantly to guide the lost and homeless), Louie ceases her natural soliciting, as the sense of self that she searches for is constructed and supplied for her by Connie's continued references to Tom, Louie's husband who is away in the army. Stella also influences Louie's habits, the latter seeing in the older woman an icon of 'refinement' that she envies, as well as regarding her as a virtuous or pure version of her own wandering self. Although they only meet once, in the harshly lit café in Piccadilly, walking home together afterwards Louie recognizes Stella as a fellow wanderer, 'a soul astray' (248), someone who is 'out of her sphere here, nonplussed, a wanderer from some better star' (306). Stella too notes some affinity with Louie, commenting that 'she and I have no idea where we are' (241), and, some days later, Louie experiences an almost psychic connection with her. It is as if Stella's spirit seeks Louie for support as much as Louie's does the older woman, and she finds herself 'clutched, compelled, forbidden to leave the spot' (292) on Stella's street where she stands. In response, she remains 'pacing to and fro, to and fro, like a last searcher for somebody said to be still alive' (291). Louie's emulation of Stella stops, however, when she reads the newspaper reports of Robert's death and the descriptions of Stella's involvement with him and other men in her luxury flat. Stella no longer seems the virtuous wanderer that Louie imagined and the latter returns to seeking identity through her 'vagrant habits'. When she falls pregnant at the end of the novel, however, she suddenly finds a sense of place and purpose. Bewildered at first at the consequences of her sexual freedom, Connie's angry judgement that she is only 'one of many' prompts a new self-realization in Louie, and an identification with others: '[t]his Louie seized upon. "Well, I *am*, only, aren't I—just one of many?" A sort of illumination widened over her features [...] this settled into a look of inward complacency, even sublimity' (324–5).[13]

This achievement of self-possession through motherhood seems rather prosaic, however, and the conclusion of the young girl, who wandered the wartime city seeking an identity that she could not satisfactorily express, as a mother pushing a pram in the countryside, is somewhat simplistic. Indeed, after the intimation of spiritual female affinity between Louie and Stella that Bowen develops through the novel,

[13] Illegitimate births more than doubled between 1939 and 1945, a large proportion being born to married women, particularly servicemen's wives. Braybon and Sunnofield, *Out of the Cage*, 216.

their respective ends as mother and wife of a brigadier are extremely conventional. Perhaps Bowen felt that the post-war city landscape was no longer a conducive environment for the connective feminine spirit of the *flâneuse*, and wanted to indicate that it once more became a male domain, with women losing their legitimate presence in the city streets and returning to traditional domestic roles. The dominant emphasis at the end of the war was that 'change was temporary, that women were "really" wives and mothers and their place was at home'.[14] The female London landscape of the war years, characterized by change, displacement, and strangeness, was to be replaced by a regimented and impersonal rebuilding plan.

Dreamscapes in the War-Torn City

The attachment to the street environment that is characteristic of the natural *flâneur* pervades Bowen's writing. Indeed, in her essay 'The Writer's Peculiar World', she distinguishes between two types of writer, 'the intellectual novelist, building upon a framework of ideas' and 'the aesthetic-intuitive, working mainly on memories and impressions'.[15] This latter type, with which Bowen herself would seem to identify, is suggestive of a literary *flâneur*. Bowen describes this writer as possessing a 'roving eye' and 'some faculty free to veer and wander', thus associating the perspective of the writer with the urban walker. Amidst the flux of modern life, the writer perceives like a child, with no presuppositions and with 'a perpetual, errant state of desire, wonder, and unexpected reflex'. Notably, it is with imagery from the city landscape that Bowen describes the writer's practice, stating that certain aspects of life stand out with vision-like significance: '[t]he one face standing forward out of the crowd, the figure in the distance crossing the street, the glare or shade significant on a building, the episode playing out at the next table'.[16] Bowen's own peculiar world is the wartime, cosmopolitan world of the London blitz.

The distinctions that Bowen notes between the generic forms of the novel and the short story can be seen to parallel those between the intellectual and the intuitive writer, and it is with the short story that the latter would seem to come into his own. In her preface to the collection

---

[14] Ibid. 281.

[15] Collected in *The Mulberry Tree: Writings of Elizabeth Bowen*, ed. Hermione Lee (London: Virago, 1986), 61.

[16] Ibid. 63.

Stories by Elizabeth Bowen, she states that, whereas the novel form is
ethically and socially based, the short story is psychologically based and
therefore 'must be more concentrated, can be more visionary', creating a
constant 'electrical-imaginative current'.[17] The short story is thus particularly suited to the impressionistic writer who relies, like Bowen, on the
'immediacy and purity of sensation'.[18] Moreover, she argues in the 'Postscript' to her collection of wartime stories in *The Demon Lover* that the
short story is the most appropriate literary form for expressing the
experience of wartime, urban existence. For the war is a hallucinatory
experience that can only be rendered in 'disjected snapshots' (*DL* 223).
Bowen asserts that 'especially in London, in wartime many people had
strange intense dreams' (219), best captured through the psychological
emphasis of the short story. It is the representation of a dreamlike city
that characterizes Bowen's writing, the imaginative perspective not only
pervading her short stories but also her novels. It is my argument that
this dream-London, like the utopian city in the story 'Mysterious Kôr', is
a particularly female urban landscape, walked and imagined by the
wartime *flâneuse.*

The experience of dislocation and loss of self is the continual subject
of Bowen's wartime writings and reminiscences. Bowen herself directly
experienced the homelessness and nomadism of London life during
periods of bombing, her house at 2, Clarence Terrace in Regent's Park
suffering successive damage, although never completely destroyed. She
remained living in the city throughout the war, however, working as an
ARP warden, a job which gave many women a new position of legitimate
authority to walk the city streets at night.[19] As the quote that I used as an
introduction to this discussion, as well as the essay 'London, 1940',
indicate, Bowen's work as warden involved a literal walking of the city
amidst a terrain of bomb craters and desecrated buildings. The city she
observed was a deserted night city, blacked out and lit only by moonlight
and the rays of searchlights, or a morning city of the smoking, broken
remains of streets and houses, about which the homeless wandered.
Virginia Woolf, in her essay 'Street Haunting', describes her sense of
losing the fixed shell of the self when she is outside her house, and of
experiencing a loss of differentiation between herself and others in the
city streets. She becomes no longer an 'I' but a bodiless, roving 'enormous eye'. Bowen too notes this identification with others in the city

---

[17] Collected in *The Mulberry Tree: Writings of Elizabeth Bowen,* ed. Hermione Lee
(London: Virago, 1986), 128.
[18] Ibid. 130.
[19] Angus Calder, *The People's War* (New York: Pantheon, 1969), 226–7, notes that one-
sixth of air-raid wardens were women.

streets, the tendency of the *flâneuse* seeming to be not so much the careful detachment from the crowd practised by her male counterpart but rather a merging with it to the extent of loss of self. Moreover, Bowen's city is literally peopled by 'haunters'—the ghosts of the dead, the shadowy figures wandering over the ruins of their homes, the women who linger in the streets of the moonlit city.

Whereas Woolf's 1930 essay concentrates on the light and enjoyable superficiality of the dallying eye, however, Bowen's version is the direct result of conditions brought about by the war: 'Walking in the darkness of the nights of six years (darkness which transformed a capital city into a network of inscrutable canyons) one developed new bare alert senses, with their own savage warnings and notations' (*DL* 223). Houses are destroyed in the wartime city, and their inhabitants forced into the streets without either a metaphorical or literal protective 'shell' for the self, all thus becoming the wandering I/eye. When Bowen walks the city streets in her capacity as warden, she therefore becomes one with a whole city of displaced wanderers. As she states in *The Demon Lover*: '[d]uring the war I lived, both as a civilian and as a writer, with every pore open; I lived so many lives, and, still more, lived among the packed repercussions of so many thousands of other lives, all under stress [. . .] It seems to me that during the war the overcharged subconsciousnesses of everybody overflowed and merged' (217). Emphasizing that her stories are of war*time* rather than *war*, she goes on to state that what pervaded the wartime psyche was this experience of wandering in both city and identity. She repeats that, during the war, the 'feeling of slight differentiation was suspended: I felt one with, and just like, everyone else. Sometimes I hardly knew where I stopped and somebody else began. The violent destruction of solid things, the explosion of the illusion that prestige, power and permanence attach to bulk and weight, left all of us, equally, heady and disembodied' (217–18). This is the experience of the *flâneur*, for whom the streets and social spaces of the city are the home and drawing-room, and the Woolfian *flâneuse*, for whom differentiation from the urban crowd breaks down. In Bowen's London, however, urban wandering is no frivolous *flânerie* but instead a restless and desperate search for self. The wartime city is populated by exiled foreigners and women (single, widowed, elderly), examples of the marginal *flâneur* who return to their bombed homes and, like the Baudelairian rag-picker, go 'to infinite lengths to assemble bits of themselves—broken ornaments, odd shoes, torn scraps of the curtains that hung in a room—from the wreckage' (220). It is these experiences that inflect the style and tone of her writing. The senses awakened to hypersensitivity as she walks the night streets require experimentation in translating them into language.

Where Richardson turned to a stream-of-consciousness style to interpret the extended perceptions of Miriam Henderson, Bowen, in the precious time of the war, turns to supernaturalistic short stories. It is with these literary 'fragments' that she reflects and reassembles the mind disparated by war.

It is in this respect that Woolf and Bowen can be contrasted as observers of the urban scene. Woolf, as pre-war *flâneuse* of the 1920s and 1930s, could flit in and out of other identities and relish the surface spectacle of the city, yet still needed to retain a sense of self-continuity. In the preface to *Stories by Elizabeth Bowen*, Bowen too asserts that she might become imbalanced as a writer if it were not for the fact that half of her work 'is under the steadying influence of the novel, with its calmer, stricter, more orthodox demands'.[20] Woolf's novelistic style itself is lyrical and vision- ary, however, and she was frequently emotionally and mentally exhausted after writing difficult works. Her mobile consciousness, if taken to ex- tremes, could end up fragmented and unable to piece itself together, and she thus fought a constant battle throughout her life with a tendency to mental breakdown. It is the mobile observer or 'street-haunter' that pervades her fiction, and it was from writing and the expression of this perspective that she was required to rest when recovering from bouts of mental illness. In particular, the loss of self experienced in the street, that is a mark of freedom for the *flâneuse* of 1930, becomes an intensified and unrelenting condition in the wartime city. Houses now become places of security for Woolf, when they are yet threatened by destruction. In June 1940, for example, she writes in her diary that 'the war [...] has taken away the outer wall of security. No echo comes back. I have no surroundings', a feeling repeated a month later when she writes that '[a]ll the walls, the protecting and reflecting walls, wear so terribly thin in this war'. She fears that the war destroys the secure echo of identity: 'the writing "I" has vanished. No audience, No echo.'[21] Having freely merged with the urban crowd in the pre-war years, she turns with horror from the wartime propaganda machine. Through propaganda people are dictated into a crowd of communal feeling and, although the traditional *flâneur* likes to mingle amidst and even merge with the crowd, his impulse is always ultimately to remain separate from it.[22] Adam Piette notes Woolf's rejec- tion of public feeling in her diary entries of 1940 and suggests that it is the result of a desperate grasp to retain private, individual identity.

[20] Bowen, *The Mulberry Tree*, 130.

[21] Virginia Woolf, *The Diary of Virginia Woolf*, vol. v: *1936–1941*, ed. Anne Olivier Bell (London: Hogarth Press, 1984), 299, 304, 293.

[22] That this distinction is not necessarily possible is similar to the traumatizing experi- ence of the narrator-observer in 'The Man in the Crowd'.

Whereas for Virginia Woolf the psychological impact of the war impeded creativity, for Bowen the wartime city provided a force of aesthetic inspiration. Indeed, Bowen herself claimed that she 'would not have missed being in London throughout the war for anything: it was the most interesting period of my life'.[23] *The Heat of the Day*, being a novel, offers an extended depiction of the effects of war on the civilian psyche and the role of women in society, and combines passages of impressionistic urban representation with comment on the political and propagandist structure of wartime society. Bowen's writings from within the war period, however, mainly in the form of short stories and essays, are necessarily more concentrated and imagistic pieces. Within them she develops her own idiosyncratic London scene. For Bowen, the intuitive writer-observer holds in his mind an inner environment, an impressionistic rather than purely geographic space. In the autobiographical 'Coming to London', in which she recalls her first impressions of the city as a child, Bowen states that 'the magic of a city, as of a person, resides in its incapacity to be known, and the necessity therefore that it should be imagined'.[24] The urban environment thus influences and creates the *flâneur*, but the latter in turn can be seen to create the urban environment through the subjectivity of his perceptions. John Lehmann described wartime London as the combination of two cities, the daytime and 'the other London', into one, 'the new, symbolic city of the blackout', and it is this place that becomes the environment for Bowen's short stories and that she depicts as the special domain of the female imagination.[25] The London described in *The Demon Lover* is the combination of an actual city and a mythical vision created by Bowen's imagination and the selective processes of her memory. This vision she associates with the walking perspective: '[t]he search for indestructible landmarks in a destructible world led many down strange paths. The attachment to these when they had been found produced small world-within-worlds of hallucination—in most cases, saving hallucinations' (*DL* 220–1). Within Bowen's fiction, it is noticeably female characters who construct these hallucinatory worlds. She depicts wartime London from the perspective of the *flâneuse*, women who occupy new positions in the city as a result of the war and whose response to it differs from that of men.

In *The Demon Lover*, Bowen notes that the collection follows 'a rising tide of hallucination' (*DL* 218). Accordingly, in the final story 'Mysterious Kôr', a young woman dreams of the city of Kôr, from H. Rider

---

[23] Glendinning, *Elizabeth Bowen*, 127.
[24] Bowen, *The Mulberry Tree*, 86.
[25] John Lehmann, *In My Own Time* (1955; Boston: Little, Brown, 1969), 235.

Haggard's *She*, within a city landscape that is itself depicted by Bowen as a surreal fantasy world. Kôr belongs along with Troy, Alexandria, and Knossos as a legendary great city that has been destroyed. Dead cities have a special imaginative power. They are one of the myths that feeds into the image of ruin and ephemerality in the concept-city, and already correlated with London by Haggard himself. Bowen's sense of geography had always been influenced by fantasy and she remembered, as a child, the disillusioning emphasis on actuality in her education. She approached geography with a pioneering passion that then 'shrivelled and shrank' as 'there was no undiscovered country, they told me, now'. As a child, Bowen searched for an abiding and undiscovered country, finding it in Kôr. Reading *She* at the age of 12, Bowen had visualized Kôr in her mind before ever seeing London, and the notion of 'city' thus involved for her a white ruin, 'an extinct, deserted city under the moon' (108). This image remained with her as a founding feature of her perception of a great city, to return from her subconscious memory when she walked the sepulchre city of wartime London. It helped her to visualize an abiding city within an undiscovered London to which the eyes of most were closed. And moreover, realizing that the power of Kôr was controlled by the 'power of the pen. The inventive pen' (113), she found that she could adjust to the experience of wartime London through her own writing.

Bowen's London is a cratered world glistening in moonlight, deserted except for a few wanderers; three French soldiers who have lost their way, two expressionless wardens, and Pepita and her boyfriend Arthur, who 'by their way of walking, seemed to have no destination but each other and to be not quite certain even of that' (197). Pepita compares this fragile city to Kôr, ' "a completely forsaken city, as high as cliffs and as white as bones, with no history" ', whilst yet also noting that ' "Kôr's altogether different; it's very strong; there is not a crack in it anywhere [...] the corners of stones and the monuments might have been cut yesterday, and the stairs and arches are built to support themselves" ' (198). Threatened London is supported in the female imagination by a sense of eternal strength, as represented by the imagined city, Kôr. Kôr is the fantasy landscape, accessed through dreaming, that is denied to Londoners in waking life, and as such it acts as an alternative, imaginary space—London's reflection rather than its 'other', and a dream realm where the desires of everyday life can be accommodated. Pepita does not remain trapped within this dreamworld, however, as Benjamin and Nin complained of the surrealists, but remembers it in the waking world, translating it onto the moonlit London around her. In the same way, Bowen perceives London as a heterotopic space, merging it in her perceptions with the mythic urban landscapes stored in her memory and imagination.

Both urban visions are essentially female perceptions, arising from the inadequacy of the language of male society to express the fantastic conditions of war. As Bowen states, these conditions were 'out of all proportion to our faculties for knowing, thinking and checking up' (219). In response, therefore, both Pepita and Bowen, who as women observe this unnatural landscape with 'childishly innocent' eyes, compensate by constructing 'saving illusory worlds' (221). Giving up on trying to express her perceptions through language—she asserts that '[w]hat it tries to say doesn't matter: I see what it makes me see' (199)—Pepita turns instead to the visual image of her dream, a hallucinatory inner terrain that Bowen creates with her characteristic skill for evoking the psychological landscape. Her female view is contrasted to that of Arthur, for whom Kôr is unreal because it cannot be marked on a map. Arthur is representative of a common male type in Bowen's wartime, expressing a fatalistic view of society as a result of the loss of past traditions. According to his masculine perspective, Pepita should think about him for emotional support rather than Kôr and, moreover, when humouring her fantasy, he cannot imagine her new world without the order of calculated time or the idea of traditional relational structures such as the family. Actually she does need him, but in terms of a different relationship to that she has with the city itself: '[h]e was the password, but not the answer: it was to Kôr's finality that she turned' (215).

Male observers could take up this perspective of the androgynous *flâneur*, but it was notably the outsider who did and could therefore still be exhilarated in the wartime city streets. The everyday London experience of the Canadian diplomat Charles Ritchie, Bowen's lover during the war years, was conducted within the masculine spaces and political arena of his office at Canada House in Trafalgar Square, his flat near Pall Mall, the clubs of St James Street, and the social rooms at the Dorchester Hotel. As the cosmopolitan *flâneur* who loves women and the city as objects of spectacle he notes in his diary for December 1941:

I enjoy my walks to the office in the mornings—the elegance of Grosvenor St, the Maisons de Haute Couture behind their ageing façades, Jacqmar's interior seen through the long plate-glass windows with the soignées salesgirls drifting about among the lengths of patterned silk. It looks as a temple of fashion should look—dimly lit and solemn, but luxurious—a proper place to stir the imagination of the passing women.[26]

---

[26] Charles Ritchie, '17 December 1941', *The Siren Years: Undiplomatic Diaries 1937–1945* (London: Macmillan, 1974), 129.

This could be Haussmann's Paris in the Second Empire as much as it is London during the Second World War. Yet Ritchie also observes London with the mystical passion for the city of the outsider-*flâneur*. He notes the silence of the streets of battered stuccoed houses at night, and the lakes of swept up broken glass during the day, and his description of a musical interlude in Hyde Park in 1939 startlingly prefigures Bowen's treatment of a similar occurrence in the opening of *The Heat of the Day*.[27] Later entries record other Bowenesque symbols; the dismantling of iron railings, the burning of leaves, a wartime population composed of women and outsiders (female clerks and secretaries, ATS girls, widows, prostitutes, Polish soldiers).[28]

Without the influence of Bowen, however, and her quest for an 'abiding city', Ritchie still conceives of a city in terms of destructibility, a view which is implied as gendered in an anecdote that he relates: 'What nonsense the woman was talking the other day when she said that it did not matter if a city were destroyed physically, if its soul lived. Cities are nothing without their bodies. When you have destroyed Paris and Oxford what happens to their souls?'[29] This belief in the continuing soul of the city is common to women's art of the period. Perhaps the subtlety of Bowen, and later H.D. and Macaulay's position, however, is that rather than deny that London has any identity as a physical entity, they deny that that physical entity is ever completely destroyed. For the physical city is a palimpsestic city, layers of which remain beneath the surface buildings of the present. Although the Blitz may have toppled many of the Regency, Victorian, and Edwardian buildings of London, for example, at the same time it revealed the relics of Londinium and fragments of the wall of the medieval City of London. Having met Bowen, Ritchie did acknowledge the influence of her particular aesthetic perspective and sense of the continuing mystical power of the city. After a walk in Regent's Park in 1941, for example, he recorded that

As we walked together I seemed to see the flowers through the lens of her sensibility. [...] the misty river, the Regency villas with their walled gardens and damp lawns and the late September afternoon weather blended into a dream—a dream in which these were all symbols soaked with mysterious associative power—Regent's Park [...] the deserted Nash house with its flaking stucco colonnade.[30]

The deserted area of Regent's Park is Bowen's habitat and in the essay 'London, 1940', literally becomes her own world: 'At nights, at my end of the terrace, I feel as though I were sleeping in one corner of a deserted

---

[27] '5 March 1939', ibid. 31.   [28] '27 October 1941', ibid. 124.
[29] '22 Sept 1940', ibid. 68.   [30] '29 September 1941', ibid. 118.

palace. I had always placed this Park among the most civilized scenes on earth; the Nash pillars look as brittle as sugar—actually, which is wonderful, they have not cracked [...] Illicitly, leading the existence of ghosts, we overlook the locked park.'[31] The moonlit Nash pillars stand as testimony to the fortitude of London and the tenacity of its nomadic inhabitants. Place is always crucial in Bowen's work and she experienced a strong identification with London during the war years, as Pepita does with Kôr. In fact Pepita herself seems a fictional equivalent of Bowen herself as urban writer portraying an atmospheric landscape, and for Bowen too 'dreams by night, and the fantasies [...] with which formerly matter-of-fact people consoled themselves by day were compensations' (219). Pepita's description of her vision, for example, suggests Bowen's assertion that the observer partially creates the environment; '[t]his war shows we've by no means come to the end. If you can blow whole places out of existence, you can blow whole places into it. [...] By the time we've come to the end, Kôr may be the one city left: The abiding city' (199). Bowen herself finds, in the landscape of destruction that is wartime London, a vision of an abiding city.

Elizabeth Bowen's wartime London is thus a personal terrain observed from walking in a city made strange by the effects of war. In terms of traditional, patriarchal society, it is an inexpressible non-place and, consequently, the site of utter disorientation for the male characters portrayed in her urban works. Women characters, attempting to express their perceptions of this world through the masculine language system, do not really fit anywhere either, as they cannot correspond to the identity types available. There is an implicit connection between Bowen as writer-walker of the city and her female characters, however, with their sensitive, 'childlike' or 'stereoscopic', fresh perceptions of the urban environment. This female landscape is notably one that combines the imagination and the real. As an ARP warden, Bowen walked at night and observed the visual impact of the play of moonlight and searchlights on the white houses and bomb-cratered streets around Regent's Park, as well as, by day, the effects of sunlight and smoke lingering around the broken glass and fallen walls of bombed buildings. As a writer she 'followed the paths [she] saw or felt people treading, and depicted those little dear saving illusory worlds' (221). Bowen's London is the result of the combination of this literal and imaginative *flânerie*, and of impressionistic and surrealistic perceptions. It is a twilight 'theatre of war' in which life is concentrated in the open spaces of the street, houses are paper backdrops, and where all inhabitants are observers waiting in

---

[31] Bowen, *The Mulberry Bush*, 24.

eerily deserted darkness for something to happen, occasionally high-lighted by the focus of the searchlight.

Rag-Pickers in the Wilderness

Bowen writes the climate and landscape of war, rather than its history. Regarding war 'more as a territory than as a page of history', she maps wartime London through its moonlit parks, deserted night streets and broken Regency façades, in a way that resembles Benjamin's definition of Second Empire Paris through the grand boulevards and public buildings of Haussmann's Paris.[32] The ruined city is an important emblem for Benjamin in his extended work on Paris in the *Passagen-Werk*, and an image that pervades the surrealist urban perception. As Susan Buck-Morss describes, the ruin is 'an emblem not only of the transitoriness and fragility of capitalist culture, but also its destructive-ness'.[33] For Baudelaire, the landscape of rubble during the rebuilding of Paris mirrors the ruins of the great classical city, Troy, as, crossing the new Place de Carrousel in 'The Swan', he is struck by the image of Hector's widow, Andromache. With this reference the '[n]ew palaces, scaffolding, blocks' of Imperial Paris are reduced to a fallen city. As Benjamin describes, the 'overtones audible in Baudelaire when he con-jures up Paris in his verse are those of the ruinousness and fragility of this great city'.[34]

Obviously man too could, and did, regard destruction as a precursor to a new order—Haussmann's Paris, the slum clearance of St Giles at the end of the nineteenth century, and the rebuilding of London after the Second World War, are all examples. Yet this cyclical destruction and construction process differs from the idea of a palimpsestic city built on layers of persistent ruin, at least on Benjamin's terms. In 'Central Park', for example, Benjamin describes the concepts of destruction and con-struction as essentially alike:

The course of history as represented in the concept of the catastrophe has no more claim on the attention of the thinking than the kaleidoscope in the hand of a child which, with each turn, collapses everything ordered into new order. The

[32] Elizabeth Bowen, *Ivy Gripped the Steps and Other Stories* (New York: Alfred A. Knopf, 1946), p. viii.

[33] Susan Buck-Morss, *The Dialectics of Seeing: Walter Benjamin and the Arcades Project* (Cambridge, Mass.: MIT Press, 1989), 164.

[34] Walter Benjamin, 'Central Park', trans. Lloyd Spencer, *New German Critique* 34 (1985), 32–58, p. 44.

justness of this image is well-founded. The concepts of the rulers have always been the mirror by means of whose image an 'order' was established.—This kaleidoscope must be smashed.[35]

The masculine perception of history—in terms of great events and disasters rather than the everyday—is identical to that of the city. The feminine perception, however, is sensitive to the influence of the every-day features of time and place that go into the identity of a city and its inhabitants. The perfect example is the cafe owner, Iris, in Doris Les-sing's *The Four-Gated City* (1969), who is one of a 'million brains, women's brains, that recorded in such loving anxious detail the histories of windowsills, skins of paint, replaced curtains and salvaged baulks of timber, in other words 'the everyday', and create a 'a sort of six-dimen-sional map which included the histories and lives and loves of people, London—a section map in depth' (*FGC* 21). Buck-Morss notes that, for Benjamin, 'the collector, the ragpicker, and the detective wander through the fields of the fossil and ruin', in opposition to 'the prostitute, the gambler, and the flâneur' who find their home in the phantasmagoria. The wandering female observer perhaps merges these two fields. Iris, as well as Bowen's Stella and Pepita, for example, collect fragments from the ruins of a blitzed London that has become for them a phantasmagoric world—a city as dream-ruin.

The young protagonist in Rose Macaulay's *The World My Wilderness* is a fictional version of those women artists who create art out of the London rubble. Barbary is a child artist-*flâneur* who lives daily in the wreckage of the city, turning the blown open shells of buildings into her own living, dining, and bedrooms. Just as the *flâneur* of the Parisian boulevards, such as Baudelaire and the new journalists, shrewdly anti-cipated their audience and wrote lucrative vignettes of life for the expanding periodical market, Barbary paints postcards of bomb ruins to sell to affluent tourists. They combine the impressionistic with the surrealistic; in one postcard, 'out of the flowering jungle shells of towered churches sprang, shells of flats soared skyward on twisting stairs, staring empty-eyed at desolation' (*WW* 159). Macaulay was a close friend of Bowen, having been instrumental in promoting her career after they met at the University Women's Club. Living in London during the war, and working for the Auxiliary Ambulance Service, she developed a similar perspective on the city, gleaned from the tense, nocturnal lifestyle: 'if your job calls you out to it, as mine sometimes does, you do at least get an eyeful, and see something you don't see as a

---

[35] Benjamin, 'Central Park', 34.

rule in the London streets.'[36] Again like Bowen, she aestheticizes these sights:

For aesthetic pleasure you must wait until dark. London nights, once garish, have become beautiful: black, with tiny lights like glow-worms faintly piercing the blackness—and on a clear night, the stars. Or, on a moony night, magically black and silver, an ivory city sharp with shadows and deep lanes of night. And always the long lances of light that sweep the skies, crossing, seeking, probing.[37]

The World My Wilderness, although written in 1950, addresses the social and psychological experience of living in this landscape in the transitional period between the end of the war and the start of rebuilding. Barbary and her step-brother Raoul are children of the war, young *maquis* or revolutionaries, who are natural wanderers. Coming to London from France, a country that has been appropriated from its inhabitants by occupation, Barbary cannot feel at home in her father's elegant Regency house in the Adelphi either. Truanting from college and walking randomly through the city, she finally finds a bombed site in Cheapside, in the shadow of St Paul's, where her spirit can take refuge. For Barbary and Raoul, whose adopted motto of the *maquis* is, like that of the rag-picker, 'we take our wilderness where we go' (210), 'these broken habitations, this stony rubbish, [seem] natural' (52). Young 'rag-pickers', they create their own city in miniature within the larger space of London itself and out of its waste and forgotten ground.

Like Kôr this bombed part of London is a 'fantastic, ruined city' (61) of 'haunted, brittle beauty' (57), and also the children's own self-contained city, made up of the shells of houses, offices, a church, and a café, surrounded by weed 'gardens'. As with Kôr it is this surreal landscape that Barbary can connect to, as opposed to the ordered streets that she regards as part of an improbable world. It is the ruin that is familiar; 'it had the clear, dark logic of a dream; it made a lunatic sense, as the unshattered streets and squares did not; it was the country that one's soul recognized and knew' (61). Importantly it is also a palimpsestic city, in which the bomb damage has torn open the ground to reveal evidence of an 'abiding city', continuing through various layers back to the past. It was largely Second World War bomb damage that allowed for the excavation of the foundations of past buildings by archaeologists, and

[36] Rose Macaulay, 'Consolations of the War', *The Listener*, 16 Jan. 1941, repr. in Jenny Hartley (ed.), *Hearts Undefeated: Women's Writing of the Second World War* (London: Virago, 1994), 222–25, p. 224.
[37] Ibid. 223.

Barbary's bomb site in Cheapside stands on the location of the early City of London. Under the rubble of the nineteenth-century city and its buildings of commerce, destroyed by the bombing, lies evidence of an earlier city and its buildings of trade, destroyed by the Great Fire. It is an underground world of 'vaults and cellars and deep caves, the wrecked guild halls that had belonged to saddlers, merchant tailors, haberdashers, waxchandlers, barbers, brewers, coopers and coachmakers, all the ancient city fraternities' (128), in which Barbary can walk through both the geographic and historical 'abiding city' of London.

A city torn open to reveal its past is also the image of London presented in H.D.'s 'The Walls Do Not Fall', her elegy to the bombed city written in 1944. The ruined landscape recalled for H.D. the excavations of the ancient world that she had visited with Winifred Bryher two decades before, and she dedicated the poem 'for Karnak 1923 I from London 1942', immediately paralleling the ruins of the ancient and the modern city. 'The Walls Do Not Fall' is split into forty-three sections, mainly memories of the ancient city framed by the view from a walk through blitzed London. H.D. described the connection of the two in a letter to Norman Holmes Pearson in 1943: '[t]he parallel between ancient Egypt and "ancient" London is obvious [. . .] we see so much of our past "on show", as if it were "another sliced wall where poor utensils show like rare objects in a museum".'[38] Bearing certain similarities with T. S. Eliot's *The Wasteland*, it develops an etymology of the landscape and psyche of the modern urban world through allusion to myths of ruin and rebirth. The first section clearly describes the London scene of 1942, with the familiar features of the dismantled railings, ruined buildings, and the natural vegetation that creeps insidiously into this city over which man has lost control. Yet H.D. notes a freedom in this ruined landscape, and experiences a spiritual response to it that prefigures that of Barbary in *The World My Wilderness*, as 'the fallen roof I leaves the sealed room I open to the air' and 'through our desolation I thoughts stir, inspiration stalks us' (*T* 3). The broken city awakens and inspires the aesthetic eye.

At times the walking poetic persona is unsure of how to respond to the battered but resilient city—does she want the walls to fall and thus allow for rebirth, or, in Eliot's terms, does she prefer to collect up the fragments from the ruins? The latter option would finally seem to be favoured, and is certainly the process taken up by H.D. for the purposes of the poem. The new city that H.D. creates is a palimpsest of the stony

---

[38] H.D. (Hilda Doolittle) letter to Norman Holmes Pearson, 1943, quoted in his preface to H.D. *Trilogy* (London: Carcanet Press, 1973), p. vii.

rubble of ancient cities with that of 1940s London, an imaginative dream-ruin. In section twenty she notes, like Elizabeth Bowen, the role of the dream in imagining a new world; 'that way of inspiration | is always open, ...and open to everyone; | it acts as go-between, the interpreter, ...it explains symbols of the past | in to-day's imagery, ...it merges the distant future | with most distant antiquity' (29). For H.D. too it is through the conflation of dream and reality that she can create a vision of the 'abiding city'. For in H.D.'s London it is the roof but not the walls that fall—the city is opened up but not levelled—and despite the 'Apocryphal fire' and the dismembered husk, tendons, and muscles of the city, she notes that, crucially, 'the frame held' (4). Yet this frame is tenuous and no longer orders or supports movement in the city. The observer is a wanderer in limbo, walking in 'thin air' amidst pavements that sag and leave the walker 'like a ship floundering' (59). Perhaps, however, the relaxing of the frame is a positive feature. Elizabeth Bowen, in her essay on *She* remembered her disillusionment when she was told that all spaces on the world map had been discovered, occupied, and recorded. The wilderness of the wartime landscape can be seen as an undiscovered space in which various women artists walked and found the aim of their pilgrimage. 'The Walls Do Not Fall' ends with a new ethic of spatial discovery:

> we know no rule
> of procedure,
>
> we are voyagers, discoverers
> of the not-known,
>
> the unrecorded;
> we have no map;
>
> possibly we will reach haven,
> heaven.   (59)

The London of the *flâneuse* in women's wartime art is continuous from its predecessor, held in a palimpsest of memories within the female mind but also in the evidence of the everyday if, like the rag-picker, one knows where to look. Mavis in *The World My Wilderness* and Iris in *The Four-Gated City* both lived and worked in the city before the bombing and possess an intimate knowledge of their respective areas, still mapping the ruins by the names and purposes of the streets and buildings that had previously stood there. This is where a particular response to the city can be noted that accords frequently with the perceptions of the female. For the city that derives from the amalgamation of the dream and the real—London viewed through the mystery of Kôr—is abiding, only the social world that forms the uppermost layer of its palimpsest is ever destroyed.[39] The city of imagination and memory is persistent and continuing, always a city of ruin that is continually erased to the ground and then rebuilt.

[39] Except perhaps in the nuclear apocalypse, the threat of which pervades post-war novels such as Lessing's *The Four-Gated City.*

Epilogue: Re-envisioning the Urban Walker

> Put her brain, together with the other million brains, women's brains, that recorded in such tiny loving anxious detail the histories of windowsills, skins of paint, replaced curtains and salvaged baulks of timber, and there would be a recording instrument, a sort of six-dimensional map which included the histories and lives and loves of people, London—a section map in depth.[1]

Martha Quest, the protagonist of Doris Lessing's visionary *The Four-Gated City*, seems an appropriate consummation of the social and literary genealogy of the *flâneuse* that I have attempted to construct. Like Miriam Henderson, Martha is undertaking a private pilgrimage, like Sasha Jensen she moves '[f]rom room to room, cheap hotel to hotel, a bed in the flat of a man whose name she could not remember' (*FGC* 16), like Stella Rodney she dwells in a city uprooted by war. Walking in a post-war city of ruin, imagining its past and prophesying its future, she develops her own female *flânerie*, observing the fragments of urban life through its past, its present, and the minds of its inhabitants.

Walking the Palimpsest

Having left her native Africa to enjoy the freedom and anonymity of being an outsider in London, Martha is portrayed in the first third of the novel as a wandering and placeless figure, predisposed to a vagrant migrancy and drawn to,

> that current of people, that tide, which always flows in and out of London through the home-owners, the rate-payers, the settled: people visiting, holidaying, people wondering if they should settle, people looking for their ancestors and their roots, the students, the travellers, the drifters, the tasters, the derelicts and the nonconformists who must have a big city to hide themselves in. (16)

[1] Doris Lessing, *The Four-Gated City* (London: MacGibbon and Kee, 1969), 21.

214

The first weeks of Martha's urban life are spent in idle *flânerie*, in 'enjoyable lazy drifting on her inclination through London'. The novel opens at a turning point, however, when she has decided to choose some direction in her life, reflected metaphorically in her decision during her urban walk 'to walk across the river, walk into a decision; not loiter and dally' (20). Traditionally a wanderer, 'travelling with her life in a suitcase', Martha only alights for brief periods. She stays with the café owners Iris and Jimmy for example, in a need for rest, 'by chance flopping down in the café for a cup of tea, her legs having collapsed from hours of walking' (22). It is this vagrant lifestyle that makes her a natural connoisseur of the city, in contrast to Iris who 'limpet on her rock, had known that Martha had drifted and eddied around this city which she would never visit, never know' (22).

Taking a mammoth journey from the south to the north of the city, crossing the Thames, taking a bus up Fleet Street, walking through Piccadilly Circus and along Oxford Street, Hyde Park, and Bayswater Road, she epitomizes the female urban pilgrim. A latter-day Miriam Henderson in her ardour for walking and her receptive observations, she seems a culmination of the female identification with, and manipulation of, the figure of the *flâneur*. At first, in the modern city of the 1950s Martha's gender does not hamper her movement and she can easily observe others whilst 'loitering, but not obviously so, among people window-shopping' (47). This changes at Bayswater Road, however, where men prowl amidst the trees, although along the prostitute-lined Queensway she actually feels quite free and safe in her obvious distinction from these other 'streetwalkers'. Being an outsider, Martha is 'walking always as a watchful critic' (50), very much the detached observer who observes and registers the dynamics of urban space. She is not an objectifying and fixing *flâneur*, however. For example, her walk creates an invisible but instinctive map (part of that six-dimensional female plan) marked by '[i]nvisible boundaries, invisibly marked territories' where 'here the corner of a street, or the hour of a day could say: Here a certain kind of order ends' (48), but by this very act, Martha also crosses these boundaries, connecting the different areas through her movement between them.

Lessing continues the fictional code of women writers who counter women's historical exclusion from the city and appropriate it for women, portraying in her novel women who have greater connective relationships with the city than men. Although Iris may not have a panoramic knowledge of London as a whole, she knows her surrounding area intimately. Stella, 'the wife, mother and daughter of dockers' (24) cherishes a dream of foreign travel but still ultimately enjoys her role as 'the matriarchal boss of her knot of streets' (25). Both women find in Martha something of the vagrant or unwanted object that can yet be surrealistically endowed with value. Thus, for Iris, Martha arouses 'the same emotion as she felt for a baulk of timber hauled up out of the tides of the river or a yard of curtain material got off the ration, or teaspoons found among rubble after a bomb had dropped', and for Stella she is 'a heady wind from countries she would never visit' (29). Part of the refuse of the city themselves, they and Martha, the alien immigrant, mutually attract and understand each other. She discovers London through her own wanderings, but her perception of it is structured by the significance its landscape has for the two working-class women Iris and Stella. For them the city is not a flat concept like Martha's imaginary city, but instead a palimpsestic site built from years of history. As the quotation which heads this epilogue indicates, through Iris, Martha observes the area of bomb-damage with the double vision of both the outsider and the intimate, observing a London that exists through the memories and perceptions of the mind. Martha's walk through London becomes also a walk in memory, but one that gives expression to the memory of the city itself. Across the blitzed landscape objects are unearthed that express a past unrecorded by official monuments and architecture.

Martha's ultimate satisfaction is to 'walk down streets interminably, to walk through mornings and afternoons and evenings, alone. [...] Her body was a machine, reliable and safe for walking; her heart and daytime mind were quiet.' Wandering the city at night with her senses alert, Martha moves into a state of heightened awareness common to that depicted by the other women writers in this study. Her body merges into one with the city as she walks, and she becomes just a 'soft dark receptive intelligence' for the collecting and filtering of 'impressions: a tree, an intensely variegated mass of light; a brick wall picked out in a flood of glowing orange' (51). She is reduced from an autonomous entity to an observing sense organ moving through the crowd, '[a] tiny entity among swarms [...] this was what she was, a taste or flavour of existence without a name. Who remembered. Who noted. And not much more' (27). The condition of hunger and fatigue that induces Miriam's more hallucinatory and impressionistic perceptions of the city or Pepita's dream of Kôr, also takes Martha into a visionary realm, and she learns to recognize and control her symptoms, able to command them at will. The experience of walking in London alone, '[f]ar from being an enemy [...] was her friend', it is a state that 'had been in fact the surprise of her being in London, its real gift to her. She had learned that if she walked long enough, slept lightly enough to be conscious of her dreams, ate at random, was struck by new experience throughout the day, then her whole self cleared, lightened, she became alive and light and aware' (47). It is a subjective awareness of the city that Martha retreats into, finding it ideal. At the same time there is something unnerving in this loss of ego, described by Virginia Woolf in 'Street Haunting' as a vulnerable observing eye without the protection of identity and the stabilizing demands of the home.

From Dream City to Urban Utopia

This subjective city differs from another dream city that Martha builds, however. Jack is another alien *flâneur*, a South African with whom Martha has an informal sexual friendship. Jack is a man who does not curtail Martha's natural wandering, the only person she knows 'who could allow her to go on living as she was now, rootless, untied, free' (50). Their attachment is not persistent but Jack does perform a function for Martha similar to that of Pepita's fiancé in Bowen's 'Mysterious Kôr'. He gives her access to a fantasy place, 'a very different place in herself again' (50). In a moment of successful, almost visionary, sex, Martha finds herself in a new place. Her words are reminiscent of those of Pepita: 'with Jack there's this special place: nothing to do with Jack the person, he's the instrument that knows how to reach it' (72). In her sexual acts with Jack, Martha achieves a state of combined bodily and sensory stimulation, 'like walking down the street in a high vibrating place'. Her mind fills with scenes of 'places she had not been to, faces she had never seen, gardens, rivers, the flash of a city she had never been in' (72). It is her dream city that then shifts to a nightmare of London in the future, full of faces that are 'tortured and hurt' (73). For it is this state of trancelike detachment that is a sign of Martha's latent psychic capacity, as, rather than dallying *flâneur*-like in the minds of others, she becomes a host mind, collecting the fragmentary thoughts jostling on the urban airwaves.

After her move into the Coldridge household, Martha's walking is suddenly curtailed and she is seemingly voluntarily caught within the family, constantly making futile plans to leave that are repeatedly postponed. This physical immobility contrasts strikingly with her early wanderings. Moreover, the house itself is structured by clearly defined boundaries. Martha is most confined in physical locale, however, when exploring the landscapes of her psyche to the full, contained within the darkened and enclosed world of Lynda's subterranean basement room. Here Martha retreats from the tangible city of London to the abstract archetypal city of her visions. Significantly, the fable she uses to inspire

Mark's creative enterprise is transformed by him into an example of 'Ivory Tower' literature, and although Martha recognizes and repudiates this, she herself turns away from interaction with the urban landscape around her to that within.

Convinced that human society is heading towards self-induced destruction, Lessing forecasts an apocalyptic end in *The Four-Gated City*. What she and Martha seem to 'quest' for is a model of society that is ideal and will avoid or grow phoenix-like from this catastrophe. The mythic cities that form a recurrent motif in Martha's imagination throughout the *Children of Violence* series, have predominantly been interpreted by critics as this ideal goal. Hence, Mary Ann Singleton, in *The City and the Veld*, describes three landscapes in Lessing's œuvre—the Rhodesian veld, the Armageddon-like London, and the visionary utopia—arguing that it is only in the latter that the individual is free from the claustrophobia and restrictions of convention and the status quo, both of which are fragmentary forces. More recently, however, critical focus has shifted the value of Lessing's various cityscapes. Ideal cities are ubiquitously flawed in utopian fiction (the notion of a utopia necessarily implies its non-existence, that it is a chimera), and Martha's versions are no exception. Her adolescent dream of a wondrous ancient city is exclusionary, both explicitly, as Martha positions a gate-keeper to bar entry to people who do not fit her requirements, and implicitly, in her class and race assumptions. For although Martha imagines a city where 'white and black and brown lived as equals, and there was no hatred or violence', the landscape that she describes is built according to a Western, upper-middle-class model. The 'white-piled, broad-thoroughfared, tree-lined, four-gated dignified city', is reminiscent of Haussman's Paris, ordered and visually controllable.[2]

The state of existence that she searches for in *The Four-Gated City* is also described by Mark in terms of a utopian city, again as a 'mythical city, the one which appeared in legends and myths and fairy stories, and [...] was a hierarchic city' (*FGC* 150). This again is a grand Le Corbusian inspired city of arterial roads and tributary arcs, all lined with trees and converging on a central point. Mark and Martha envisage what seems intended to be a multi-purpose architecture in which 'functions [are] not over-defined', '[p]eople might teach in the market' and where 'in what looked like a temple, or a place of worship, goods could be bought or bartered for' (150). However, this only seems to repeat urban planners in the late nineteenth-century world cities who aimed to employ devotional architectural forms in the design of department stores, railway

[2] Doris Lessing, *Martha Quest* (London: Picador, 1952), 134.

stations, and other commercial public buildings. The new utopia is also described as 'a gardened city' (151), a common ideal of reformist urban planners from the beginning of the rapid growth of the metropolitan city.

Yet the mythopoeic city that Martha and Mark construct is not so much a vision for the future but a fable of the past, a story of the degeneration and destruction of the city. For, according to Martha, a shadow city grows up concentrically, to be the habitat of the 'hungry and dirty and short-lived people' (151) who were unfit for entry to the ideal city. Extending and adding detail to turn the fable into a novel, 'A City in the Desert', Mark describes the outer city as becoming powerful and wealthy yet unable to achieve the harmony and order of the inner city. Attempting to find the secret of the inner city's superiority, the rulers of the malignant growth attack and overcome it. It is at this point that the city becomes known and forms a part of history. The tangible city that is lived in and known, that 'reached a great climax of fame and power [...] spread out into a kingdom and then an empire [...] had a fine literature, and an art of its own' (152), is thus the excrescent city. The original city is forgotten, vestiges of its character being retained only in pre-history myth 'based on legends which persisted', gaining a spiritual cultural aura as 'the old lost city' (152). In his account of the ideal city, Mark is drawing on a tradition of reverence for a lost, urban Eden that pervades our culture. This imagined city is therefore far from being a vision of a new world. In its pure phase it is meant to be harmonious and ordered, but this results in an ultimately static atmosphere. Once the outer city has taken over, the principles of the original fall to ruin. Perhaps ironically, it is because of the hierarchical model of a city that Martha adopts, excluding those who do not fulfil certain requirements, that the over-throw of the original city occurs. The ruin of the city is not only inevitable, but the result of its own inherent characteristics. After the unspecified catastrophe at the end of the novel, the recovering human race unites in the creation of gardened private enclosures that recall the 'city in the desert'. Already, however, these enclosures are exclusionary, their doors barred to those living in 'Contaminated' areas. In fact Mark, now disillusioned with the prospect of a future world, repudiates the idealism of the concept of a mythic or dream city: '[w]e said Nineveh and Tyre, and Sodom and Gomorrah, and Rome, Carthage, Balkh and Cordoba—but that never meant anything. A desert which was a grave-yard becomes a place where cities are not built. That is all' (666).

The next time Martha walks extendedly in London's streets is several years later, when 'that dirty, ruinous, war-soaked city she had arrived in [...] was gone' (314), rebuilt after the war into a commercial modern city. She responds to this new city much as Iris did to the war-torn landscape a decade before, superimposing it over the image of the old city she had known previously: '[s]he walked through this city and kept that other one in her mind, so that a long street of fashionably bright houses had behind it, or in it, an avenue of nightmare squalor [...] there was a surface of freshness, hiding weights of shoddiness that threatened to crumble and lean' (314). Lessing contrasts this rapidly changing London to the notion of the abstract city such as that delineated by Mark:

Somewhere in our minds there is an idea of a city. A City, rather! a solid, slow-moving thing, not far off that picture of a city presented by Mark, where streets ran North and South and East and West and known landmarks could be referred to through generations. But London heaved up and down, houses changed shape, collapsed, whole streets were vanishing into rubble. (314)

This *idea* of a 'City' (and note that Lessing does not use the word *ideal*) is that handed down mythic city that Lessing seems to suggest is part of a formative pre-history. Yet it is this ever-changing London that has vitality and life, and at the same time continues a palimpsestic relationship with its past. For Martha describes it not as a separate 'new' city but as one that is another layer on the old; layers of memory register the rebuilt city, the war-torn city and the Edwardian city, in the same way that the layered wallpaper that Martha finds registers different periods in the history of a house. Moreover, this movement suggests the continued life of the city, in contrast to the deadening impression of the 'solid, slow-moving' city in the desert: '[t]he old city was all movement. Exhilarating' (315). Certainly London exudes a dominant presence in the novel, and it is importantly one that is sensual and physical, that demands the involvement of the observer by walking in its streets.

Like her protagonist, Martha, Lessing is also a 'builder of imagined cities'.[3] Critics have drawn attention to the shift from a realist to a fantastic tone in her later novels, in which the utopian city is a persistent feature. Whereas the first novels of the *Children of Violence* series are semi-autobiographical and written in a conventional narrative voice, Lessing's fiction from the 1960s onwards has taken an apocalyptic and utopian perspective. Thus, *The Four-Gated City*, the fifth and final part of the sequence, is quite different in its latter half to the earlier 'Martha' novels, and its visionary emphasis corresponds rather to the 'space fiction' of the *Canopus in Argos: Archives* series. The golden city of Martha's imagination and the archetypal cities that Lessing creates in

---

[3] Claire Sprague, *Rereading Doris Lessing: Narrative Patterns of Doubling and Repetition* (Chapel Hill, NC: University of North Carolina Press, 1987).

her galactic series, both by definition unrealizable ideals, have a sterility and coldness about them. Abstract city plans, they do not have the vitality that marks the depiction of London in the first section of *The Four-Gated City*. Martha's golden city is mapped into harmonious order, with its inhabitants all fulfilling a necessary function in a necessary place, but there is no sense of the rushing movement, rapid change, and infinite variety that ultimately is what constitutes urban experience. There is no physical, sensory interaction with the abstract city—its observer is an omniscient overseer rather than a moving *flâneur*.

In *Flesh and Stone*, Richard Sennett has complained of such sensory deprivation in the present-day city, partly the result of 'modern architects and urbanists having somehow lost an active connection to the human body in their designs', partly stemming from 'deeper historical origins' (16).[4] In the *Canopus* series Lessing herself is perhaps comparable to this modern architect, conceiving abstract cities through myth rather than 'a history of the city told through people's bodily experience' (15). In *The Four-Gated City*, however, the lengthy and insightful depiction of the actual city of London, in comparison with the fable of the 'city in the desert', suggests an engagement with those 'historical origins' that form our urban perceptions. For, whereas the golden city in the desert becomes a degenerate city, a dead city, and finally a non-existent city of legend, post-war London, flawed and devastated, is yet alive; in the flower that sprouts on the timber baulk in the bomb-site, in the cyclical social rhythms of its days and seasons, in its persistent process of demolishing and rebuilding. Martha contrasts walking in the African bush or English country lane, over the roots of trees and shrubs, to walking in London 'through unaired rootless soil, where electricity and telephone and gas tubes ran and knotted and twined' (18), where these cables are the life currents of the city.

Similarly to H.D., who in 'The Walls Do Not Fall' described the streets of London as unstable, shifting walkways, Lessing also implies that walking in London means walking on a rootless and thus unsteady surface, however. The trees that are so prominent a part of female urban topography have been heavily decimated in Martha's post-war London, and with them seem to have gone the roots of the city itself. The plight of both tree and city is symbolized by the massive hulk of timber left in the bomb-site on the south side of the river. Although '[t]his object had been a tree', it is no longer recognizable as such, having been polluted by the greyness, damp, and fumes of London; '[w]ood had never meant a great baulk of greyish-brown substance that smelled of

---

[4] Sennett, *Flesh and Stone*, 16.

wet, of damp, of rot, and of the gas which must have soaked everything in this street' (19). Yet it has taken on a new meaning and value as part of the memories of the city. A flawed and unwanted object, for Iris and Martha the piece of rotten timber is a poignant symbol of the tenacity and continuation of the ever-changing city.

The current trend towards the value of the tangible city advocated by Sennett is manifest in contemporary work on Lessing. Christine Sizemore devotes a chapter of her excellent *A Female Vision of the City* to 'The City as Palimpsest' in the fiction of Doris Lessing, and Claire Sprague also argues that Lessing's interest in London should not be overlooked in favour of her 'newer sacramental imagination'.[5] Sprague captures the power of Lessing's London when she states that '[t]he evocation of the historical London of the 1950s and 1960s, in all its brilliant detail and protean force, represents a different kind of triumph. It denies perfection and celebrates change, validating the palimpsestic nature of history and human experience.' It retains the fragments of urban history, exposing the past in the palimpsest of the war-torn landscape. It is the palimpsestic city, manifest in the scrap of layered wallpapers, Iris's memories, and Martha's observation of the bombed-open ground that both Sizemore and Sprague associate with Lessing's representation of London. This palimpsest is the result of human interaction through and in the city, however, revealing its significance to the walkers in its streets.

Conclusion

Carthage, Rome, Ninevah, cries T. S. Eliot at the end of *The Waste Land*. The city is so often the epic text of modernity, a phantasmagoria where heroism is acted out by outcasts amidst the refuse of everyday life, creating modern myths of a Ulysses on the Liffey, or an 'Odysseus on the pavement'.[6] Literary modernism silences and conceals the female presence in the city by such mythologizing, however. Women are rarely present in the city of myth; rather they are personified as the mythic city itself, a landscape for the hero to explore and conquer. Only Troy is dominated by a woman—Helen, the beauty and whore who is the cause of its destruction. The 'heroic' women of modern London and Paris thus

---

[5] Christine Sizemore, *A Female Vision of the City: London in the Novels of Five British Women* (Knoxville, Tenn.: University of Tennessee Press, 1989). Sprague, *Rereading Doris Lessing*, 180.

[6] Gilloch, *Myth and Metropolis*, 151.

do not act out a pretence at heroic ancient myth as they have none to follow.[7] Rather they create their own heroism, stepping out on their own pilgrimages. For Levy, Richardson, and Woolf, the city of London was a stimulating lover; for Bowen, a visionary ruin. For Rhys, Paris became an intoxicating narcotic; for Flanner, a haven for the exiled. All these women wrote as *flâneuses*, for whom the city was irresistible. For these writers, the cities of London and Paris become mythic presences but this does not mean that they are rendered as inert ruins, as the mythologizing of the city is always kept in interplay with a focus on the particular life that takes place within them. In fact, London and Paris can be conceived as 'abiding', palimpsestic cities precisely because of the exhilaration that these women experience in walking amidst the buildings, streets, inhabitants, cries, and traffic of their contemporary environments.

That Walter Benjamin's 'Arcades Project', the theoretical point of departure for discussion of the *flâneur* in the city, is itself a work of written *flânerie* has been frequently noted.[8] The text is regarded as labyrinth, a building site, a site of fragments, expressed through montage. As readers, therefore, we have to pick our way through the conglomeration of images, myths, commodities, and types that people the pages of the text as they do the streets of a city. The *flâneur* is one of these figures, who constantly wanders away from interpretation and eludes definition in just the same way as the *passante*. Between the essay 'The Flâneur' and its revision as 'On Some Motifs on Baudelaire', Poe's 'The Man of the Crowd' and Benjamin's own reworking of the themes and images of his earlier *Berlin Childhood*, the *flâneur* wanders away and reappears in different guise. As a result, what can be extrapolated from Benjamin's account of the *flâneur* is equivocal. What is certain, however, is that the *flâneur* must be conceived in relation to his place within the city itself, and as a specifically walking figure. However much he operates for Baudelaire and Benjamin as an allegorical object, it is the socio-geographic landscape of the city that gives him purpose and meaning.

What I have attempted to do in this study is to move beyond rather abstract discussions of the *flâneur* derived solely from Benjamin's writing, retaining his methodological framework of relating the structural motifs of urban and aesthetic form but expanding the subject to focus on how this structural equation can be played out by women writers in expression of their socio-historical position with regards to the urban

---

[7] The exception is H.D., who actually reconstructs mythic tradition to incorporate the female, notably in *Helen in Egypt* (New York: Grove, 1961).

[8] Graeme Gilloch is the most recent. He describes it as 'a description of the urban (text-as-city)', *Myth and Metropolis*, 94.

environment. In particular I have looked at the coincidence of Richardson's demand for a new mode of aesthetic sensibility and representation to record female experience with the need for a new mode of perception brought about by the turn-of-the-century city. Baudelaire described the *modernité* of mid-nineteenth-century Paris as 'the ephemeral, the fugitive, the contingent', to be appreciated by equally transient wandering urban figures that we can loosely group under the term *flâneur*. By the time that Benjamin reconceptualizes Baudelaire's work in the 1930s, he is influenced by the structure and atmosphere of cities that are fifty, seventy, and eighty years on from the birth of the French poet's conception of *modernité*; by the Berlin of his childhood, the Moscow of his political and geographical exploratory travels in the 1920s, and the Paris of his exile in the 1930s. The city of modernity has become largely a place to retreat from in a frantic attempt at order, rather than a space in which to idly and randomly wander. It is precisely into the modern cities of these later years, however, that women emerge, keen for freedom and autonomy, seeking to understand the city on their own terms and ready to express their experiences in their own voice. Benjamin's cultural study of the metropolis is an implicit critique of 'history', that practice that constructs an illusory sense of the past in terms of the ideology of bourgeois modernity. A reanalysis of the historical depiction of the urban environment is also what is required for women to be recognized as observing subjects in the city. Moreover, just as Benjamin argues for an understanding of the city based in the memory and preservation of abandoned or unvalued objects, and a dialectical awareness of the interaction of past and present, the urban perspective adopted for such feminist revisioning is one that retains everyday but obsolete images and objects from the past, in so doing constructing a palimpsestic city that belies its apparently ever-changing and fragmenting surface.

Benjamin conceives his locale of discussion—the metropolis—on several different levels: as phantasmagoria, site of modern capitalism, a remembered childhood fairground, a historical ruin. His means of access to this metropolis, the manifestation of his practice of cultural and sociological philosophy, is the *flâneur*, who himself shifts between these palimpsestic layers of representation as, variously, myth, metaphor, and social phenomenon. The *flâneur* is a moving observer, indeed more specifically a *walking* observer, whose movement has autonomy even if not direction. As urban historians have noted, the idea of movement in urban space was a formative feature in the formation of nineteenth-century cities and their social organization. Richard Sennett describes, for example, how John Nash's regency London and Baron Haussmann's imperial Paris, both habitats for the leisured male urbanite, were designed 'to create a crowd of freely moving individuals, and to discourage the movement of organized groups through the city'.[9] They are cities based around networks of arterial roads and wide adjacent pavements. Moreover, the urban experience of isolation or individualism was largely the direct result of an environment planned on a principle of fluid movement rather than static place, for Sennett continues that '[i]ndividual bodies moving through urban space gradually became detached from the space in which they moved, and from the people the space contained [...] space became devalued through motion'.[10] A defining feature of the pure concept of the *flâneur* is thus detachment during movement (and hence a mental detachment during physical connection), to which other models of authoritative, 'masculine' observation of the city such as the panopticon or the panorama, in which the observer is stationary, are only subsidiary.

The *flâneur* is a hypersensitive and observant type of the indifferent individuals who co-exist as the urban crowd. He is physically part of this crowd yet also mentally detached from it; it is in no way a socio-political collective. Describing Nash's scheme, Sennett explains that the 'pressure of linear pedestrian movement on Regent Street made, and still makes, it difficult for a stationary crowd to form [...] Instead both street and park privileged the individual moving body.'[11] However, according to Sennett, what can result from this isolation is a lack of connection with the social world of the city, and it is perhaps this circumstance that accounts for the common confusion in which the *flâneur* is conflated with the static, panoramic spectator and becomes embroiled in the discourse of observation and visual control in and of urban space. Walter Benjamin's late nineteenth-century *flâneur*, who retreats to the balcony or the window for authoritative control, is just such a figure who has lost the involved sensation of walking: '[i]ndividualism and the facts of speed together deaden the modern body; it does not connect.'[12] This was the more prevalent and considered aspect of Benjamin's urban writings. Yet a fascination with the realm of the metropolis never left him, and indeed was tied up with the paradoxes of this 'magical place where the wonderful and the terrible existed simultaneously'.[13]

The attempted socio-political function of the *flâneur* as Benjamin defined him was to observe, differentiate, and classify the individuals that made up the urban crowd, to be a 'botanist' of the asphalt habitat. Common to sociological and literary representations of the urban scene

[9] Sennett, *Flesh and Stone*, 323.   [10] Ibid.   [11] Ibid.   [12] Ibid. 324.
[13] Linda Hoffman, 'Walter Benjamin's Infernal City', *Washington State University Research Studies* 52/3–4 (1983), 146–55, p. 147.

is a preponderance of certain types of individuals, however, who can be designated under the term the 'other'; the prostitute, the immigrant, the elderly, the sexual invert, the rag-picker. What is particularly provocative about Sennett's philosophy of the city is that he regards it as a positive site for the 'other' and the exile, innovatively suggesting that the city should be regarded not as a sanctuary but as an open space 'in which people come alive, where they expose, acknowledge, and address the discordant parts of themselves and one another'.[14] Simmel and Freud's study of the modern, urban individual as an organism highly receptive of stimuli and yet detached from this stimuli by a protective crust offers a sense of the urban environment as a threatening place. Yet Sennett draws on Freud's countering insight that 'if protection rules, if the body is not open to periodic crises, eventually the organism sickens from lack of stimulation'.[15] As he perceptively reminds us, the fact that 'Regent Street [for example] was itself, and remains, anything but lifeless' is the result of the movement of many such disconnected modern bodies.[16]

Sennett warns that it is too easy to view the moving urban crowd pessimistically, as Benjamin came to do, as a force of uniformity, passivity, self-extinction. Interestingly, it has been a persistent masculine response to the crowd to define it as a brutal and engulfing mass; for example, the late nineteenth-century stereotype of the New Woman and the Odd Woman as part of a degenerate female herd stampeding over London, or Benjamin's bourgeois and Fascist masses dehumanizing Paris and Berlin. The crowd is a quagmire, against which the *flâneur* asserts heroic resistance. The *flâneuse* too defines herself as an individual amongst the crowd, and as the female urbanites of this study manifest, they do this in numerous ways. Miriam Henderson jealously guards the individuality she is accorded by her isolated urban existence and resists any hint of classification—she is the elusive *flâneur/passante* extraordinaire. Cecilia Summers, in Bowen's *To the North*, likes to objectify her individuality within the city, cherishing an obsession for mirrored restaurants that reflect her self, a practice that is continued by Bowen's later male protagonist Harrison, the spy who at once uses but subverts the supposedly concealing veil of the urban crowd. Janet Flanner and Romaine Brooks adopt the Parisian tradition of dandyism in a studied and self-conscious pose of individualistic indifference. All these women flirt with the quintessential characteristics of the bourgeois *flâneur*. They

---

[14] Linda Hoffman, 'Walter Benjamin's Infernal City', *Washington State University Research Studies* 52/3–4 (1983), 146–55, p. 354.

[15] Ibid. 372.

[16] Ibid. 324.

adapt to the crowd and move in accord with its tempo, rather than attempting to hold out against it like Benjamin's dawdling and hence finally extinct aristocrat. Indeed, for women, the crowd is never quite an amorphous body anyway, but instead a differentiated collectivity. It is made up of people as individual as the observer herself, who yet cross paths and group together periodically over the cycle of the urban day and year, creating the flowing life-blood and heart rhythms of the city. Moreover, the women of this study, isolated *flâneuses* or 'women of the crowd', find an external anonymity in the crowd that then allows them the freedom to conduct a female pilgrimage, both the 'voyage out' and the 'voyage in'. As an elusive figure in the crowd, the woman can deny voyeuristic objectification—what seems threatening and disconcertingly unclassifiable to the observing male, therefore, is protective and usefully concealing for the urban woman.

The women writers that I have considered recognize both the exhilaration that the city can offer and the isolation that it demands, and, even if they mourn the latter, they tend to see it as the basis for the former. Women writers and artists based in the city frequently constructed their own networks of connection within the overall atmosphere of isolation and fragmentation. Moreover, many of these spaces act in reverse to the impulse towards interiorization that Benjamin defines as characteristic of the (male) bourgeois urban temperament, and become means of access to the public world of the city. They could take the form of private rooms where Richardson could enjoy debate with other independent 'new women', the social club where both she and Levy met friends and publishers, the ABCs where working women such as Mary Datchet or Emmeline Summers could meet colleagues for lunch, and the aesthetic salon where Natalie Barney could shepherd the financial and emotional fortunes of her creative associates. Such places were linked by the street, bus, or underground rail map. Non-mappable networks also existed however, such as the unspoken awareness of back-street abortionists that Olivia Curtis joins, the series of unexclusive and accommodating (both socially and sexually) Parisian bars that Jean Rhys's heroines can sniff out, or the communities of ambulance, air raid, and fire wardens known to Elizabeth Bowen and Rose Macaulay in the blitz.

Obviously, to generalize the experiences of such socially diverse women as Levy, Richardson, Woolf, Rhys, and Bowen, for example, into the character of the *flâneuse*, is to risk overlooking the specific and particular influences of their race and class, as well as the period in which they live. The actual and metaphoric use of the description *flâneur* come into tension. This is exactly the criticism that is levelled at

Benjamin; for example, Graeme Gilloch complains that '[t]he relationships and correspondences posited by Benjamin between the *flâneur* and
the sandwichman, the gambler and the assembly-line worker, the poet
and the prostitute, sometimes reveal a perplexing and unfortunate lack
of discrimination'.[17] Ultimately, however, Benjamin is never equating
these figures as social actualities. What he does do is use the *flâneur*
for theoretical and historiographical means, as a model for both his own
methodology and the cultural climate that he studies. Common to the
women writers of my study, however, is a self-conscious positioning of
themselves as living and working in relation to a tradition of urban representation based on just such a tropic understanding of the urban
walker observer. As such they engage with and against the *flâneur*
metaphor, identifying with it as a model of urban freedom and stimulation, but in terms of the actual experience of this freedom in the social
environment. The atmosphere of urban space becomes all-pervasive in
the texts of the most formally experimental of the women writing within
them, the urban consciousness they produce translating into the very
style of writing. The city is frequently enabling, sometimes difficult,
always irresistible, providing spaces in which these women can explore
their identities and their writerly voices. Richardson, Woolf, and Rhys, in
seeking a narrative form for the representation of cities, create texts that
are themselves shaped by the experience of the urban environment. Thus
the vast sections of flowing interior monologue in *Pilgrimage*, coupled
with moments of linguistic claustrophobia when language seems inade-
quate for the expression of experience, correspond to Miriam Henderson's long, perceptive walks, and her sensation of stifling enclosure in a
room that is sometimes a place of repose but more often a tangible
reminder of the economic conditions of her freedom. The aesthetic style
of Rhys operates in a similar way, psychological experience paralleling an
urban environment of streets and rooms, yet generally reverses Richardson's value system to find an agoraphobic openness in the all-too-
familiar street and protection in the unknown room. Nin and Bowen
also interrelate city and text, both searching urban wastelands which,
when perceived through certain conditions, offer a magic that can lead
to the creation of a mystical utopia. Djuna Barnes struggles to record the
experience of her urban night world through a language of allusion,
fragmentation, fantasy, and ultimately silence.

Significantly, the influential urban environment is one that is familiar,
if not always expressible within the limits of the conventional language-
meaning system. The *flâneur/flâneuse* is not lost or a stranger to the city

---

[17] Gilloch, *Myth and Metropolis*, 15.

and, hence, the city is rarely portrayed as a labyrinth. The impulse of Richardson, Woolf, and Rhys is not to give the city the order of a graphic map. In their fiction the perspective of the *flâneuse* operates both thematically and structurally, as the sociological and the aesthetic coalesce. Thus Richardson and Woolf present impressionistic images of the city through a literary style sensitive to the atmospheric and psychological urban atmosphere, and Rhys surrealistically depicts a city of human and material refuse through a montage of carefully collected symbols of decay and degradation. Their writing of the city *in* texts result from their walking of the city *as* text. They embody the surrealist notion of modernity as 'mythology in motion'. Benjamin's *flâneur* is incompletely defined and thus a paradoxical figure. Perhaps this is intentional, reflecting the elusive nature of the urban walker him/herself. Certainly the image of the urban walker as it has developed in women's fiction has actually been defined *as* elusive and ambiguous, as the *flâneuse* or *passante* who walks away from the categorizing, possessing gaze of the masculine observer.

Bibliography

APPIGNANESI, LISA, *Femininity and the Creative Imagination: A Study of Henry James, Robert Musil and Marcel Proust* (London: Vision Press, 1973).

APTER, EMILY, *Feminising the Fetish: Psychoanalysis and Narrative Obsession in Turn-of-the-Century France* (Ithaca, NY: Cornell University Press, 1991).

ARMSTRONG, ISOBEL (ed.), *New Feminist Discourses* (London: Routledge, 1992).

—— *Victorian Poetry: Poetry, Poetics and Politics* (London: Routledge, 1993).

BAIR, DEIDRE, *Anaïs Nin: A Biography* (London: Bloomsbury, 1995).

BARNES, DJUNA, *Nightwood* (1936; London: Faber and Faber, 1996).

BARROWS, SUSANNA, *Distorting Mirrors: Visions of the Crowd in Late Nineteenth-Century France* (New Haven: Yale University Press, 1981).

BAUDELAIRE, CHARLES, *My Heart Laid Bare and Other Prose Writings*, ed. Peter Quennell, trans. Norman Cameron (London: Soho Book Co., 1986).

—— *The Flowers of Evil*, trans. James McGowan (Oxford: Oxford UP, 1993).

—— *Parisian Prowler*, trans. Edward K. Kaplan (Athens, Ga.: University of Georgia Press, 1989).

BECK, EVELYN TORTON (ed.), *Nice Jewish Girls: A Lesbian Anthology* (Boston: Beacon Press, 1989).

Bedford College, London, *Educating Women: A Pictorial History of Bedford College, University of London 1849–1985* (Egham, Surrey: Alma 1991).

BENJAMIN, WALTER, *Charles Baudelaire: A Lyric Poet in the Era of High Capitalism*, trans. Harry Zohn (London: Verso, 1989).

—— *One Way Street and Other Writings*, trans. Edmund Jephcott and Kingsley Shorter (London: Verso, 1992).

—— 'Central Park,' trans. Lloyd Spencer, *New German Critique* 34 (1985), 32–58.

—— *Illuminations*, ed. Hannah Arendt, trans. Harry Zohn (London: Jonathon Cape, 1970).

—— *Das Passagen-werk*, 2 vols. (Frankfurt: Suhrkamp, 1983).

BENSTOCK, SHARI, *Women of the Left Bank: Paris 1900–1940* (London: Virago, 1986).

BLAU DUPLESSIS, RACHEL, *H.D.* (Brighton: Harvester, 1986).

BOWEN, ELIZABETH, *To the North* (1927; London: Gollancz, 1932).

—— *The Demon Lover and Other Stories* (1945; London: Jonathon Cape, 1952).

—— *The Heat of the Day* (1949; London: Penguin, 1987).

—— *Ivy Gripped the Steps and Other Stories* (New York: Alfred A. Knopf, 1946).

—— *The Mulberry Tree: Writings of Elizabeth Bowen*, ed. Hermione Lee (London: Virago, 1986).

BOWLBY, RACHEL, *Just Looking: Consumer Culture in Dreiser, Gissing and Zola* (New York: Methuen, 1985).
—— *Shopping With Freud* (London: Routledge, 1993).
BRADBURY, MALCOLM, and JAMES McFARLANE (eds.), *Modernism: A Guide to European Literature, 1890–1930* (London: Penguin, 1991).
BRAND, DANA, *The Spectator and the City in Nineteenth Century American Literature* (Cambridge: Cambridge UP, 1991).
BRAYBON, GAIL, and SUGGERFIELD, PENNY, *Out of the Case; Woner's Experiences, in Two World Wars* (London: Pandora Press, 1987).
BRETON, ANDRÉ, *Nadja* (1928; trans. Richard Howard, New York: Grove Press, 1960).
BROE, MARY LYNN (ed.), *Silence and Power: Djuna Barnes, a Revaluation* (Carbondale, Ill.: Southern Illinois University Press, 1986).
BRONTË, CHARLOTTE, *Villette* (1853; Harmondsworth: Penguin, 1983).
BUCK-MORSS, SUSAN, *The Dialectics of Seeing: Walter Benjamin and the Arcades Project* (Cambridge, Mass.: MIT Press, 1989).
BURGIN, VICTOR, 'Chance Encounters: *Flâneur* and *Détraquée* in Breton's *Nadja*', *Qui Parle* 4/1 (1990), 47–61.
CALDER, ANGUS, *The People's War* (New York: Pantheon, 1969).
CARR, HELEN, *Jean Rhys* (Plymouth: Northcote House, 1996).
CAWS, MARY ANN (ed.), *City Images: Perspectives from Literature, Philosophy, and Film* (New York: Gordon and Breach, 1991).
CHADWICK, WHITNEY, *Women Artists and the Surrealist Movement* (London: Thames and Hudson, 1985).
CHEYETTE, BRYAN, *Constructions of 'the Jew' in English Literature and Society: Radical Representations, 1875–1945* (Cambridge: Cambridge UP, 1993).
CHISHOLM, DIANE, 'Obscene Modernism: *Eros Noir* and the Profane Illumination of Djuna Barnes', *American Literature* 69/1 (1997), 167–206.
CLARKE, GRAHAM (ed.), *Henry James: Critical Assessments* (Mountfield: Helm Information, ed., 1991).
CLARKE, T. J., *The Painting of Modern Life: Paris in the Art of Manet and his Followers* (London: Thames and Hudson, 1984).
COHEN, MARGARET, *Profane Illumination: Walter Benjamin and the Paris of Surrealist Revolution* (Berkeley: University of Los Angeles Press, 1993).
CONNOR, STEVEN, 'Cultural Sociology and Cultural Sciences', Bryan S. Turner (ed.), *The Blackwell Companion to Social Theory* (Oxford: Blackwell, 1996).
COWLEY, MALCOLM, *Exile's Return: A Literary Odyssey of the 1920s* (New York: Viking, 1951).
CRARY, JONATHAN, *Techniques of the Observer: On Vision and Modernity in the Nineteenth Century* (Cambridge, Mass.: MIT Press, 1990).
CREWS, F. C., *The Tragedy of Manners: Moral Drama in the Later Novels of Henry James* (New Haven: Yale University Press, 1957).
DAVIDOSS, LEONORA, *The Best Circles: Society, Eliquette and the Season* (London: Croom, Helm, 1973).
DE CERTEAU, MICHEL, *The Practice of Everyday Life* (1974; Berkeley: University of California Press, 1984).

Bibliography

DELEUZE, GILLES, and FÉLIX GUATTARI, *Anti-Oedipus*, trans. Robert Hurley, Mark Seem, and Helen R. Lane (New York: Viking Press, 1977).

DOANE, MARY ANN, 'Film and the Masquerade: Theorising the Female Spectator', *Screen* 23: 3–4 (1982).

DOOLITTLE, HILDA (H.D.) *Trilogy* (1942–4; London: Carcanet Press, 1973).

DREISER, THEODORE, *Sister Carrie* (1900; London: Penguin 1981).

EDEL, LEON, *The Psychological Novel, 1900–1950* (New York: J. B. Lippincott, 1955).

EISENSTEIN, ELIZABETH L., *Grub Street Abroad: Aspects of the French Cosmopolitan Population, from the Age of Louis XIV to the French Revolution* (Oxford: Clarendon Press, 1992).

ELIOT, T. S., *Collected Poems 1909–1935* (1936; London: Faber and Faber, 1959).

ELLMANN, MAUD, *The Poetics of Impersonality* (Brighton: Harvester, 1987).

ELLMANN, RICHARD, *Oscar Wilde* (Harmondsworth: Penguin, 1988).

EMERY, MARY LOU, *Jean Rhys at 'World's End': Novels of Colonial and Sexual Exile* (Austin, Tex.: University of Texas Press, 1990).

EVENSON, NORMA, *Paris: A Century of Change, 1878–1978* (New Haven: Yale University Press, 1979).

FELDMAN, DAVID, and GARETH STEDMAN JONES (eds.), *Metropolis. London: Histories and Representations Since 1800* (London: Routledge, 1989).

FELDMAN, JUDITH, *Gender on the Divide: The Dandy in Modernist Literature* (Ithaca, NY: Cornell University Press, 1993).

FELSKI, RITA, *Beyond Feminist Aesthetics: Literature and Social Change* (Cambridge, Mass.: Harvard University Press, 1989).

FLANNER, JANET, *Paris Was Yesterday 1923–1939*, ed. Irving Drutman (London: Angus and Robertson, 1973).

FOUCAULT, MICHEL, *Discipline and Punishment*, trans. Alan Sheridan (London: Allen Lane, 1977).

FRICKEY, PIERRETTE (ed.), *Critical Perspectives on Jean Rhys* (Washington: Three Continents Press, 1990).

FRIEDBERG, ANNE, 'Les *Flâneurs* du Mal(l): Cinema and the Postmodern Condition', *PMLA* 106/3 (1991), 419–31.

FRISBY, DAVID, *Fragments of Modernity: Theories of Modernity in the Work of Simmel, Kracauer and Benjamin* (Cambridge: Polity Press, 1985).

—— *Simmel and Since* (London: Routledge, 1992).

—— *Sociological Impressionism: A Reassessment of Georg Simmel's Social Theory* (London: Routledge, 1992).

GILLOCH, GRAEME, *Myth and Metropolis: Walter Benjamin and the City* (Cambridge: Polity Press, 1996).

GISSING, GEORGE, *The Odd Women* (1893; London: Sidgewick and Jackson, 1911).

—— *In The Year of Jubilee* (1894; New York: Dover Books, 1982).

GLENDINNING, VICTORIA, *Elizabeth Bowen: Portrait of a Writer* (London: Weidenfeld and Nicolson, 1977).

GODDARD, CONSTANCE, *Come Wind, Come Weather* (London: Cape, 1945).

GOLDSMITH, MARGARET, *Women at War* (London: Lindsay Brummond, 1943).

HANSCOMBE, GILLIAN, and VIRGINIA, L. SMYERS, *Writing for Their Lives: The Modernist Women 1910–1940* (London: The Women's Press, 1987).

HARTLEY, JENNY (ed.), *Hearts Undefeated: Women's Writing of the Second World War* (London: Virago, 1994).

HEILBRUN, CAROLYN, *Reinventing Womanhood* (New York: Norton, 1979).

HEMINGWAY, ERNEST, *A Moveable Feast* (New York: Scribners, 1964).

HOBSBAWM, E. J., *The Age of Empire 1875–1914* (London: Weidenfeld and Nicolson, 1987).

HOFFMAN, LINDA, 'Walter Benjamin's Infernal City', *Washington State University Research Studies* 52/3–4 (1983), 146–55.

HOOKS, J., *British Policies and Methods of Employing Women in Wartime* (Washington: US Goverment, 1944).

HUGHES, MARY V., *A London Family 1870–1900* (London: Oxford UP, 1946).

HUYSSEN, ANDREAS, *After the Great Divide: Modernism, Mass Culture and Postmodernism* (London: Macmillan, 1986).

JACOBS, JANE, *The Death and Life of Great American Cities* (London: Penguin, 1994).

JAMES, HENRY, *The Princess Cassimassima* (1886; Harmondsworth: Penguin, 1977).

—— *What Maisie Knew* (1897; Oxford: Oxford UP, 1966).

—— *The Ambassadors* (1903; New York: Norton, 1994).

—— *The Notebooks of Henry James*, ed. F. O. Matthieson and Kenneth B. Murdock (Oxford: Oxford UP, 1961).

KAPLAN, CAREN, 'Deterritorializations: The Rewriting of Home and Exile in Western Discourse', *Cultural Critique* 6 (1987), 187–98.

KENNEDY, J. GERALD, *Imagining Paris: Exile, Writing, and American Identity* (New Haven: Yale UP, 1993).

KOLKER, ROBERT PHILLIP, and PETER BEICKEN, *The Films of Wim Wenders: Cinemas as Vision and Desire* (Cambridge: Cambridge UP, 1993).

KOUIDIS, VIRGINIA M., *Mina Loy: American Modernist Poet* (Baton Rouge, La.: Louisiana State UP, 1980).

KRACAUER, SIEGFRIED, *Jacques Offenbach and the Paris of his Time*, trans. G. David and E. Mosbacher (London: Constable, 1937).

KRISTEVA, JULIA, *Powers of Horror: An Essay on Abjection*, trans. Leon S. Roudiez (New York: Columbia UP, 1982).

LASSNER, PHYLLIS, 'Reimagining the Arts of War: Language and History in Elizabeth Bowen's *The Heat of the Day* and Rose Macaulay; *The Word My Wildernass*; *Perspectives in Contemporary Criticism* 14 (1988), 30–8.

LEACH, WILLIAM R. 'Transformations in a Culture of Consumption: Women and Department Stores 1890–1925', *Journal of American History* 71/2 (1984), 319–42.

LE BON, GUSTAVE, *The Crowd* (London: T. Fisher Unwin, 1897).

LE CORBUSIER, *The City of Tomorrow* (1924; trans. Frederick Etchells, Cambridge, Mass.: MIT Press, 1971).

LEDGER, SALLY, 'Gissing, the Shopgirl and the New Woman', *Women: A Cultural Review* 6/3 (1995), 263–74.

LEHMANN, JOHN, *In My Own Time* (1955; Boston: Little, Brown, 1969).

Bibliography

LEHMANN, ROSAMOND, *Invitation to the Waltz* (1932; London: Virago, 1981).
—— *The Weather in the Streets* (1936; London: Virago, 1981).
LESSING, DORIS, *Martha Quest* (London: Picador, 1952).
—— *The Four-Gated City* (London: MacGibbon and Kee, 1969).
LEVY, AMY, *The Complete Novels and Selected Writings of Amy Levy 1861–1889*, ed. Melvyn New (Gainesville, Fla.: Florida UP, 1993).
LEWIS, PETER, *A People's War* (London: Thames Methuen, 1986).
LOY, MINA, *The Lost Lunar Baedeker*, ed. Roger L. Conover (New York: Farrar, Straus and Giroux, 1996).
MACAULAY, ROSE, *The World My Wilderness* (London: Collins, 1950).
MELLOWN, ELGIN W., 'Character and Themes in the Novels of Jean Rhys', *Contemporary Literature* 1/3 (1972), 103–17.
MOERS, ELLEN, *The Dandy in Literature: Brummell to Beerbohm* (London: Secker and Warburg, 1960).
NALBANTIAN, SUZANNE (ed.), *Anaïs Nin: Literary Perspectives* (Basingstoke: Macmillan, 1997).
NIETZSCHE, FRIEDRICH, *The Portable Nietzsche*, ed. Walter Kaufmann (New York: Random House, 1967).
NIN, ANAÏS, *Winter of Artifice* (1945; London: Peter Owen, 1991).
—— *Under a Glass Bell* (1948; London: Penguin, 1979).
—— *Children of the Albatross* (Chicago: Swallow, 1959).
—— *Seduction of the Minotaur* (Chicago: Swallow, 1961).
—— *The Journals of Anaïs Nin: 1939–1944*, ed. Gunther Stuhlmann (London: Peter Owen, 1969).
—— *A Woman Speaks* (London: Penguin, 1975).
—— *The Early Diaries of Anaïs Nin*, 4 vols. (San Diego: Harcourt Brace Jovanovich, 1985).
—— *Fire: The Unexpurgated Diary of Anaïs Nin 1934–1937* (New York: Harcourt Brace, 1995).
NOCHLIN, LINDA, and TAMAR GARB (eds.), *The Jew in the Text: Modernity and the Construction of Identity* (London: Thames and Hudson, 1995).
NORD, DEBORAH, *Walking the Victorian Streets: Women, Representation, and the City* (Ithaca, NY: Cornell UP, 1995).
OLSEN, DONALD, J., *The Growth of Victorian London* (London: Batsford, 1976).
—— *The City as a Work of Art: London, Paris, Vienna* (New Haven: Yale UP, 1986).
PACTEAU, FRANCES, 'The Impossible Referent: representations of the Androgyne', in Victor Burgin, James Donald and Cora Kaplan (eds.), *Formations of Fantasy* (London: Routledge, 1986), 62–84.
PETRUSO, T. F., *Life Made Real* (Mich.: University of Michigan Press, 1991).
PIETTE, ADAM, *Imagination of War: British Fiction and Poetry 1939–1945* (London: Papermac, 1995).
PINKNEY, TONY (ed.), *The Politics of Modernism: Against the New Conformists* (London: Verso, 1989).
POE, EDGAR ALLAN, *The Portable Poe*, ed. Philip Van Doren Stern (New York: Viking, 1945).

POLLOCK, GRISELDA, *Vision and Difference: Femininity, Feminism and the Histories of Art* (London: Routledge, 1988).

PRATT, MINNIE BRUCE, 'Identity: Skin Blood Heart', in Elly Bulkin, Minnie Bruce Pratt, and Barbara Smith (eds.) *Yours in Struggle: Three Feminist Perspectives on Anti-Semitism and Racism* (Brooklyn, NY: Long Haul Press, 1984).

PRENDERGAST, CHRISTOPHER, *Paris and the Nineteenth Century* (Oxford: Blackwell, 1992).

PROUST, MARCEL, *Remembrance of Things Past*, 3 vols., trans. C. K. Scott Moncrieff, Terence Kilmartin, and Andreas Mayor (1954; London: Chatto and Windus, 1981).

REILLY, CATHERINE W. (ed.), *Chaos of the Night: Women's Poetry and Verse of the Second World War* (London: Virago, 1984).

RHYS, JEAN, *The Left Bank and Other Stories* (1927; New York: Arno Press, 1970).

—— *Quartet* (1928; London: Deutsch, 1969).

—— *After Leaving Mr Mackenzie* (1930; London: Deutsch, 1969).

—— *Voyage in the Dark* (1934; London: Deutsch, 1967).

—— *Good Morning, Midnight* (1939; London: Deutsch, 1967).

—— *Jean Rhys: Letters 1931–1966*, ed. Francis Wyndham and Diana Melly (London: Deutsch, 1984).

RICHARDSON, DOROTHY, *Pilgrimage* (1915–67), 4 vols. (London: Virago, 1979).

—— 'Yeats of Bloomsbury', *Life and Letters Today* (Apr. 1939), 60–6.

—— *Windows on Modernism: Selected Letters of Dorothy Richardson*, ed. Gloria Glikin Fromm (Athens, Ga., and London: University of Georgia Press, 1995).

RIFKIN, ADRIAN, *Street Noises: Parisian Pleasure, 1900–40* (Manchester: Manchester University Press, 1993).

RITCHIE, CHARLES, *The Siren Years: Undiplomatic Diaries 1937–1945* (London: Macmillan, 1974).

RIVIÈRE, JOAN, 'Womanliness as a Masquerade', *International Journal of Psychoanalysis* 10 (1929).

ROBINSON, JEFFREY C., *The Walk: Notes on a Romantic Image* (Norman, Okla.: University of Oklahoma Press, 1989).

ROSE, GILLIAN, *Feminism and Geography: The Limits of Geographical Knowledge* (Cambridge: Polity Press, 1993).

ROSE, JACQUELINE, *States of Fantasy* (Oxford: Clarendon Press, 1996).

SENNETT, RICHARD (ed.), *Classic Essays on the Culture of Cities* (Englewood Cliffs, NJ: Prentice Hall, 1969).

—— *Flesh and Stone: The Body and the City in Western Civilization* (London: Faber and Faber, 1994).

SHARPE, WILLIAM, and LEONARD WALLOCK, *Visions of the Modern City: Essays in History, Art and Literature* (New York: Columbia UP, 1983).

SHERINGHAM, MICHAEL, *Parisian Fields* (London: Reaktion Books, 1996).

SHIFF, RICHARD, *Cézanne and the End of Impressionism* (Chicago: University of Chicago Press, 1984).

SHOWALTER, ELAINE, *A Literature of Their Own: Women Writers from Charlotte Brontë to Doris Lessing* (London: Virago, 1978).

Bibliography

SHOWALTER, ELAINE, *Daughters of Decadence: Woman Writers of the Fin-de-Siècle* (London: Virago, 1993).

SIZEMORE, CHRISTINE, *A Female Vision of the City: London in the Novels of Five British Women* (Knoxville, Tenn.: University of Tennessee Press, 1989).

SMITH, GARY (ed.), *On Walter Benjamin: Critical Essays and Recollections* (Cambridge, Mass.: MIT Press, 1988).

—— *Benjamin: Philosophy, Aesthetics, History* (Chicago: University of Chicago Press, 1989).

The Spectator, vol. 1, ed. Donald F. Bond (Oxford: Clarendon Press, 1965).

SPENDER, SHARON, *Collage of Dreams: The Writings of Anaïs Nin* (New York: Harcourt Brace, 1981).

SPRAGUE, CLAIRE, *Rereading Doris Lessing: Narrative Patterns of Doubling and Repetition* (Chapel Hill, NC: University of North Carolina Press, 1987).

SQUIER, SUSAN, *Virginia Woolf and London: The Sexual Politics of the City* (London: University of North Carolina Press, 1985).

STEIN, GERTRUDE, *Paris, France* (New York: Scribner's, 1940).

TARDE, GABRIEL, *On Communication and Social Influence*, ed. Terry Clark (Chicago: University of Chicago Press, 1969).

TESTER, KEITH (ed.), *The Flâneur* (London: Routledge, 1994).

THOMSON, JAMES, *The City of Dreadful Night* (1874; Edinburgh: Canongate Press, 1993).

VALMAN, NADIA, 'Women and Jews in an Age of Emancipation (1845–1900),' MA diss. (University of Leeds, October 1991).

VICINUS, MARTHA, *Independent Women: Work and Community for Single Women 1850–1920* (London: Virago, 1985).

VIDLER, ANTHONY, *The Architectural Uncanny: Essays in the Modern Unhomely* (Cambridge, Mass.: MIT Press, 1992).

WALKOWITZ, JUDITH, *City of Dreadful Delight: Narratives of Sexual Danger in London* (London: Virago, 1992).

WATTS, CAROL, *Dorothy Richardson* (Plymouth: Northcote House, 1995).

WEINSTEIN, DANA, and MICHAEL A., 'Georg Simmel: Sociological flâneur bricoleur' in Dana and Michael A. Weinstein (eds.), *Postmodern(ized) Simmel* (London: Routledge, 1993).

WESTBROOK, MAX, 'Dreiser's Defense of Carrie Meeber', *MFS* 23 (1977), 381–93.

WILLIAMS, RAYMOND, *The Country and the City* (London: Chatto and Windus, 1973).

WILSON, ELIZABETH, *The Sphinx in the City* (London: Virago, 1991).

—— 'The Invisible *Flâneur*', *New Left Review* 191 (1992), 90–110.

WINEAPPLE, BRENDA, *Genêt: A Biography of Janet Flanner* (New York: Tickner and Fields, 1989).

WOLFF, JANET, 'The Invisible *Flâneuse*: Women and the Literature of Modernity', *Theory, Culture and Society* 2/3 (1985), 37–46.

—— *Feminine Sentences* (Cambridge: Polity Press, 1990).

Woman's World 1, ed. Oscar Wilde (1888).

WOOLF, VIRGINIA, *Night and Day* (1919; Oxford: Oxford UP, 1992).

—— *Mrs Dalloway* (1925; Oxford: Oxford UP, 1992).

WOOLF, VIRGINIA, *Collected Essays*, 4 vols, ed. Leonard Woolf (London: Chatto and Windus, 1967).

—— *A Room of One's Own* (1929; London: Chatto and Windus, 1984).

—— *The Years* (1937; Oxford: Oxford UP, 1992).

—— *Women and Writing*, ed. Michele Barrett (London: Women's Press, 1979).

—— *The Diary of Virginia Woolf*, ed. Anne Olivier Bell (London: Hogarth Press, 1977–84).

—— *The Crowded Dance of Modern Life* (Harmondsworth: Penguin, 1993).

ZATLIN, LINDA, *The Nineteenth-Century Anglo-Jewish Novel* (Boston: Twayne, 1981).

ZOLA, ÉMILE, *The Ladies' Paradise* (1883; Berkeley: California UP, 1992).

Index

abjection 177
accommodation 110, 111–12
Addison, Joseph 18–19, 22, 35
Adorno, Theodor 34
advertising 47
agoraphobia 30
alienation 22, 28, 39, 50, 105, 137
  in Rhys's writings 140
Aliens Act (1905) 103
Allen, Grant 83
ambivalence 97
  in Gissing's *In the Year of Jubilee* 84
  in Nin's writings 173
androgyny 26, 42, 81
  in Proust's *A la recherche du temps perdu* 67
  in Richardson's *Pilgrimage* (*Revolving Lights*) 75–6
angels 91, 92
Appignanesi, Lisa 68
Apter, Emily 48 n.
Aragon, Louis 10
arcades project 10, 33, 208, 223
  flâneur in 3, 34, 37
  rag-picker in 36
Armstrong, Isobel 89–90
'artist of modern life' 22, 24, 32
artist-*flâneur* 22, 31, 62, 97, 209

B. V. (pseudonym of James Thomson) 88–9
Baedeker, Karl 182
Bair, Deidre 178 n.
Baker, Josephine 154
Barnes, Djuna 7, 15, 153, 154, 155, 183
  Nightwood 178–82
  on the rag-picker 152
  on the urban night world 228
Barney, Natalie 135, 149
Barrows, Susanna 44 n. 1, 45 n. 6

Baudelaire, Charles Pierre 3, 19, 21, 22, 23, 224
  A une Passante 72–3, 81
  on the dandy 20
  on elderly women 27–8
  Le Peintre de la Vie Moderne 4 n. 5
  on women 25, 26
Beaumont Trust 88 n. 6
Benjamin, Walter 2–4, 9–10, 208–9, 224, 225, 228
  'angel of history' 91
  arcades project 223
  on Baudelaire 23, 24, 25, 29, 34–6
  city geography 7
  on the *flâneur* 19, 31, 32, 33, 34–7, 79, 80
  on the rag-picker 152
Benstock, Shari 7, 139, 149, 150, 151, 186
  on Barnes 178
  on Flanner 154, 155
Bentham, Jeremy 8 n. 12
Berlin 31, 123, 178
Bildungsroman 122, 125, 133, 150, 163, 186
  as journey 88, 124, 130
  in Rhys's writings 135
Blitz 191, 199, 206
boarding-houses 110, 112
Bonheur, Rosa 40
Booth, Charles 86, 102
Bowen, Elizabeth 7, 15, 52, 98, 147, 172, 228
  The Demon Lover 192, 201, 203–4
  The Heat of the Day 107, 188, 190, 193, 194–9, 203
  To the North 125–7, 130, 226
Bowlby, Rachel 5, 47, 49, 50, 74
Bradbury, Malcolm 123 n. 2
Brand, Dana 20
Breton, André 173–6
  Nadja 180
Broderick, Catherine 170, 172 n. 47

,

239

Index

Index

Index

Index